THE PIG FARMER'S
DAUGHTER
AND OTHER TALES OF
AMERICAN JUSTICE

THE PIG FARMER'S

DAUGHTER

AND OTHER TALES OF

AMERICAN JUSTICE

⋙⋘

Episodes of Racism and

Sexism in the Courts from 1865

to the Present

MARY FRANCES BERRY

 ALFRED A. KNOPF   NEW YORK   1999

THIS IS A BORZOI BOOK
PUBLISHED BY ALFRED A. KNOPF, INC.

Copyright © 1999 by Mary Frances Berry
All rights reserved under International and Pan-American
Copyright Conventions. Published in the United States by
Alfred A. Knopf, Inc., New York, and simultaneously
in Canada by Random House of Canada Limited, Toronto.
Distributed by Random House, Inc., New York.

www.randomhouse.com

Knopf, Borzoi Books, and the colophon are registered
trademarks of Random House, Inc.

Library of Congress Cataloging-in-Publication Data
Berry, Mary Frances.
The pig farmer's daughter and other tales of American justice :
episodes of racism and sexism in the courts from 1865 to the
present / by Mary Frances Berry. — 1st ed.
p.   cm.
"This is a Borzoi book"—T.p. verso.
ISBN 0-679-43611-1
1. Afro-Americans—Legal status, laws, etc.
2. Sex crimes—United States. 3. Discrimination in criminal
justice administration—United States.   I. Title.
KF4757.B44 1999
342.73'0873—dc21   98-38233   CIP

Manufactured in the United States of America
Published April 16, 1999
Second Printing, May 1999

Contents

THE PIG FARMER'S
DAUGHTER
AND OTHER TALES OF
AMERICAN JUSTICE

INTRODUCTION

⇌

When I was four I had my first encounter with the law. An open field lay next to the house of my mother's middle brother and his family, where my many Southall cousins played ball to while away lazy summer days. One afternoon a uniformed white man on a motorcycle rode into the field, kicking up a cloud of dust. He called out to us youngsters as we watched our older cousins' ball game, "What day is this?" Someone answered, "Monday." We scattered in all directions when suddenly the man on the motorcycle drove at us, yelling angrily, "Call me *Mr.* Monday!" and then raced away up the road. This man, the older cousins told us, was a police officer who frequently patrolled the community. To this day, if a white uniformed officer approaches me, I see in my mind's eye Mr. Monday on that Nashville summer's day.[1]

This story has a rich history, dating from the days of slavery. Then, any white person had the authority to stop a slave to ask for his pass, or to correct any slave who he thought was misbehaving. A white man deputized for slave patrol could even kill a slave at his discretion. The story of Mr. Monday also fits within the tradition of Night Riders and White Cappers who intimidated and terrorized African Americans after slavery to keep them from voting or to punish those who prospered economically or seemed "uppity." This tradition of keeping African Americans in their place, through the awful and unpredictable power of the white man to harass and abuse them at any time—a power supported by the white community and the legal system—this reality was imprinted on my mind at an early age. Imprinted also by that one encounter was what years of teaching about the law and worrying about the enforcement of the law has only reinforced: the law has the force of violence, and the law can be irrational and prickly in the hands of its enforcers.

But I now know that everyone has stories, including lawyers, judges, and jurors. Stories provide a frame of reference that determines what each of us believes is true about the law. They also shape law and how it is enforced. The stories of African Americans like me and my cousins—our cultural frame of reference—rarely prevail. Rather it is white Americans' stories that judges and lawmakers accept, and that determine legal outcomes. William Pickens described in 1933 how the stories of those in control dictate legal results: "For generations in this country when a Negro came into court facing a white opponent, he had to settle not only the question involved in the charge against him as an individual, but also all the traditional charges against his race—in fact the whole race question. Like Socrates before his accusers, he had to face a jury which was influenced not only by the evidence just presented, but also by the 'evidence' that had been taught to them in their infancy, in their growing up, in literature, taverns, shops, and from a million other sources."[2]

Whose story counts in legal decisions rests heavily on who controls political and economic power, in a process that is circular and progressive. The stories of the powerful are the only ones that count, and the counting further enhances the power of the tellers in the economic and political arena. The exclusion of their stories reflects the historical silencing of African Americans. Because of slavery and Jim Crow, only in recent years have African Americans served on juries, been able to testify freely, been admitted to leading law schools or published in major law reviews or served on state and federal courts. Hearing and responding to African American stories is a radically new experience for many white Americans.

Another early experience embedded a narrative of class and racial paternalism in my consciousness. My uncle Lincoln was a scamp who teased and poked fun and played rough with his children and all the cousins. His playful pinches were so hard that they frequently brought us to tears. But he always had jokes to tell and pockets filled with an endless supply of candy kisses. When drunk, he was likely to end up in a fight and then in jail. Always, his wealthy white employer would obtain Uncle Lincoln's quick release with a phone call to the sheriff. Lincoln, his employer told everyone, was his "boy" and was just having fun; when sober, Lincoln was the best worker you could find.

Uncle Lincoln also fit within a historical tradition—the protection given the valuable black slave by his master. Such a slave could be punished—or, for a dire offense, put to death—only with his master's complicity and if legal officials adequately compensated the master. After slavery, paternalism still played a role. For example, African Americans could easily gain release on parole if some white person expressed interest in using them. Letters were regularly received by parole officials inquiring: "I can use a Negro full time. . . . I understand that the state is letting out prisoners on parole, if so I would like to get a Negro named— G—— W."[3]

Most Euro-Americans have not experienced motorcycle policemen trying to run them over, or the racial paternalism that protected Uncle Lincoln as the white man's boy. White Americans have their own stories, but these do not include African Americans' profoundly racist and discriminatory experiences with the law. They generally do not include police who are anything other than guardians. Their stories presume a system of evenhanded justice and of equality before the law. Court TV and other media of modern America have begun to familiarize white viewers with stories of African Americans. But white Americans, who have the power to control most legal decisions, only reluctantly credit stories that differ radically from their own.

Courts are a theatrical venue where disparate stories interact. In their halls, we hear the stories of the officers of the court—judges, prosecutors, and defense attorneys. These stories are shaped by thousands of years of common-law tradition and by intense professional training. They are the stories of an educated elite. But other actors fill the courts telling very different stories. Jurors— middle-class and working-class; male and female; black, white, yellow, and red—all have their own stories, as do the police, as do social workers, victims, and those who stand accused, who again represent a variety of classes and colors. The courts constitute an intense and dramatic microcosm of American society in which issues of life and death often hang in the balance.

Polls tell us what stories influence judges and lawmakers, who know the same stories they believe everyone else knows. Euro-Americans often think the poor are, for the most part, lazy welfare cheats and that women are primarily responsible for children and are weaker and less effective on the job than men. Polls also show that white Americans believe African Americans are less intelligent, less patriotic, less interested in work than they are; more interested in sex and a good time; and more prone to violent behavior.[4]

The O. J. Simpson criminal trial exemplifies the ways in which different racial experiences with the law produce conflicting stories about the law. It demonstrates as well the difficulty different groups have communicating through and around the stories they have learned. White Americans' responses to the Simpson trial were rooted in age-old stories of black male assault on white women, stories that date from the bloody Klan and the lynchings that followed the abolition of slavery. They were also influenced by a growing chorus of stories about domestic violence—male violence against women—stories that were about sexism and power, not racial antagonism. These stories intersected and reinforced white visions of the violent, sexually consumed black man. The polls show us that the confluence of racist stories and domestic violence stories—combined with the threat affluent blacks pose to the existing racial balance—led many white Americans to see the Simpson verdict as the story of a rich black man able to afford a pride of clever lawyers who, playing on a black racist jury, secured Simpson's acquittal.5

Christopher Darden, the black prosecutor in the Simpson case, acknowledged the importance of the injustice stories shared by African Americans in downtown Los Angeles. Of the majority-black jury pool for the case, he said, "It was a nightmare jury pool, a stagnant, shallow pool of bitterness and anger, and I couldn't say that I was the least bit surprised. The system itself had forged this jury. . . . In the molten anger of a million indignities and injustices, some collective and historical, some deeply personal, I knew where this jury came from." He understood, however, that the case needed to be tried in that venue, and insisted that "to move it would have been unethical and manipulative."6

Because the black jurors, like all jurors, would see the case in view of the stories they knew and told, Darden saw the problem as the system that conjured what they saw. The jurors' historical memory and present reality included white racist police who tamper with and even invent evidence or, like Officer Monday, set up situations that allow them to harass and convict African Americans, or even justify police assault on them, to reinforce their own stories of African American culpability. As Christopher Darden said: "We can't have a system that creates the prejudices and beliefs of these jurors—emotions that run much deeper than the Simpson jury pool—and then hope they won't show up when we call for a jury of peers." The prosecution hoped to appeal to the African American jurors by telling some different stories. Because of the Fuhrman tapes, the gloves that did not fit, and problematic blood evidence, their strategy failed. Even without the Fuhrman tapes, race would have been in the room, as it is whenever blacks encounter the legal system. However, without the tapes the word might have gone unspoken. In the Simpson case, as in any other case, the stories that judges and juries believe, the prevailing narratives, ultimately inform the decisions. Whatever view one takes of the Simpson verdict, controversy continues unabated because, in this high-profile case, the minority African American narrative of injustice prevailed—necessarily a novel, and to many Euro-Americans, shocking, enraging experience.[7]

The importance of racial stories was highlighted in February 1997, when a civil jury from the west side of Los Angeles awarded the Goldman and Brown families $8 million in actual damages and $25 million in punitive damages in their suit against Simpson for liability in the murders of Ronald Goldman and Nicole Brown Simpson. There were no African Americans on the jury, and the lone African American alternate, a woman who heard all the evidence, said afterward that she thought Simpson had been mistreated: "For the most part I felt Simpson was pretty credible." Reaction to the civil verdict split along racial lines; President Clinton urged everyone to respect the decision but said he was "troubled" that "Americans see the world differently, generally based on their race." He acknowledged the importance of stories—of the different racial experiences that make us see the world in different ways. What the President did not say is that the very same stories—stories based on different experiences—that divided public opinion also influenced the jurors, which helped to account for the different verdicts.[8]

Gendered frames of reference also determine verdicts, because they, too, provide stories judges and juries know and believe, and think everyone else knows and believes. In handing down a decision in his Baltimore courtroom on October 17, 1994, Judge Robert Cahill Sr. openly stated his views concerning appropriate male and female sexual behavior and psychological responses. After a plea bargain, prosecutors asked for only a three- to eight-year term for defendant Kenneth Peacock, who killed his wife several hours after he found her in bed with another man. Judge Cahill agreed that the sentence should be short; in fact, he reduced it to eighteen months. He sympathized with Peacock: he could not "think of a circumstance whereby personal rage is uncontrollable greater than this for someone who is happily married." The judge proclaimed that without a special-interest group such as Mothers Against Drunk Driving in the courtroom to monitor his behavior, he was free to sentence Peacock "in anonymity": "The chances are, this case will not even be written up."

Cahill soon discovered, however, that his gendered assumptions, which permitted killing a philandering wife, did not match everyone else's story. The press reported his actions, and there were public protests from women's groups. But the state's judicial commission held to Cahill's old story, finding that his behavior did not amount to judicial misconduct. Proving that the inclusion of women in the judiciary did not automatically establish a different story, one female member, Judge Marjorie L. Clagett of the Calvert County Circuit Court, agreed with Cahill's decision. However, two other women on the seven-member judicial commission dissented. Judge Teaette Price, of the Baltimore District Court, and Sandra Gray, a lay commission member, said the comments reflected "a stereotypical view of the proper or expected behavior of a husband who finds his wife engaged in infidelity." Cahill, unrepentant, blamed the media for stimulating unnecessary criticism.[9]

Those who want changes in the law must understand the impact of stories upon its operation. If the law is regarded only as a series of formal rules, reformers will focus their energies on changing the rules. They will then wait in vain for different results in the legal process. For example, rape-law reformers who opposed forcing women complainants to testify about their prior sexual activities worked to change the rules so as to exclude such questions. Despite the new rules, jurors and judges brought the same old stories about gender with them into court. Even after reformers thought they had succeeded, rapes continued and rapists went unpunished, even when the questions they had complained about were forbidden. Police, prosecutors, juries, and judges continued to act upon their prejudices about how women should behave.[10]

William Kennedy Smith's trial is a case in point, informed not only by gendered expectations but by class assumptions and stories. We must remember that gender is always "raced" and "classed." Men and women are always white, black, Hispanic, Asian, or Native American, and upper-, middle-, or lower-class. In December 1991, a Florida jury acquitted Smith of raping a twenty-nine-year-old woman at his family's Palm Beach estate. She reported returning to the family compound with Smith after dancing and drinking at a club where Smith had gone with his uncle, Senator Edward Kennedy, and the senator's son, Patrick. She said Smith walked with her on the beach, went for a swim by himself, and then, as she was walking back to the house, tackled her by the pool and raped her. The police report listed her injuries as cuts, bruises, and a possible fractured rib. Smith insisted the sex was voluntary and said the woman became annoyed when he called her by the name of a former girlfriend. The defense lawyers persuaded the judge to exclude the testimony of other women who had charged Smith with harassment. They then supported Smith's story by presenting two separate narratives, which were equally attractive to white middle-class America. First, they emphasized the story of Smith, the hardworking medical student. Second, they deployed class prejudices to paint his accuser as a promiscuous working-class woman. This was a woman who went to nightclubs rather than staying home with her children, then accompanied a man to his home, and, out for a good time, falsely cried rape.[11]

Eighteen-year-old African American beauty pageant contestant Desiree Washington's July 1991 charge that former heavyweight champion Mike Tyson raped her evoked different stories and a contrasting result. Tyson's defenders insisted that Washington's story was no more persuasive than that of William Kennedy Smith's accuser. Washington, who went to Tyson's hotel room voluntarily, was depicted by African American clergy and other political leaders who supported Tyson as a promiscuous woman and as a Jezebel. They believed that the jury could just as easily have found "exploitative sex, not rape." Tyson was convicted in February 1992, and sentenced to six years in prison. He was released from prison in March 1995.[12]

The Tyson case presented two narratives. The first was one that the legal system usually ignored, a black woman's complaint of male sexual abuse; the second was one that the legal system usually endorsed, the stereotype of the black male rapist, but this time the conflict was "unraced," because accused and victim were both African Americans. A story of class influenced the outcome: Tyson was seen as not just a black man but as a powerful black man being punished by the patriarchal racial system and tagged with the label of the sexually consumed black man.[13]

Sexual harassment suits show clearly that a mix of rules and personal beliefs and stories constitutes the law. When a jury or a judge decides whether a woman should prevail, the rules require an assessment of her speech and dress. They determine whether she appears as a sexually "aware" woman who welcomes sexual overtures. However, the meaning of "welcomeness" is determined by individual beliefs or stories about appropriate female behavior. The juror or judge who believes that women want sex from every man who might find them attractive may find polite conversation or wearing anything short of a shroud as "welcomeness" to men's advances. A judge who expects a woman to wear and say whatever she wants, without inviting sex or touching unless she asks for it, will be more discerning. When the woman is African American, the relevant stories have a cultural as well as gendered frame that evokes beliefs about black licentiousness. When the woman is poor, assumptions about the loose morals of the poor may affect the decision.[14]

The legal consideration of same-sex marriages provides another example of the importance of gendered frames of reference in the law. When the Hawaii Supreme Court decided in May 1993 that denial of a marriage license to a same-sex couple appeared to violate the equal protection clause of the state's constitution and that same-sex marriage might be permitted if officials could find no compelling state interest in rejecting it, a political firestorm erupted.[15]

The Hawaii court saw the denial of the marriage license as similar to bans against interracial marriage, bans outlawed by the 1967 U.S. Supreme Court decision in *Loving v. Virginia*. They saw the issue as equal rights rather than homosexuality. Same-sex couples could not use and acquire property in ways Americans who are free to marry come to expect. They were denied access to benefits obtainable by spouses in a legal marriage, including filing joint tax returns, sharing health insurance policies, being presumptive heirs, even obtaining a discount on a health club membership. The court explained that homosexual and same-sex marriages are not synonymous. There may be persons who are attracted to someone of the same sex but who are married to people of a different sex. There may also be people who are attracted to someone of the opposite sex who are in relationships with someone of the same sex. A married heterosexual may or may not be actually homosexual and parties to a same-sex marriage could be either homosexual or heterosexual. Thus, equality of rights should not depend on the sexuality of marriage partners. The Hawaii court used the rhetoric of the civil rights movement rather than the old story of man-woman marriage and patriarchal privilege. The state could not outlaw same-sex marriage as necessarily not "rooted in the traditions and collective conscience of our people that failure to recognize it would violate the fundamental principles of liberty and justice that lie at the base of all our civil and political institutions." This analysis only prevented the parties from claiming a fundamental right of privacy. However, they could claim a right to equal protection of the laws. Hawaii would no longer be permitted to refuse marriage licenses to couples merely because they are of the same sex, because the state constitution expressly prohibits discrimination against persons in the exercise of their civil rights on the basis of sex. The court concluded: "Constitutional law may mandate, like it or not, that customs change with an evolving social order."[16]

Daniel Foley was the lawyer for the first two plaintiffs in the Hawaii case, Joseph Melillio and Patrick Lagon. In explaining the decision, Foley underscored how the stories judges believe can influence court decisions. He thought a change in the frame of reference of the judges on the Hawaii Supreme Court led to his clients' victory. When he began the case in 1990, "the court was five men approaching seventy." But by 1994, there was "a changing of the guard." The result was a "baby boomer court with one woman, and that was a major difference." In addition, the political profile of Hawaii made it unlikely that these new members would have traditional, inflexible, gendered expectations. Hawaii was one of the first states to legalize abortion and approve the Equal Rights Amendment. Hawaii's voters were telling their judges and lawyers new nontraditional stories. The new judges heard the new stories. They sent the case back to the lower court for reconsideration based on their decision. The lower court reviewed the evidence and, in December 1996, decided same-sex marriages must be permitted. Its decision was scheduled for review by the Hawaii Supreme Court. However, opponents succeeded in passing a ballot initiative in November 1998 that permits the state legislature to ban same-sex marriages. Perhaps the judges were actually ahead of the story the public is willing to accept.[17]

Similar changes in stories involving the relationship between homosexuality and equal rights led the U.S. Supreme Court to strike down an antigay amendment to the Colorado constitution in 1996. A statewide antigay referendum adopted the amendment, which precluded all legislative, executive, or judicial action at any level of state or local government to protect people from discrimination based on their "homosexual, lesbian or bisexual orientation, conduct, practices or relationships." The referendum was adopted after several Colorado municipalities passed ordinances banning discrimination based on sexual orientation. In the Colorado case, *Evans v. Romer,* the Supreme Court decided that the antigay amendment violated the equal protection clause of the Fourteenth Amendment to the U.S. Constitution. Furthermore, the Colorado amendment raised the inevitable inference that it was obviously based on animosity toward homosexuals and had no identifiable legitimate purpose.

A Supreme Court majority consisting of Justices Frank Kennedy, David Souter, Ruth Bader Ginsburg, Stephen Breyer, Sandra Day O'Connor, and John Stevens thought it unfair that homosexuals alone were prohibited from seeking to protect their legal rights. This was a clear departure from the approach of the majority in *Bowers v. Hardwick,* which had upheld the punishment of homosexual sodomy under Georgia's laws ten years before. The *Bowers* majority had been replaced by justices who brought different stories to the court. Byron White, Warren Burger, Lewis Powell, Sandra Day O'Connor, and William Rehnquist made up the *Bowers* majority. (After he left the court, Powell publicly lamented what he regarded as his wrong vote in the case.)

Stevens had dissented in *Bowers,* while O'Connor switched to vote with Kennedy, Breyer, and Ginsburg. Her change of position is puzzling. Perhaps her views were affected by her affinity with Kennedy in almost every civil case, including the abortion decisions refusing to overturn *Roe v. Wade,* and by the perspectives of the new justices.

In *Evans v. Romer,* Justice Antonin Scalia, in dissent, joined by Rehnquist and Clarence Thomas, tried to foreclose any legal support for same-sex marriages. Scalia described Colorado's action as merely showing moral disapproval of homosexual conduct and put homosexuality in the same category as polygamy, which has long been illegal. His dissent relied on an 1885 decision rejecting a constitutional challenge to a U.S. statute that barred those who engaged in polygamous cohabitation from voting in federal territories. Scalia's story linked social order, liberal democracy, and a Western culture dependent on a traditional patriarchal nuclear family. He exposed his underlying assumptions concerning true social order by declaring: "Certainly no legislation can be supposed more wholesome and necessary in the founding of a free, self-governing commonwealth, fit to take rank as one of the coordinate States of the Union, than that which seeks to establish it on the basis of the idea of the family, as consisting in and springing from the union for life of one man and one woman in the holy estate of matrimony; the sure foundation of all that is stable and noble in our civilization; the best guaranty of that reverent morality which is the source of all beneficent progress in social and political improvement." His old patriarchal story is of the social contract—of the liberal republic formed by sovereign heads of households to protect the head's rights and authority. It goes back to Locke and even Aristotle, and it excluded homosexual relationships from equality of rights, unlike the new story accepted by the Hawaii courts.

Scalia's story proceeded uninfluenced by reality, ignoring the experiences of homosexuals and of social workers who pointed to the existence of happy homosexual families. He also ignored women's complaints and police stories of domestic violence and sexual abuse of wives and children in heterosexual marriages. He refused, as well, to engage the view of the Hawaii Supreme Court that equal rights, not homosexuality, are the issue. In the congressional debate over the Defense of Marriage Act (DOMA), which bans federal recognition of same-sex marriages and allows states to ignore gay marriages performed in other states, proponents used the patriarchy defense as their principal line of argument. The traditional family has stood for five thousand years, it was argued. "Are we so wise today that we are ready to reject 5,000 years of recorded history?" Senator Phil Gramm asked his senatorial colleagues shortly before they passed DOMA. Proponents were wedded to defining the issue as homosexuality rather than equality of rights.[18]

To counter the old stories, gay rights advocates described gays and lesbians as family oriented and no different from heterosexuals. Their attempt to gain tolerance and even acceptance of homosexual rights by presenting well-documented stories of lesbian and gay families with children is reminiscent of the successful suffragist argument for the Nineteenth Amendment: proponents of suffrage argued that nothing would change because women would vote like their husbands. The gay-family strategy is also reminiscent of the "politics of respectability" adopted by bourgeois African Americans after slavery, who hoped that by self-consciously adopting white middle-class values they would end discrimination and negative images of African Americans. (Even today this culture of respectability is seen in African Americans who will not go to the grocery store, even on vacation, without dressing as if they are on their way to church or a business appointment.) However, the use of such a strategy by gays and lesbians risks silencing those for whom homosexuality *is* an alternative lifestyle, which may include casual sexual contact with no committed relationships. In effect, the individual rights of gays whose personal stories emphasize their difference are marginalized and silenced in gay public pronouncements seeking same-sex marriages. In this sense, the new stories may be no more all-inclusive than the old.[19]

Anyone who doubts the importance of stories in the law should recall the confirmation of Clarence Thomas to the U.S. Supreme Court. Thomas used historical images of black men being lynched for alleged sexual transgressions to deflect Anita Hill's sexual harassment charges. The response to her charges showed the importance of gendered and cultural frames of reference discussed earlier. Even before his Senate confirmation hearings, the "Pin Point story" used by the Bush administration to sell Thomas to the public effectively insulated him from serious criticism. So effective was the strategy that Thomas's public record as a government official was almost totally ignored. The administration managed to cloak his black story with an extremely popular white story: a poor boy who rose from rags to riches through hard work and native talent, like Horatio Alger's heroes. Superimposing the Horatio Alger story on Thomas, the Republicans presented a positive racial experience, reinforcing the "anyone can make it in America" myth. In short, Thomas's Republicanism and his legal conservatism effectively "whitened" him for Euro-American consumption.[20]

Thomas's story, beginning with his birth in rural Pin Point, Georgia, a town of about two hundred residents that remains poverty-stricken like much of the rural South, was a publicist's dream. He was delivered by a midwife; the family lived in a five-room board house without a toilet or a telephone. Before he was two, his father abandoned them and left for Philadelphia. His mother, Leola Williams, supported her children on $30 a week, earned from picking crabmeat for five cents a pound. The family commonly ate grits, sprinkled with a little butter and egg or shredded crab. Shortly after their house burned down when he was about eight, Clarence and his younger brother, Myers, were sent to live with their grandparents in Savannah. Actually, he grew up in the home of his maternal grandfather, Myers Anderson, a well-off businessman, whom he came to call Daddy. Anderson had started a coal delivery business by fastening an iron axle and wheels onto a large wooden box: he later expanded into delivery of wood, ice, and fuel oil and the construction of cinder blocks used to build homes.[21]

The administration's "Up from Pin Point" saga highlighted Thomas's attendance at a now-closed Roman Catholic school for black children run by white Franciscan nuns. Thomas, a bright student, an altar boy, patrol boy, and athlete, who still contributes money to help support the nuns' retirement, is part of the story. Thomas was seen choking back tears on national television as he thanked the nuns shortly after being nominated to the Supreme Court. His mother's remark that this was the only time she could recall seeing him cry adds luster to the story. The story includes the incident when Thomas dropped out of seminary preparatory school because of anger over Martin Luther King's assassination. Abbot James Jones's recollection that Thomas "just felt he didn't want to be a priest" is ignored as a deviation from the story line. As the narrative proceeds, Thomas successfully negotiates elite institutions—Holy Cross and Yale Law School. The "Up from Pin Point" story was particularly attractive to white Americans, whose European immigrant grandfathers struggled like Thomas's grandfather to achieve the American dream. Thomas's *old* rags-to-riches story was infinitely more acceptable than Anita Hill's new feminist story of sexual harassment of a black woman. Whites and blacks could share in rejecting her claims, just as a working-class woman's rape claims against William Kennedy Smith were rejected, and just as black women's pleas against sexual abuse have been rejected through the centuries. Relatively unscathed, Thomas took his place as a lifetime Supreme Court justice.

The interaction between stories and the interpretation of legal rules is a process. We change the law not by focusing exclusively on formal legal rules but by changing the experiences, and eroding the myths and stereotypes, that underlie each person's stories. In this way we can make everyone's stories count. If we want to insure justice we must give voice and power to previously silenced narratives, remembering that what the law does is a part of everyone's personal stories. Otherwise the law has no validity and is an illegitimate exercise of power.

To change the stories requires action, not just analysis. The Fourteenth Amendment has been on the books since 1868, but has been used primarily to promote property rights rather than to protect human rights. World War II, with the threat of Nazism and communism, produced alternative stories, making it possible in *Brown v. Board of Education* for justices to reinterpret the Fourteenth Amendment and thus foster the civil rights movement. Gradually, jury composition was modified and new judges took the bench. What was previously screened out of the dialogue began to be heard. But the traditional racist stories Euro-Americans told one another were so powerful that they were not successfully displaced; the decline of the civil rights protest movement left the symbolism of formal rules changed while the reality of positive social change with respect to race was stalled. The modern women's rights movement imprinted different stories about gender, which led to *Roe v. Wade;* but much work to change gender assumptions remains. The gay rights movement has a long way to go in establishing new stories about sexual orientation.[22]

In order to secure justice we must work to undo our internalization of the Euro-American master's narrative. To do so we must understand the importance of storytelling and reconstructing history in making law. And we must be receptive to the alternative stories others tell, especially their stories about race, gender, sexual orientation, and class.[23]

This book aims to draw Americans' attention to storytelling and to expand the repertoire of stories we consider. Still, it cannot tell everyone's story. I chose to focus on narratives that deal with the intersection of race, class, and gender in their most graphic expression, since stories of what is forbidden and permitted sexually lie at the core of self-definition *and* definition of the other, of who has power and who is denied power. The stories African Americans tell about white justice and the stories white courts tell about African Americans are particularly instructive. Racism against African Americans established the model for racism in America. African Americans are the negative other against which all other immigrant groups seek to confirm their whiteness—be they Irish in the 1860s, Italians in the 1890s, Jews in the early 1900s, or Asian and Hispanic Americans today. The disputes discussed in this book are not fictional. They show how the stories of race, gender, and class believed by judges and juries and lawyers in the state appellate courts (until the late twentieth century these people were almost exclusively white men) influence the law. They also show how stories change and how they remain the same. They should help us to understand how justice and injustice are dispensed.[24]

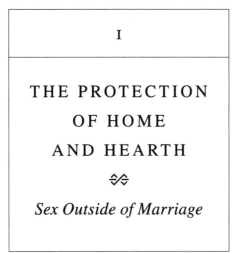

I

THE PROTECTION
OF HOME
AND HEARTH

⇌

Sex Outside of Marriage

E very legal consideration of sexuality is influenced by stories
of race, gender, and class. Judicial decisions concerning
heterosexual fornication, sex outside of marriage, have depended
on several interacting stories. They tell of the licentiousness of
African Americans, the purity of white women, the toleration of a
husband's sex with African American women, and the power of
white men to exercise control over their own sexuality and that of
African Americans and white women.

This interplay of stories was clearly displayed in the case of a
white Alabama husband, Matthew Turner. Despite the economic
hard times brought on by war and the abolition of slavery, Turner's
estate was worth nearly $400,000 in 1867. His wife of fourteen
years, Ann G. Turner, had brought little capital into the marriage
except for her excellent reputation. Everyone agreed, she was
"a chaste, . . . useful and obedient wife." One Sunday evening
in 1867, Mrs. Turner went to visit a near neighbor. When she

returned, "probably sooner than her husband expected," she found him "in adulterous association with . . . Sally, his former slave" in their bedroom. Mrs. Turner forgave her husband, but he kept Sally working at the house despite Mrs. Turner's "request to have her removed." Supported by the authority of her master, Sally became "insolent" to Mrs. Turner, who chastised her. Thereupon, Mr. Turner "upbraided his wife" and "forbade her to correct Sally in the future." Mrs. Turner replied that if Sally remained in the household, she, Mrs. Turner, would punish her for any insolent behavior. Matthew Turner's infidelity, Ann Turner's jealousy, and Sally's defiance created a drama of race, class, and gender dynamics that was played out in the courtroom.[1]

Turner, outraged at his wife's threat to disrupt his sexual access to Sally, "threatened to whip" her. He had Sally "go out and get switches for that purpose." He was a reputed wife batterer, but he did not actually strike Ann Turner on this occasion; instead, he made her "stand on the floor before him and his paramour, the colored woman Sally, and cower under the switches, which the latter had brought for the chastisement of her, the mistress!" Mrs. Turner now filed for divorce, on the grounds of adultery, cruelty, and abandonment.

Turner admitted having sex with Sally but insisted, despite voluminous testimony sustaining his wife's story, that Mrs. Turner condoned it. A lower court refused to grant Mrs. Turner alimony or even a divorce. The Alabama Supreme Court overturned the lower court's decision. Meanwhile, Turner went to Indiana, at the time a haven for easy divorce, and sued successfully to dissolve the marriage. To insure the payment of alimony, the Alabama court enjoined the couple's son, who sided with his father, from removing Turner's assets from the state and established a lien on the property.[2]

The Alabama judges drew upon a number of narratives as they implemented the formal legal rules that outlawed fornication. One narrative viewed sex between a white man and a black woman as of no consequence—indeed, as the continuation of an old practice condoned under slavery. A second story, that well may have influenced the judges, told of the chaste white woman, pure, faithful, and frail, in need of her husband's protection. White Madonna and black Venus mirrored one another in white men's sexual fantasies. Familiar with such stories, the Alabama judges saw no need to challenge Turner's concubinage with Sally.

They did, however, challenge his treatment of Mrs. Turner. She won her case because Mr. Turner deviated from the well-accepted story that gentlemen protected the honor of their families by treating their wives with respect and shielding them from knowledge of their extramarital, cross-racial affairs. Turner insisted on more than his wife's tolerance of his concubine. He demanded her acknowledgment of the situation—and more, her submission to Sally. He let his sexual passions turn the South's system of race privileges upside down. By repeatedly humiliating his wife in the presence of his black concubine, Turner had inverted well-established social and racial norms. He had crossed the line between acceptable and transgressive behavior. Having violated the script of Southern chivalry, he was duly rebuked by the court.

The legal treatment of heterosexual fornication depended on the intersection of stories of gender, race, and class in the shaping of sexual behavior. Such narratives, fusing sexual myths and fantasies, floated forward in time on a sea of assumptions that incorporated stories from slave pens in Africa, from the Middle Passage, slavery, emancipation, and the days of Jim Crow until they resurfaced in modern discussions of unwed pregnancy and family values, best encapsulated in the 1965 Moynihan Report. The rationale of African racial inferiority as a basis for disparate treatment has persisted from the colonial period to today.

By the late eighteenth century, distinctions of race and sexuality were firmly entrenched. In his *Notes on the State of Virginia*

(1781), Thomas Jefferson recapitulated the reigning narrative concerning the subhuman character of African Americans. Jefferson, a slaveholder, had an intimate basis for his conclusions. African Americans, he claimed, exhibited lower-order animal traits, with little intellectual capacity and a strong desire for sexual satisfaction. Their childish emotionality made them more concerned with "sensation than [with] reflection." For "love seems with them to be more an eager desire, than a tender delicate mixture of sentiment and sensation." His unsubstantiated conclusions accurately reflected the dominant story of African American sexuality.[3]

In the new American republic, stories filled with sexual imagery reinforced the subordination of women and African American men to the domination of propertied white males. In the 1800s, white middle-class women became defined as passionless creatures rather than as incarnations of Eve the temptress. Allowing themselves sexual license, white men defined respectable white women as the carriers of family virtue. The men feared, however, that white women regarded black men as their binary opposites, sweet but forbidden fruit. Therefore, they especially emphasized the sexual threat posed by African American males, and the need to control them. In keeping with their own desires, white men portrayed working-class white women as but one step removed from African women, that is, as sexually passionate and available. Working-class white women became increasingly vulnerable to male abuse. Black women, represented as excessively passionate enticers and seducers of white men and "oversexed black men," remained available and therefore "unrapable." The persistent interest in black male sexuality gained expression in the 1781 observations of a Pennsylvania military officer in Virginia concerning young black boys waiting on table, their "whole nakedness" exposed. The officer thought "it would Surprize a person to see . . . how well they are hung."[4]

The way white masters presented African Americans in public

and the limited control slaves had over the way they appeared embellished the stories. Black bodies signaled black subordination. White men displayed black women on the auction block, their bodies exposed, their flesh handled as beasts were handled. Black female slaves working in the fields, bodies visible through worn and tattered clothes, confirmed white portrayals of black women's lasciviousness. The African American male often appeared in a similar posture, physically exposed, represented as a stud on the auction block.[5]

The willingness of some white women to consort with black men was shocking to white sensibilities—but not unknown. A Virginia woman in 1815 refused to apologize for giving birth to a mulatto, saying that "she had not been the first nor would she be the last guilty of such conduct, and that she saw no more harm in a white woman's having been the mother of a black child than in a white man's having one, though the latter was more frequent." The 1830 U.S. census for Nansemond County, Virginia, reported eight white "wives" of free "Negroes."[6]

The antebellum North Carolina court chose with difficulty from among narratives of race and gender when two white men sought to divorce their wives because each gave birth to mulatto children shortly after their marriages. Both husbands had apparently had premarital sex with their wives.[7]

In 1832, North Carolina Chief Justice Thomas Ruffin denied the husband in one of those cases a divorce. He explained that persons who marry agree to take each other as they are. Nothing would be more dangerous than to sever marriage vows because of spousal disagreements or fights. Ruffin acknowledged that his decision for the wife collided with societal feeling against the acknowledgment of interracial relationships, which made "contempt for the husband so marked and unextinguishable." The stigma was so indelible that he had "not been able, without a struggle," to reach a conclusion. However, Ruffin explained, the circumstances made his decision easier. The couple married in December and the infant was born in May. Ruffin thought the husband must have known his wife was pregnant and had therefore had sex with her. His complaint, then, was not her pregnancy but the fact that the child was not white. By knowingly marrying a lewd woman, he became an accessory to his own "dishonor." He wanted a divorce because her "infamy" had become "notorious, though he could reconcile himself in secret to the crime which makes her infamous." Finding refuge in a biblical story, Ruffin explained that since the days of Solomon, "he who marries a wanton, knowing her true character, submits himself to the lowest degradation."[8] The court decision brought a storm of public protest. Thereafter, in the second divorce case, Ruffin aligned himself with white male power: it was unspeakable to expect a white man to keep a wife who bore a mulatto child. Concluding that the wife had engaged in nuptial fraud, he refused to deny the divorce. The outcome became a cautionary tale to warn white women against crossing sexual and racial boundaries.[9]

Stories of differential punishment based on race transformed perceptions and thus reconstituted reality. Characterizing sexual relations between white women and African American men as unnatural and therefore taboo, and ignoring sexual relations between white men and African American women, taxed reason though not custom: the visible fruit of interracial sex abounded. The 1850 U.S. Census included a multiracial category for the first time; it found 406,000 mulattoes, 11 percent of the country's 3,639,000 African Americans. By 1860, about 50 percent of the nonwhite population in New Orleans, Baltimore, and St. Louis consisted of mulattoes. While some mulattoes had mulatto parents, interracial contacts constituted a central part of their lineage. Interracial sex, though formally forbidden, was a story everyone knew.[10]

Mary Chestnut described households in which husbands abided

by convention while fornicating with slave women: "Like the patriarchs of old, our men live all in one house with their wives and concubines; and the mulattoes one sees in every family partly resemble the white children. Any lady is ready to tell you who is the father of all the mulatto children in everybody's household but her own. Those, she seems to think, drop from the clouds."[11]

Another powerful myth reinforcing stories of black sexuality became widespread: the notion that black men possessed massive genitals. White pornography reveals clearly the prevalence of white male penis envy. Studying this literature, two psychologists, Eberhard and Phyllis Kornhausen, found numerous scenes describing sexual relations between black males and white females in which the males always had a massive penis and were lovers par excellence. The books they examined illustrated the belief popularly held by Euro-Americans that blacks "are extraordinarily virile, sensuous, and given to all kinds of perversions." Believing that black males had more physical prowess, inexhaustible sexual appetites, and uncontrollable passions, many white males also believed they were sexual predators. In life and literature, it might be said without much exaggeration, the black male became America's phallic alter ego.[12]

Whites defined African Americans' sexuality to reinforce the validity of their subordination. However, at the same time African Americans sexually fascinated them. Many a white man's sexual fantasies, dreams, and desires were projected onto blacks, most clearly in fantasies about black women; for example, a white supervisor in a 1993 Louisiana case projected his desire for a black woman worker into asking her, repeatedly, if she had "gotten any," as he tried to fondle her. She concluded that he thought all black women "stayed in bed." James Baldwin describes the effect of such fantasies on the psyche of the racist sheriff in *Going to Meet the Man* who, impotent with his wife, lay there while "the image of a black girl caused a distant excitement in him." The image of the black woman as sensual, exotic, mysterious, and voluptuous predominated in the traditional sexual and racial mythology of the United States. Most white women were understood to be quite the opposite. While some white women might behave erotically, like African American women, those who did so, white men told one another, were most commonly foreign born, poor white trash, or just plain perverted—in short, evil, bad girls, who consumed male power. By creating antithetical mythological figures, the black Venus and the white virgin, the white man dehumanized both. He made the lusty black woman an animal and the frail, cold white woman a statue, the mere representation of a woman. The white woman became, in this story, endlessly prone to rape by that other black animal, the stud.[13]

The Mississippi Supreme Court held in 1859 that "masters and slaves can not be governed by the same system or laws; so different are their positions, rights and duties." The rape of a black female was not indictable "at common law or under our statutes." The case involved the rape of a black girl by a black male slave, but the same reasoning applies to the rape of an African American woman by anyone, black or white. The decision supported the idea that neither black nor white men were required to show sexual restraint with black women.[14]

By the end of the Civil War, these narratives of whiteness and blackness, of gender, power, and sexuality, were firmly imprinted in the public mind. Whites worried, however, that they would be erased. Some saw marriage as a way to channel black sexuality and to induce discipline in the lives of freedpeople. State laws legalized existing relationships, and Freedmen's Bureau officials urged African Americans to marry. Some did in group weddings, often picking from among spouses with whom they had established serial relationships during slavery. The churches played a major role in encouraging marriage; black and white ministers performed ceremonies. White acceptance of the story of licentiousness as part of "negro" behavior, however, left adultery among African Americans mostly ignored unless African Americans pressed for legal intervention themselves.

African Americans had another story: they accepted as valid the society's public pronouncements affirming the sanctity of marriage and keenly desired to legalize their relationships. The bigamy charges they instigated showed their concern. In Virginia between 1870 and 1883 twenty-two blacks convicted of bigamy were incarcerated at the state penitentiary. However, governors pardoned some offenders who did not understand the need for legal affirmation of divorce. In any case, most whites did not care what African Americans did among themselves so long as they worked hard.[15]

Even after Reconstruction, whites perpetuated the old myths of black sexuality to maintain the taboo against sex between white women and black men. White Southerners attributed an apparent increase in promiscuous interracial mixing to the emancipation of African Americans. To keep blacks in their place, they sought to reinforce the old story and to retain in force laws forbidding such relationships.[16]

The narratives that the law enforced received additional encouragement from "scientific" evidence concerning race and class inferiority. Throughout the nineteenth century, scientists offered theories to reinforce these stories. The English psychologist Francis Galton in his 1869 study, *Hereditary Genius,* contended that there were a large number of "half-witted men" among blacks who made "childish, stupid, and simpleton-like mistakes." Nineteenth-century scientists measured skulls to show that the brains of African Americans weighed less than those of whites.

During the nineteenth century, thirty-eight states enacted miscegenation statutes at one time or another to prevent the mixture of inferior and superior races. The main target of these laws' enforcers was not fornication but interracial marriage. The period around the Civil War saw the repeal of intermarriage bans in nine Northern states. By 1887, Indiana was the only Northern state east of the Mississippi with such a ban on its books. In the South, Alabama, Georgia, Texas, and Tennessee outlawed both intermarriage and fornication; however, Mississippi lacked a ban on interracial marriage between 1870 and 1880, as did Louisiana between 1870 and 1894. South Carolina made intermarriage illegal in 1865, then legalized it by implication under the 1868 constitution; the state legislated an intermarriage prohibition in 1879, but passed no law prohibiting interracial fornication. South Carolina did not punish simple fornication, although interracial marriage was illegal. Relationships between white women and African American men were reportedly rarer than those between African American women and white men.[17]

White male legislators continued to focus on white women who had relationships with black men. South Carolina's legislators banned interracial marriage in 1879, when reports reached their ears that twenty-five or thirty white women with African American husbands lived in the state; the couples had come from North Carolina, where the marriages were already outlawed. The state constitution of 1895 also outlawed intermarriage; however, fornication by white men with African American women remained unpunished. Virginia, Florida, Arkansas, Mississippi, North Carolina, and Tennessee banned interracial marriage, but no laws prohibited interracial fornication. Texas prohibited interracial marriage or cohabitation in 1858 and 1879. The courts in several states decided cases in which mixed-race couples were charged with cohabiting without benefit of marriage. There was no particular interest, except in Alabama and Georgia, in identifying interracial sex outside marriage as a crime distinct from living together without being married.[18]

Some African Americans and whites found bans on interracial marriage inimical to the new freedom story. In defiance of the bans, interracial marriages before and after the Civil War were numerous. In 1880 New Orleans, 176 white men reported their marriages to African American women. Most of the men were skilled craftsmen and professionals; only 15 percent were laborers; ninety-seven of the group were foreign born, twenty-eight from France. Also, by comparison, in 1880, twenty-nine white women reported marriages to black men. Seven of the black men were laborers; others were cigar makers, brokers, merchants, ministers, and gardeners; ten of the women and three of the men were foreign born.[19]

After the Union victory, observers in Mississippi reported a few interracial marriages. For example, a daughter of a slave owner insisted on marrying a former slave. When the quadroon mistress of a Mississippi planter refused to continue their relationship unless he married her, he complied. These marriages were quickly banned. The state law enacted in 1865 punished interracial marriages with life imprisonment. The 1871 Revision contained no intermarriage provision. However, the 1880 code included a ban with a fine of up to $500, or up to ten years' imprisonment in the penitentiary, or both.[20]

Interracial marriages also caused great concern in Virginia. In November 1870 a local newspaper reported that in a rural county a "disturbance" had occurred over an interracial elopement. A "negro" and the daughter of his employer began a liaison and eventually disappeared. One of her brothers took fifteen to twenty white neighbors to the "negro's house where they thought to find them." As they neared the house, someone yelled for them to stop. When they did not, some "negroes" inside fired on them. In the subsequent exchange of fire, seven whites and two blacks were wounded. The persons inside the house fled. Afterward, "wiser heads prevailed," ending the violence. The woman was "about 18 and handsome," and was "engaged to a respectable white man." The African American man was "much older, ginger and homely."

Local whites expressed amazement that a white woman would engage in such disreputable behavior.[21]

From 1878 to 1901, the Virginia state prison received seven prisoners convicted for interracial marriage in violation of the state law. Besides state laws several cities in the South had ordinances that outlawed interracial marriage, fornication, and cohabitation as a matter of local concern. Despite the laws, arrests for interracial cohabitation averaged thirteen couples a year in Nashville in the 1880s. Some had married; others had extramarital liaisons.[22]

To reinforce the laws banning interracial marriage, whites fostered stories of the natural unfitness of African Americans, explaining that antimiscegenation laws prevented the birth of disabled mixed-race children. A Georgia court expressed this rationale in an 1869 intermarriage case: "The offspring of these unnatural connections are generally sickly and effeminate, and . . . are inferior in physical development and strength to the full blood of either race." In 1881 the Alabama Supreme Court, in upholding the conviction of Tony Pace, a "negro," and "Mary Cox a white woman" for adultery or fornication, announced similar views. Pace and Cox were sentenced to two years in prison, while intraracial fornicators only paid a fine. The court feared that interracial copulation might produce "a mongrel population and a degraded civilization, the prevention of which is dictated by a sound public policy affecting the highest interest of society and government."[23]

Constraints on interracial marriage were not related to contemporaneous state initiatives, aiming to insure marital fitness as a public health measure. Legislatures enacted restrictions concerning age, kin ties, and mental and physical health. However, there was no evidence that unfitness resulted from interracial sex. The large mulatto population showed no particular signs of unhealthiness. The myth that interracial sex would produce a "bad seed" provided a convenient rationale for promoting the ideology of genetic inferiority and segregation.[24]

State supreme court judges, like the people whose views they reflected, perpetuated the story that mixed-race relationships undermined the social order. The targets of law enforcement were not elites. Those arrested for interracial sex, like those arrested in other sexual behavior cases, were mostly from rural areas, where everyone knew everyone else, and they were poor. The judges who decided their cases extended the antebellum story of good white women, bad white women, and inferior blacks.

Alabama courts provide one example of how Southern judges used antebellum, Reconstruction, and post-Reconstruction stories in their decisions. In an 1868 case, *Ellis v. State,* the unreconstructed Alabama state supreme court declared that racial intermarriage, illegal before the Civil War, remained illegal. The justices rejected the notion that either the abolition of slavery or the Civil Rights Act of 1866, which prohibited discrimination in the making of contracts, affected interracial relationships.[25]

The *Ellis* decision upheld the conviction of a black man and a white woman for violating the interracial marriage ban and applied differential punishment based on race. For same-race fornication, the law imposed a fine, permitting a prison term only if the fornication was committed three times. For an interracial offense, the punishment was more severe. The statute required imprisonment for not less than two nor more than seven years for the first offense. The court rejected the fine of $100 imposed on Thornton Ellis and Susan Bishop and instructed the trial court to order their imprisonment for not less than two or more than seven years. The Alabama Supreme Court explained that there was no discrimination, since a white man who fornicated with a black woman received the same punishment as the black woman, and a white woman was punished in "precisely" the same way as the black man with whom she had an "adulterous connexion." Ellis and Bishop erred in comparing their punishment with that of fornicators of the same race.[26]

The Southern Republican appointees who served as judges

during Reconstruction, however, were influenced by the new freedom story. They believed that emancipation and civil rights for African Americans included an end to bans on interracial sex. In *Burns v. State,* an 1872 case, new Alabama justices, who were Southerners but not ex-Confederates, controlled the bench. They declared the *Ellis* decision wrong. The race-mixing statute was unconstitutional under the Fourteenth Amendment and the Civil Rights Act of 1866, which prohibited inequality of treatment. By the reasoning of the *Ellis* court, said the decision in *Burns,* laws prohibiting the races from suing each other would be permissible so long as blacks could sue blacks, and whites could sue whites. But if blacks had the right to make and enforce contracts, they could do so with anyone. And "contracts" included the marriage contract.[27]

A local newspaper, expressing white reaction to the decision, urged another change in the court and the overthrow of Reconstruction. The *Selma Argus,* in a September 1874 article reprinted in other cities, complained that the valid fears about African Americans, which led to interracial sex bans, were discounted by Republican political aims. The paper complained that the "Radical judges" had voided the racial intermarriage laws of Alabama and that "Alabama had too many Negro voters"; it recommended that two of the offending judges, on the ballot for reelection, be rejected. Not only had a disreputable white woman degraded herself by marrying Burns but, the writer complained, the judges had also "prostituted" their offices for partisan purposes by refusing punishment. They had pandered to black voters, and now they were asking white men to vote to continue them in office although they had done "so much to bring reproach upon the state and shame upon the people." In the 1874 election, removing black political influence became the dominant campaign issue. After winning the election and redeeming the state, the legislature acted quickly to ban marriages between black and white persons.

"Redemption" turned the pages of law and history back to the old story of black inferiority and subordination.[28]

In 1877, the newly elected Alabama Supreme Court, consisting of Southern ex-Confederate judges, upheld the conviction of Aaron Green, a black man, and Julia Atkinson "alias Green," a white woman. The couple had defied convention by living together for several years as laborers on the premises of a white plantation owner. They possessed a marriage license signed by a local minister and by the local probate judge, who had held office during Republican Reconstruction. They had acted on the freedom story and would be made to suffer.[29]

In explaining the *Green* decision, the court claimed the interracial marriage ban benefited everyone. Without it, the "mongrels" born of such marriages would "overburden the poor," who already had too many problems. Furthermore, in the court's story, marriage created homes, the "nurseries of States," in which the family congregated and the young became "imbued" with ideas that "[gave] shape to their characters." Race mixing would introduce elements so "heterogeneous" that they would cause "shame, disruption of family circles and estrangement of kindred." The more "humble" a family, the more they needed protection of home and hearth from alien influences. In addition, the ban protected weak masters from the wiles of their nefarious employees. It deflected "all the secret arts, practices, and persuasions of servants or others upon the weak-minded or froward." Therefore, interracial marriage bans contributed to the "peace and happiness of the black race, as well as of the white." The court's decision fit within the framework of "diseased and seductive servant" stories, perpetuated since the beginning of time.[30]

The Georgia Supreme Court agreed with the Alabama judges. In 1869 they concluded that "the fortunes of war have compelled us to yield to the freedmen" many legal rights. "But we have neither authorized nor legalized the marriage relation between the races, nor have we enacted or placed in the power of the legislature hereafter to make laws, regulating the social status, so as to compel our people to meet the colored race on terms of social equality." No Northern states enforced social equality laws, the court said, and none would be desired by the "thoughtful" people of either race. Georgia behaved no differently from the other Southern states in outlawing interracial marriage.[31]

White men could have sexual access to African American women, but class played a role in whether the male's desire drew the attention of the law. Poor whites and blacks might find common cause in political movements if the ideology of black inferiority and segregation was undermined. Acting in a way consistent with this understanding, the appellate courts might punish poor white men charged with interracial fornication. They did not have the benefit of the license extended to privileged white men with greater resources. For example, Mississippi justices upheld a joint conviction of a poor white man and a "colored" woman for unlawful cohabitation in an 1887 case from Yazoo County. Witnesses saw them together in bed. Also, she had two mulatto children, and he "had been heard to call them his children." The court believed that such relationships threatened the narrative of "proper relations between the races."[32]

In 1870, the Texas Supreme Court took a similar approach, upholding the conviction of a poor married white man who lived in the same house with an African American woman and her small child. Everyone who visited could see that the house only had one bed—strong evidence of cohabitation. The Arkansas Supreme Court, however, tilted toward another side of the race and sex story when a man of higher social status was involved. They chose to endorse his patriarchal rights by ignoring evidence that a relationship involved sexual access. A unanimous court in 1877 reversed the conviction of Sullivan, a white man, and revoked his $100 fine for cohabiting with a "colored woman." Whatever the character of their relationship, the court concluded, it seemed harmless to the public morals. The "colored" woman, Laura Durham, worked as the cook and housekeeper for Sullivan's father. One witness testified that he had slept at the father's house. The next morning, after Sullivan left, the witness saw Laura Durham sitting on the side of his bed in a loose robe or gown, putting on her stockings. Another witness testified that their demeanor toward each other was curious. He saw Sullivan "help her on her horse, and had seen them take horse-back rides together."[33]

Given the difference in their stations, neighbors found their behavior "unseemly." Witnesses observed the two of them walking arm in arm; on another occasion, Sullivan held an umbrella over Durham. One witness testified that Sullivan's father asked Durham to leave "on account of her conduct with the defendant, and the defendant boarded her at various places where he visited her." After his father's death, Sullivan brought her back to the house. The local jury convicted the defendants, but the Arkansas Supreme Court found nothing illegal or fearsome in their behavior. The cohabitation law had two purposes—to prevent "public scandal and disgrace . . . but also to promote the institution of marriage." A privileged white man's sexual practices were a private affair. Public representations of sexuality, on the other hand, were subject to public scrutiny. Public displays had to conform to the accepted story of racial subordination.

To local people, the problem was not sex; it was that Sullivan's treatment of Laura resembled the respectfulness prescribed only for white women. The high court, however, emphasized that no one had presented evidence that Sullivan, even if he was having sex with Laura, sought public acknowledgment of their relationship. The court decided to fit the case within the principle that "the relationships and sleeping arrangements of households and servants were left to the employers to handle." The court found a way to give Sullivan latitude without rejecting an important mechanism of social control.[34]

Open defiance of the conventional story, however, could prove fatal. Robert Yerby's interracial fornication and respect for his lover were used to justify his murder. He "got into a row" in July 1875 with some of his Arkansas friends, who teased him about his African American concubine. He angrily responded that she was as good as any white woman and, "stung by the taunt regarding the negro woman," sent a written challenge to one of his tormentors. That night, during a "ruckus" between the comrades, Yerby was killed. The jury found his assailant guilty of manslaughter, but the appellate court disagreed. The justices thought that the circumstances justified acquittal on the grounds of self-defense. The state supreme court weighed the behavior of the deceased, declaring that he "had unfortunately put himself out of the pale of society by subjecting himself to the general opinion in the neighborhood of living in adultery with a colored woman; one who had abandoned himself to drinking, a man plainly of violent resentments and reckless of consequences." Worse, Yerby was "chafing under" his assailant's refusal to give him a meeting, and also under the "allusion to his woman." Essentially, Yerby inverted the social order. He treated his black lover as if she were a white woman; instead of accepting her status as an "object," he wanted her regarded as a person. He insisted that others give the respect reserved only for a white woman to her negative other, an African American woman.[35]

Those who challenged the narrative that pitted the black Venus against the white virgin and privileged whiteness could suffer other dire consequences. Interracial sex undermined the character and reputation of a white Texas wife and mitigated the punishment her white husband received for killing her. A court reduced the charge against him to second-degree murder, partly because she was a "bad woman" who had "lived with a Negro."[36]

When whites were charged with same-race fornication, the courtroom drama focused more directly on gender and class instead of race. Whites' cohabitation challenged several assumptions: that single women should remain chaste; that gentlemen should not seduce white women; and that a married man should avoid the insult to his marriage and wife occasioned by publicity surrounding an extramarital affair. As in interracial cases, judges strongly objected to relationships that appeared too open and thus too much resembled marriage. The 1880 case of two white South Carolinians drew this kind of negative reaction. Several citizens of the tiny town of St. Matthews, South Carolina, near Orangeburg, decided to end a long-term affair between Laura Smoak, a single woman, and Daniel Carroll, a married man. Forty-one persons "assembled in public meeting and passed resolutions" demanding that Carroll leave town or be indicted for violating the state law forbidding "habitual" sexual intercourse outside marriage. A heated dispute arose between Carroll and the complaining citizens because Dan Carroll did not want to leave town. He told the group he was willing to promise to end the relationship.

They insisted on something firm and in writing. At first, Carroll refused to sign a letter they had prepared, because he objected to the inclusion of his paramour's name. The group pressed him to sign, promising that would end the matter. Under protest, Carroll signed the letter, agreeing to "at once and forever abandon all connection with Laura Smoak."

When the couple continued their affair despite the agreement, the citizens' group had him prosecuted. The letter he had signed became a key piece of evidence for the prosecution because in it he confessed to his adultery. Carroll's brother-in-law, apparently angry at the slight to his sister, testified that Carroll had casually admitted the relationship to him. The jury found Carroll guilty and the circuit judge sentenced him to six months' imprisonment and a $200 fine. The high court affirmed his sentence. Smoak did not suffer prosecution; Carroll was married and therefore a more guilty party. Also, he had publicly insulted the honor of his wife's family. There was no duress involved; he could have refused to sign the letter, because he was "not under arrest at the time and none was threatened." Carroll had violated the code of honor, and neither he nor the Smoaks were wealthy or powerful enough to protect themselves from the wrath of the town.[37]

So important was a white woman's reputation, so critical was it to the maintenance of social order, community cohesion, and racial distinctions, that courts viewed favorably slander suits brought by white women accused of lacking chastity and therefore of being available sex objects. A North Carolina woman who had been accused of fornication or "whoring about" sued successfully in 1888. To prove her respectability, she took the precaution of having two physicians testify that, upon examination of her person, they found "all the signs of a preserved virtue."[38]

In 1889, concerned Georgia citizens brought a member of their Methodist Episcopal church in Corinth before a church committee on adultery charges in order to end his fornication with an unmarried woman. The woman's brother, a member of the same congregation, testified out of "moral and religious duty" that he saw them together. He also informed his parents of her fornication "in discharge of his domestic duty; for the good of his sister and the honor of his family." His sister successfully sued him for slander, noting that the circumstantial evidence did not prove sexual intercourse. She had to protect her social standing, which depended on her reputation for chastity.[39]

The reigning narrative that working-class and poor whites had inferior standards of moral behavior was so well accepted that judges accepted it as a defense in fornication cases. A North Carolina court overturned a conviction in the case of a man who had playfully struggled with another woman; the woman fell into his lap in the presence of his wife. The state solicitor told the trial jury this was evidence of guilt: "In refined society and [if] the female had a proper 'avenger' it would have put the defendant's life in jeopardy" to engage in such behavior. The defense counsel objected that the solicitor might be correct about the implications if the episode had happened "in high life, yet such acts of familiarity were common in that section among plain people," who regarded such behavior as "innocent sport." The judge then charged the jury, saying, "It is for you the jury to say if such acts are usual here." The high court found nothing wrong with this charge. The familiarity between the sexes confirmed the story of poor white immorality.[40]

The circle of social class and racial stories remained unbroken. Expectations that poor whites and African Americans would behave licentiously, and good white women with restraint and dignity, continued to inform basic legal and social narratives into the twentieth century. Heterosexual fornication was immune from punishment unless it challenged race and class assumptions or the sanctity-of-marriage story. Scientific racism and biological determinism reinforced and embellished the earlier stories. Increasingly, the new genetic focus tied Southern racist stories to a broader reservoir of narratives about the hereditary nature of poverty, ignorance, and immorality. Soon stories appeared that also featured Jews, the "Mediterranean races," the poor and criminal classes of Europe, and the colonized people of the world. The Italian criminologist Cesare Lombroso and others now weighed in to enlarge on the older stories and to endow them with "scientific" proof. Writing in the *South African Journal of Science* in 1929, Lawrence Fick, for example, declared that blacks demonstrated such a "marked inferiority" to Europeans that the number of Africans who could "benefit by education of the ordinary type beyond the rudimentary" was severely limited. After the Frenchman Alfred Binet developed a test in 1905 that allegedly predicted success in school, Americans quickly adopted it as a hard-and-fast measure of intelligence. Since the test questions focused on topics with which native-born middle-class white children were familiar, lower-class, undereducated blacks and the foreign-born predictably scored low. Almost immediately, scientists contended that these groups were inherently less intelligent. In 1926, Lewis Terman of Stanford University, who developed the widely used Stanford-Binet test, asserted: "Indians, Mexicans, and Negroes . . . should be segregated in special classes [because] they cannot master abstractions. . . . they constitute a grave menace because of their unusually prolific breeding."[41]

Scientific justifications for the subordination of women paralleled the support for racial stereotypes. In the early twentieth century, middle-class women pushed their way into higher education and the professions, or, as "typewriters" and store clerks, into the middle echelons of white-collar employment. With new roles outside the home and with salaries of their own, they began to experience greater social and sexual freedom. At the same time, scientists began to supply evidence to support the old story that all women were sexual predators. Circes and Salomes and, by nature, destroyers, women used the power of their sexuality to deplete the creative energies of white men. Popular culture and the movies reinforced these themes in narratives about women and African Americans. "Primitives," poor whites, laborers, and "peasants," as well as the "mentally inferior" races, were clearly evil; their social inferiority was genetically linked to their sinful lack of concern for the preservation of their spiritual capital and their indulgence in the lewd pleasures of the body. White men must act to control them, or social order and civilization would collapse. These ideas were reinforced by popular pseudoscience and the media well into the twentieth century.[42]

During the 1920s, genetics took an increasingly political turn, constituting the "scientific" underpinning of America's new racist immigration legislation. American racial theorists focused on the foreign born, but African Americans were not exempt. Racial theory was a worldwide movement, however, assuming one of its most extreme forms in Nazi Germany. As the horrors Hitler had perpetrated came to light, the scientific community withdrew its complicity. For a period, at least, biological determinism fell into disrepute. The nurture story succeeded the nature story. These new legal and political stories about human and civil rights also weighed in just in time for the Supreme Court, in *Brown v. Board of Education* (1954), to use the Fourteenth Amendment to outlaw separate but equal education.[43]

In the 1960s, prosecutors and the courts responded to changed attitudes and altered stories about sex, gender, and race. The major change involving interracial sex was to end interracial marriage bans. At the beginning of the 1950s, thirty-one states banned interracial marriages. By 1967, fourteen states had repealed such laws; only Southern and border states, including Virginia, still had them.[44]

In June 1958, the marriage of two Virginians, Mildred Jeter, "a Negro woman," and Richard Loving, a white man, in the District of Columbia, challenged the story that tabooed interracial marriage. When they returned to live in Caroline County, Virginia, they were convicted of violating the state's ban on interracial marriages and sentenced to one year in jail. The Virginia legislature had reaffirmed the state's interracial marriage ban in the Racial Integrity Act of 1924, passed during the period of extreme nativism that followed the end of the First World War. The trial court suspended the Lovings' sentence on the condition that they leave Virginia and not return to the state together for twenty-five years. In explaining his decision, the trial judge expressed familiar and long-standing attitudes expressed by courts when white men or women presumed to marry African Americans. He used a religious story, declaring: "Almighty God created the races white, black, yellow, malay and red, and he placed them on separate continents. And but for the interference with his arrangement there would be no cause for such marriages. The fact that he separated the races shows that he did not intend for the races to mix."[45]

When the Lovings appealed the order, the state supreme court let stand the trial court opinion, upholding the old story of the state's right to prevent "the corruption of blood" and "the obliteration of racial pride" by "a mongrel breed of citizens," despite worldwide repudiation of Hitler's version of that story. In 1967, the U.S. Supreme Court unanimously overruled the state supreme court's decision, calling it "obviously an endorsement of the doctrine of White Supremacy." Chief Justice Earl Warren, who wrote the decision, made clear that the old racist story had been eroded by social change. He stated that Virginia's miscegenation statutes, resting solely upon distinctions drawn according to race, were outmoded. America was now a nation "whose institutions are founded upon the doctrine of equality." To prevent marriage solely because of racial classifications violated the equal protection clause of the U.S. Constitution.[46]

Furthermore, the Supreme Court declared, the state had deprived the Lovings of their liberty without due process of law, in violation of the due process clause of the Fourteenth Amendment. They decided that the "freedom to marry or not marry, a person of another race resides with the individual and cannot be infringed by the State." In a period when sexual mores and the constraints imposed by race and gender were relaxing, interracial marriage bans had become outdated. World War II and the horrific racial misdeeds of Hitler's Nazi Germany had created a climate in which legal affirmation of black inequality was out of the question. The new environment that made *Brown v. Board of Education* and the civil rights movement possible had consolidated a new racial equality story. As a result, interracial marriage bans seemed ludicrous.[47]

Nevertheless, racial narratives continued to influence and inform judges and juries. Indeed, those who were threatened by the new stories reacted to reinforce and recycle the old inferiority stories in different forms. Intermarriage bans were unimaginable, but the old stories, it turned out, were not easily dislodged. Social scientists soon renewed the challenge to assumptions of equality. Columbia University psychology professor Henry Garrett claimed in 1961 that egalitarianism was "the scientific hoax of the century." The effort to enforce affirmative action in the 1970s gave currency to claims by the psychologist Arthur Jensen and the physicist William Shockley that blacks were naturally inferior and unqualified.[48]

Nor had the old narratives about gender disappeared, despite the second wave of feminism and the political women's movement. Gender stories remained mixed with stories of race and class; they could be seen in the new stories about unwed and welfare mothers. In 1965 the Moynihan Report on the black family popularized the thesis that African American inequality would remain an intractable problem until black licentiousness and sexual irresponsibility declined and father-headed families became the rule among the black poor. By the 1970s, increases in the number of children born out of wedlock elicited public condemnation of heterosexual fornication. The public emphasis was on black children and black unmarried mothers. Some critics decried the use of taxpayer-funded support for children born out of wedlock. Others focused on the sinfulness of extramarital sex. Single parenthood came to symbolize all that was wrong with America. Race, gender, and class stories interacted. To explain social problems, social science analyses reinforced a story of decline in "family values." During the Reagan era, pro-family rhetoric gained ascendancy as the number of divorces, remarriages, and female-headed households escalated and the youth culture eagerly embraced androgyny. Despite the availability of contraceptives, premarital pregnancy rates increased among whites and blacks alike. The religious right, reenacting the worst aspects of the nineteenth-century social purity movement, initiated a public movement against feminism, sex education, and gay liberation. They retold the old story of gender role differentiation and female respectability in a contemporary world.[49]

Their efforts to suppress the new "sexual freedom" story were only partly successful. In 1975, only 30 percent of the U.S. population objected to premarital sexual intercourse. By the late 1980s, despite concerns about AIDS, most people took premarital sex for granted. Greater equality between men and women affected popular attitudes, as did easier-to-use birth control methods. Interestingly, however, women were less accepting than men. The old, old stories about romance, love, tenderness, and intimacy, as well as the madonna/whore story, led many women to see sex as more complex than simple sexual attraction or a one-night stand.

The story of women's rights and sexual freedom influenced most state courts to decide that old fornication statutes violated the federal and state constitutional recognition of the individual's right to privacy. However, thirteen states continued to outlaw fornication between consenting heterosexuals. Courts in these states reasoned that repeal would signify approval of extramarital sex. These statutes, those judges argued, served as "sentimental signposts" representative of "better" days before the 1960s transformed sexual mores.[50]

Judge Harvie Wilkinson of the Fourth Circuit federal Court of Appeals mapped out the ways attitudes toward nonmarital and extramarital sex remained contested terrain. In a 1986 Virginia case, he noted that the courts had increasingly found that the statutes punishing fornication violated "the sacred component of privacy in sexual expression." They saw the laws as inviting the police into the "sanctity of the home or apartment" and as representing "antiquated attitudes about sex that bear little relevance to the diversity of individual lifestyles in a contemporary world."[51]

But many average citizens, judges, and juries, according to Wilkinson, saw the statutes as expressing "the value society places upon the life of the family and the institution of marriage . . .

the encouragement of sexual fidelity, and . . . the prevention of sexually transmitted disease." These people "discern in old laws renewed relevance as traditional values come under siege." Wilkinson concluded that "each view has its adherents, and the pendulum of social conscience will doubtless swing between the two indefinitely." State legislatures should make the choice, because they still bear the responsibility for public safety, health, welfare, and morals.

Rulings such as Wilkinson's honored local custom or moral symbolism above the right to privacy. They made it possible to advance race, gender, and class stories concerning appropriate behavior to harass single people and interracial couples, in particular, at the predilection of state and local police and prosecutors.[52]

In the 1990s, because of concern about out-of-wedlock pregnancy (concern built upon the edifice of the Moynihan Report) and popular rage over AIDS and drugs, the campaign against premarital and extramarital sex was extended, and the old stories, recycled by traditionalists, were reinforced. Politicians and opinion leaders promoted abstinence before marriage and redefined sex outside of marriage as an evil in itself.[53]

The legal treatment of heterosexual fornication shows how sexuality is connected to our notions of pleasure and power and to stories of race, gender, and class. We engage in sexual behavior because it is instinctual and pleasurable. Our goal of curbing it is based on our concepts of roles and relationships. Our ideal relationship is still marriage between heterosexuals of the same race and class. The easy acceptance of difference is still alien to many Americans. Anything that is contrary to or undermines the ideal is suspect. Some things, however, are more suspect than others. Deviation from the story line could result in punishment. Some people have engaged in voluntary sex outside or without benefit of marriage and remained within the boundary of toleration: poor whites having sex with other unmarried poor whites; blacks having sex with other blacks; wealthy white men and their black mistresses; husbands who were discreet. Others have suffered punishment—white women who had sex with black men; indiscreet husbands who flouted their marriage vows and insulted their wives; women who ended up pregnant, and the men responsible for their pregnancy. As social change infused more and different narratives of race, gender, and class into the discussion, the courts altered their responses and expanded the boundaries of toleration.

2

THE CRIME
THAT HAD NO
NAME

≋

*Narratives of Gay
and Lesbian Sex*

B efore the mid-twentieth century, the story of gay sex played a relatively minor role in the public imagination. Gays themselves did not press the discussion, and the legal system was no more eager to engage the behavior than society at large was to acknowledge it. When appellate judges confronted homosexuality in the postbellum period they referred to it as "that abominable and detestable crime" under the common law and statutes, too "foul" to detail in the pages of the case reporters. A Texas decision included references by the district attorney to a sodomy defendant as "a raving, vicious bull, running at large upon the highways," who should be "penned."[1]

A Louisiana court described just enough of the offense to justify a conviction, focusing on the reaction of the parties. Bourg and T. were on the front porch of T.'s house in Lafourche Parish, engaged in conversation, when Adolph Vicknair came along with his son Cyprien. In front of the house, Cyprien asked T. whether "he was trying to ruin" his family by complaining against the elder Vicknair. T. answered that he did not mean to ruin them. He had waited almost a year to report the offense, and he meant no harm to Cyprien and his mother, but Vicknair continued to misbehave. Adolph was a "damned dirty old fellow," and T. wanted to send him to jail, "where he ought to have been long ago."

When Cyprien asked what his father had done, T. replied it was so "awful" that he would rather have been murdered. When pressed by Cyprien, he responded that Adolph "s——d the ———— of my son, Ned until he has lost his mind." Adolph called him a liar and they exchanged harsh words. Cyprien insisted that his father's denial should be accepted: T. himself had admitted that Ned had "lost his mind." T. responded that Adolph had also "s——d" his other sons John and Jules, as well as one other person. Adolph admitted: "As to those three, I don't say no; I did it, but I swear on my honor, I have not done it to Ned."

Sodomy "committed with mankind or beast" had been outlawed by statute in Louisiana in 1805, and had been retained as an offense in the most recent code revision, in 1870. After 1870 there was some doubt as to whether oral sex was covered. An 1876 case gave no details of the offense. The legislative act of 1896 extended the definition of sodomy to acts committed with the sexual organs "or with the mouth." Therefore, Adolph Vicknair was convicted for "the detestable and abominable crime against nature," committed orally upon T.'s son Jules, who was fourteen years old in 1898, when the incident occurred.

The appellate court insisted that even had there been no change in the statute they would have upheld the conviction. It was "incomprehensible" that in the common-law courts, oral sex should not have been considered as much "against nature, as though the act were committed per anum." Vicknair's voluntary confession made his punishment certain.

The Louisiana court found it necessary to detail the exchange between Adolph, Cyprien, and T. to explain its abhorrence of oral sex. Their endorsement of the prevailing view of sex between men as "abominable and detestable," as sin and perversion, was clearly expressed.[2]

To apply the law to gays and lesbians, the courts had to augment the narratives of race, gender, and class among heterosexuals with an additional story of homosexual desire. Before the mid-nineteenth century, when their story was closeted—those who engaged in same-sex sex neither sought public acceptability nor threatened the values of marriage and family—their behavior evoked no sustained public attention and few attendant demands for legal intervention. Homosexual conduct was practically invisible in the courts before the 1880s. In their criminal laws, all but five of the thirty-eight states, including the eleven ex-Confederate states, prohibited sodomy. Most legislators agreed with a Delaware jurist who, in 1858, insisted that "pederasty" should not be addressed in a criminal code, because same-sex sex shouldn't be discussed at all. Only three states singled out same-sex sodomy, and the laws of thirty-two states ignored oral sex until the last decade of the nineteenth century. However, all states prohibited anal intercourse, whether homosexual or heterosexual. Male homosexual behavior has been known throughout human history; it was condemned in canon and civil law and was a capital offense in English common law. Although lesbianism was well known, the focus of the law and society was on male organs and male sex, and on the relationship of sodomy to the religious story concerning the sinfulness of men having sex with other men.[3]

In the nineteenth century, race and social-class distinctions influenced who was arrested and prosecuted for homosexual offenses. Among the small number of prisoners incarcerated for homosexual sex, African American men were disproportionately represented. Early evidence shows an inclination to sanction black men for "unmanly" behavior that undermined racial stereotypes.

The U.S. Census for 1880 enumerated the prison population, including those jailed for "the crime against nature," defined as sodomy, buggery, or bestiality. Thirty of the sixty-three prisoners were described as "colored."[4]

A similar pattern existed in the 1890 Census enumeration of offenses against public morals, including the "crime against nature." Of 224 such crimes reported, 78 were committed by "colored" violators, including 2 Chinese and 76 African Americans. Only six appellate cases were reported in digests before 1900. Judges, and not just those in Texas and Louisiana, puzzled over the inclusion of oral sex along with anal sex as a "crime against nature."[5]

Just as science reinforced public thinking about race, gender, class, and heterosexual behavior, so it played a role in developing a narrative that required urgent legal attention to homosexuality. As Michel Foucault explained, nineteenth-century psychiatry, jurisprudence, and literature advanced a whole series of discourses on the perversity of homosexuality. These nineteenth-century discourses rationalized legal action to control homosexual behavior in order to protect heterosexual relationships. In response, gays began to speak on their own behalf, to demand that their legitimacy be acknowledged; often they used the same vocabulary and the same categories by which their behavior was medically disqualified. The stories gays developed to explain their own behavior only gradually emerged into public view.[6]

In the 1880s in the United States, and somewhat earlier in Europe, physicians began writing about inverted sexual impulses, which had long been the province of law and religion. Echoing the unscientific claims of ancient writers concerning male and female homosexuality, they described sodomy and the "crime against nature" as evidence of disease. Practitioners of a new medico-scientific field of investigation, sexology, focused on the study of male homosexuality. Their approach, as one aspect of late-nineteenth-century scientific determinism, social Darwinism, and eugenics, emphasized the need to categorize the behavior.[7]

The leading spokesman for sexology in nineteenth-century Europe was the German neurologist Richard von Krafft-Ebing. He saw homosexuality as an organic disease, not as evidence of immorality or sin. In his seven-volume *Studies in the Psychology of Sex,* published between 1897 and 1928, the English sexologist Havelock Ellis explained that sex was a natural part of life and emphasized gratification instead of self-control. He tried to remove the stigma attached to homosexuality, describing it as congenital, as natural to those who were homosexual as heterosexual sex was to heterosexuals. He therefore opposed sodomy laws, and he vigorously protested the conviction of Oscar Wilde. Sigmund Freud's visit to the United States to lecture in 1909 and the subsequent dissemination of his views led to the understanding that the sexual impulse is an insistent force that demands expression and must be satisfied. However, Freudianism left the implication that homosexuality was an acquired, treatable condition.

The work of the sexologists and scientists, a new departure from the sin and perversity stories, opened possibilities for gays to express themselves. But there were also countervailing pressures against liberalization in the society. Euro-American concern about race suicide, fears of the "New Woman," who might not reproduce, and fear of the different all contributed to suppression. In a period of a gradual shift to a consumer economy and huge corporations, large-scale urbanization, and immigration, Robert Weibe explains, there was a search for order.[8]

However, the spread of a capitalist economy and the growth of large cities began to allow homosexual desires greater expression. Wage labor allowed men and women to detach themselves from families. In the cities, homosexual meeting places and an underground culture developed, supplanting the passionate friendships of the nineteenth century and the isolated female couples in which one of the women passed as a man. Between 1880 and World War I, doctors reported learning from their patients of the existence of networks in every large city. The meeting places were venues in which young people on their own were somewhat shielded from respectable society—boardinghouses, red-light districts, transvestite clubs that paid the police for protection, and military bases.[9]

Because the behavior remained mostly clandestine, the legal story of sin and perversity did not change and there was no pressure for it to change. In the few court cases concerning gay men after the turn of the century, judges routinely called gay male sex immoral, vile, and detestable. In 1916, the Georgia appeals court showed the usual tentativeness about describing homosexual behavior when it heard the appeal of Comer Jones of Sumter County, who had been convicted of sodomy. The judges noted only that Jones had performed oral sex on Ernest Walker, "who was then and there a man." Walker was not culpable: he was only enjoying the sexual services of Jones, who was the pervert. The court upheld Jones's conviction. However, the judges did not hesitate to express their pain in making explicit the grounds of the conviction: "Unpleasant as it is to discuss a case of this disgusting character, it is nevertheless necessary to some extent." A conviction could not be sustained without at least a statement on the record of what Jones had done.[10]

Same-sex sex did not yet appear to threaten marriage or gender roles enough to warrant a wholesale law enforcement campaign. During World War I, military officials court-martialed men for committing homosexual acts, and there were some egregious episodes of persecution of homosexual men. There was no effort, however, to identify homosexuals so as to exclude them from enlistment.

The story of homosexuality was of members of the avant-garde leading a risqué lifestyle, much as if getting high on illegal alcohol or drugs—a story gays themselves would not expect the public to accept. New York City gays were ubiquitous in the 1910s and 1920s in every public sphere, although they remained hidden in a shadow world of masquerades, coded gestures, and double entendres. The general air of sexual liberation and the bachelor culture of immigrants widened public space for gays. The Great Migration northward of African Americans nourished the Harlem Renaissance, and with it a uniquely African American gay and lesbian culture, during the 1920s. However, that was not the whole story. The Red scare and the banning of "un-American" foreign works by the Treasury Department, including such books as the famous lesbian novel *The Well of Loneliness*, made the post–World War I era in America a time of censorship, especially with respect to sex.[11]

The legal repression of homosexuality grew; six appellate cases had been recorded before 1870, while about two hundred cases were decided nationally in the first half of the twentieth century. The numbers remained small compared to the numbers of other offenses. For example, of the 7,721 felony arrests in Chicago in 1908, only 73 were for "the crime against nature." In 1909, there were 31 out of 6,460. The story appellate judges told still emphasized their awareness that sex—especially when perverted—should remain outside polite discourse. As in Comer Jones's case, judges were reluctant even to discuss such a "disgusting" subject.[12]

In the 1920s and 1930s, as the narratives concerning women and African Americans began to include more positive images, gender and racial distinctions became less confining. However, interest grew in making homosexual boundaries tighter. The same urbanization and war that allowed more gender and race contact allowed more interaction among mobile homosexuals. As they became more visible, homosexuals seemed to threaten appropriate gender roles and norms of sexual behavior. The rising visibility of homosexuals led to a perception that heterosexual identity needed protection. Society clung to the old story of perversion and evil rather than developing a more positive narrative.

In the small number of reported cases between 1900 and 1930 in which gays appealed convictions for "the crime against nature," the stories they presented avoided claims to the acceptability of homosexual sex or the rights of homosexuals. They insisted, instead, on due process, in accord with the emerging emphasis on civil liberties protection by the states under state constitutions or the Bill of Rights in the federal Constitution. The defendants' convictions were usually upheld. However, to insulate against reversal, judges found it necessary to permit in their courts, and to include in their opinions, expanded descriptions of the offense, even while making clear that it was "detestable." In 1915 the California Supreme Court detailed the "pederastic performance" of the accused while stating that "every consideration of decency" means that we "purposely refrain from reproducing herein the sickening results of the examination of the parts of the bodies of the two men," described to the jury by the doctors called in by the police to examine them after their arrest. A Missouri court expansively described Barto Hubbard's 1926 offense as taking "a certain negro boy" into an alley and "wickedly and feloniously inserting his penis or sexual organ into the mouth" of the victim. The Illinois Supreme Court described a defendant as "exposing his privates" to a boy. The New Jersey Supreme Court described how the defendant "wickedly, diabolically, and against the order of nature" committed the "detestable and abominable crime of buggery."13

However, courts willingly used class considerations as well as more positive stories to aid defendants. For example, in 1915 the California Supreme Court reversed a conviction for attempted sodomy upon a sixteen-year-old male. The sixteen-year-old lived in a residence large enough to accommodate his family, a grandmother, an uncle, and a housekeeper, who had separate accommodations of her own. The court described the fifty-six-year-old defendant as a friend of the family, who had frequently visited the house. He often played "innocent games" indoors and on the lawn with the teenager. The justices released the defendant, who was accused of soliciting the teenager when the two went to the bathroom together to wash their hands after playing tennis. The court also called attention to the "big brother movement," in which "thousands of men throughout the country are systematically cultivating the friendship of boys" to aid in their development of the "best qualities." A man should not be convicted of "degrading crimes upon mere suspicion," even if the youth supported the complaint. A dissenter in the case thought the majority opinion was absurd. He did not accept the new stories. The housekeeper saw the two enter the bathroom together; they locked the door, then stayed for at least five minutes more after she made a noise at the door. This judge saw no reason why the two should go to the bathroom together in the first place. Furthermore, the man told a police officer, "It is his word against my word." The dissenter believed this statement was not that of an innocent man falsely charged with an "unspeakable" crime.[14]

In the 1930s, homosexuality was still so despised that the Army and Navy used testing and induction physicals to keep homosexuals out of the military. Interviews at induction physicals included such questions as "Did you ever have a homosexual experience?" *Newsweek* reported that it was easy to identify a gay man in a three-minute interview, thanks to his "effeminate looks and behavior." Yet, the magazine complained, "scores of these inverts" slipped through. But the massive mobilization after Pearl Harbor forced the military to accommodate homosexuality, at least temporarily. The Surgeon General's Office said that homosexual relationships could be tolerated so long as they were private and consensual, establishing what amounted to a "Don't ask, don't tell" policy. However, gays could obtain their release from the service if they admitted their homosexuality and underwent special board hearings, hospitalization in the psychiatric ward, or undesirable discharges with no benefits. Those who stayed in and avoided the military police often enjoyed a better off-duty social life than they had had at home. The gay bar scene during the 1940s began to expand outside large cities, as gays and lesbians sought public space and institutions of their own.[15]

In the war years few cases were prosecuted or appealed, but those decided by the appellate courts showed the continued influence of the old story of sin and perversion. They also showed the impact of civil liberties reform, in the trend toward greater description of the offense charged in order to show that due process had been afforded the defendant. In an opinion that the Comer Jones court would have found shocking, the Georgia Supreme Court in 1949 reversed a conviction because the indictment stated only that the accused had "carnal knowledge and connection, against the order of nature, and in an unlawful manner," with another man. The court denounced the conduct with the usual pejoratives—"distasteful" and "vile." However, it stated, due process requires a "somewhat full discussion" of the crime. They would discuss it without "unnecessary indelicacy of expression." Also, courts, no matter how disgusted, could not consider "the esthetics or lack of esthetics" of a crime. The new civil liberties protection story demanded more open discussion in these cases, which were, according to the court, "fortunately rare."[16]

After World War II, gays were ushered back into the closet, just as women and blacks were forced out of occupations they had gained during the war. When Johnny came marching home after V-E Day and V-J Day, his job and the pressure to establish a heterosexual family were waiting for him. As they were pushed out of the paid workforce, women were told that a new critical job awaited them: child-rearing. Repopulating the nation after depression and war became a patriotic duty for all Americans. At the same time, the Kinsey Reports on male and female sexual behavior increased awareness of the variety of sexual experience; but the reaction to the research underscored negative attitudes toward homosexuality. The duty to produce families militated against sexual freedom for homosexuals. Unsurprisingly, the Kinsey Institute lost most of its funding in 1954, when conservatives denounced its findings—especially the report on the high incidence of homosexual behavior—as a threat to national morality. Public awareness of the subject was mixed. When a Gallup poll in the summer of 1953 asked, "Have you heard or read anything about Dr. Kinsey and his studies on sex?," 42 percent answered yes, while 58 percent said no.[17]

Some gays adopted the story of homosexuality as a perversion and illness in an attempt to avoid punishment when arrested for having sex. Controversy over commitment to psychiatric institutions for treatment of the "illness" of homosexual behavior became more prominent. There was a growing public interest in psychopathic sex crimes which began before the war, subsided for the duration, and reoccurred for a short time thereafter. Interest in sex crimes arose from heterosexual misconduct, including pedophilia and murder. Soon state and local governments passed laws transferring authority to control deviant behavior to psychiatrists and creating institutions to treat "sexual psychopaths," who were determined to engage in criminal behavior because they could not control their feelings.[18]

During the war, media attention shifted away from sex crimes, although arrest rates remained high. After the war, with the emphasis on protecting the family, a resurgence of interest in sex crimes occurred. Media discussion of sex crimes in the period after the war led Gallup to poll public opinion on the subject. A February 1953 Gallup poll asked, "Do you think the press should or should not be allowed to attend and report on all trials dealing with sex crimes?" Fifty-nine percent of respondents answered "should," 31 percent answered "should not," and 10 percent had "no opinion."[19]

After World War II, legislatures passed new "sexual psychopath" laws in response to the recommendations of legal reformers. The laws provided that when the prosecution thought an accused was a "criminal sexual psychopath," they could file a petition asking that the issue be determined. After the accused was examined by psychiatrists, the jury would decide whether he or she was indeed a criminal sexual psychopath. A person who was committed as a criminal sexual psychopath, but later was determined to have recovered, would stand trial on the criminal charges.[20]

In a typical case in which a gay man tried to use the illness story to his advantage, Russell Sellers claimed psychiatric problems to avoid punishment for sodomy. He was observed by police from behind a wall, having sex with another man through a "glory hole" in the partition between two stalls in a restroom with doorless stalls. The California courts routinely affirmed convictions in such cases until a 1973 decision accepting the civil libertarian argument that surreptitious restroom surveillance violated an expectation of privacy. Sellers based his unsuccessful appeal on the argument that the court should have allowed a physician specializing in neurology and psychiatry to examine him. He argued that a person accused of sex crimes other than sodomy could introduce evidence showing whether he had a tendency toward the claimed behavior. Therefore, Sellers claimed, the court should permit him to introduce expert testimony that he was not a homosexual. His lawyer conceded that there were no precedents supporting this argument. The California Supreme Court approved his conviction for "toilet sex" in 1951. The judges explained that the law did not distinguish between the types of persons who committed the act charged. Sodomy was a punishable offense whether the person was "normal or abnormal."[21]

Utah's high court was willing to define homosexuality as psychopathic because to do so reinforced the story of perversion and evil and threatened no family values. When the judges considered Grant Cooper's conviction for fondling an eleven-year-old boy in 1949, the justices tried to prod the legislature into passing a "sexual psychopath" law. Noting that other state legislatures had provided treatment for child abusers, whether heterosexual or homosexual, the court found that congenital and, "to a certain extent," psychopathic homosexuals could be totally "unresponsible" for their acts. The court understood that "such persons cannot be left to prey upon society, and particularly upon young children." However, "the wisdom of declaring their conduct to be criminal may be seriously questioned." The judges suggested that "in the light of advanced biological and medical knowledge, the legislature might well provide for their confinement in sanitaria for necessary treatment." Unfortunately, the legislature had not done so. So the court was forced "to accept the legislative mandate." The justices upheld Cooper's conviction.[22]

Utah's legislature did not act, but in 1952 Pennsylvania enacted a law that identified homosexuals as eligible for treatment along with other types of sex offenders. According to the law, following the defendant's psychiatric evaluation a judge could impose an indeterminate sentence if he or she found that the person might threaten bodily harm or was a habitual offender or mentally ill.[23]

During the Cold War the homosexuality story acquired embellishment: not only was homosexuality a perversion, which undermined heterosexual marriage, but it threatened national security as well. Anticommunist crusaders insisted that homosexuals in government were possible targets of blackmail. A Senate committee report in 1950 declared the presence of homosexuals in government service a security concern. In 1953, the Eisenhower administration barred gays and lesbians from all federal jobs. Police sweeps through gay bars produced large numbers of arrests. In a way reminiscent of the Red scare, as a result of intelligence investigations thousands of alleged homosexuals were discharged from the military in the 1950s. Unmarried men and women were likely to be accused of homosexual orientation.[24]

In response to harassment, gays began to speak in their own behalf, to tell their own stories. They told stories of routine lives, of social responsibility, of economic responsibility, and of their right to wear clothing styles that would not mask sexual orientation. They wanted gays to insist on their due process rights as homosexuals in the courts, rather than accept punishment in the hope of avoiding disclosure when they were harassed and arrested. After testifying before the House Un-American Activities Committee, Harry Hay and others organized the Mattachine Society in Los Angeles around 1950. Their first legal case involved one of the founders, Dale Jennings, who had been entrapped into lewd behavior in a Los Angeles park. Most gay men under such circumstances pleaded guilty and avoided trial. Jennings entered a plea of not guilty; his trial ended in a hung jury. The district attorney decided not to pursue charges.

In 1955, Del Martin and Phyllis Lyon formed the first lesbian organization, the Daughters of Bilitis (DOB), in San Francisco. Soon, chapters of Mattachine and DOB sprang up around the country. Both groups were social organizations, but they also held educational events at which lawyers and psychiatrists spoke and disseminated publications to change the narratives about homosexual behavior. DOB and Mattachine promoted middle-class respectability, not confrontation. They combined an emphasis on civil liberties with an effort to change the perception of gays by telling a different story about the reality of who homosexuals were and about the validity of their lives.[25]

Gay and lesbian activists, along with devotees of civil libertarian causes, worked hard to change the stories concerning consensual behavior. While the federal government aggressively attempted to suppress homosexuals, New York State began to decriminalize consensual sex as part of a reform package including family violence to substitute healing of the family for punishment by the courts. In some cases, the move away from punishment extended to the treatment of consensual homosexual sex that took place in venues other than bars. In a 1952 sodomy decision, the state's highest court, the Court of Appeals, began to decriminalize private consensual homosexual acts. The court reversed the sodomy conviction of a teacher who had taught in private schools for boys for twenty-five years. He was accused of an act of sodomy with one of his twelve-year-old boarding school pupils. The judges found insufficient evidence that the student did not consent to the sex; consent made him an accomplice. The teacher admitted that he was "fooling with the boy," that he "pushed him down on the bed," and that he was asked to stop but did not relent. He also admitted that he told the pupil to "go downstairs easy" so the school commandant would not hear him leave the room. There was also testimony that on several occasions the teacher gave the student money. The court concluded, however, that to convict the teacher, the boy's testimony required corroboration, which the prosecutor was unable to supply. The decision, based on legal rules of procedure and evidence, made it less likely that private consensual homosexual acts, among certain social classes, would lead to conviction in New York. Stories of consent and due process would outweigh an emphasis on the "detestable" nature of the sex.[26]

In most states, the law mainly concerned itself with men arrested for sex in toilets or other public places, and with bar owners charged with running disorderly establishments. The importance of the bar as a gay and lesbian social institution cannot be overstated. Whereas DOB and Mattachine emphasized respectability as a route to acceptance and disdained the bar culture as unseemly, bars invited nonconformity, which could lead to police harassment. In a 1951 California case, the state supreme court granted gays a major victory by declaring that bar owners could not lose their licenses for merely catering to homosexuals, without proof concerning the patrons' conduct. The law and law enforcement changed gradually in other states. However, beginning with the California decision, the story that a bar was frequented by people who were thought to be homosexual was no longer enough to bring legal retribution. Sol Stoumen, the owner of the Black Cat in San Francisco, was charged with permitting his premises to be used as a disorderly house for purposes injurious to public morals. Allen Ginsberg described the Black Cat as "the greatest gay bar in America": "All the gay screaming queens would come, the heterosexual gray flannel suit types, longshoremen, all the poets were there."[27] For fifteen years, beginning in the 1940s, Stoumen fought the state liquor board to stay open.

The California courts held in favor of the Black Cat, deciding that in order to close down a bar or punish the owner, some sex act or solicitation to commit one had to be shown. The court reasoned that if a liquor license could not be revoked because "prostitutes had dined in [the] restaurant" holding the license, and if bawdy-house convictions were rejected when based on nothing but the residence of "women of loose or immoral character," then the owner of the Black Cat could not lose his license for serving homosexuals. In bawdy-house cases, the court had found that such women are "human beings entitled to shelter and that it is not a crime to give them lodging unless it is done for immoral purposes." The Black Cat court announced that the same reasoning applied to homosexuals. Their presence in public at a bar, like the appearance of heterosexuals, needed no further explanation than a desire to drink and socialize. The court accepted a narrative that gays should be treated by a standard of behavior applied to everyone else, rather than a presumption that they were involved in illicit conduct. The court insisted upon the individual freedom story, which had gained currency through the due process revolution, rather than on the sinfulness-of-homosexual-behavior story.

When convicted of running a disorderly establishment, the owner of Bernard's Bar and Grill at 110 West Fifty-second Street in New York City won an appeal based on the new narrative expressed in the Black Cat precedent. A police officer testified that ten men at the bar were "hugging one another and rubbing their knees and arms against the private parts of one another." They also used "endearing terms in addressing each other." When questioned about the nature of the bar, the owner replied: "Some guys run a whore joint, and I run this kind of a joint." Since no solicitation took place and the police officer could not say whether those present at the bar were homosexuals, the judges would not accept the conclusion that the owner ran a disorderly place within the meaning of the statute. This court, too, applied the due process narrative rather than the sin and perversion narrative.[28]

Police in some cities continued to harass businesses that served lesbians and gay men—especially bars, restaurants, coffeehouses, and after-hours clubs, without closing them down. Many of these businesses paid off the police in return for promises of reduced harassment and warnings about raids. Police justified their surveillance and occasional arrests, like the ones at the Philadelphia Humoresque coffeehouse in 1959, as based on disorderly conduct, providing a haven for narcotics users, and disturbing the peace and quiet of the neighborhood, and not on the presence of homosexuals. However, the police apparently targeted the Humoresque because of its large gay clientele and because it became a symbol of increasing gay visibility in Center City and the Rittenhouse Square neighborhood. Its visibility threatened to slide into a de facto claim to normality in a world heavily committed to heterosexuality.[29]

The work of gay organizations and reformers to change the narrative concerning gays began to bear fruit in the 1960s. The civil rights movement and women's rights movement imprinted a concern for human rights in the public mind. In the 1960s, a climate of liberation from repression soon permitted homosexuality to come out of the closet to a greater extent. The women's movement called into question the status of women as sex objects, and despite opposition from some feminists, who feared the political cause of women's rights would be jeopardized, NOW welcomed lesbians. However, feminists were assailed by those who labeled them "dykes" engaged in "male bashing." Lesbianism remained an issue in the women's movement throughout the period. As for gay men, the opposition that developed on June 27, 1969, when a group of Manhattan police officers tried to close the Stonewall Inn, a gay bar in Greenwich Village, was a milestone. To the previous emphasis of reformers on due process protection in the courts, the gay liberation movement added an insistence on the rights of homosexuals to pursue sex and relationships.[30]

The rise of feminism in the 1970s elaborated the equal rights narrative that permitted gays and lesbians to claim status as subjects and to repudiate the old discourse of sin and perversity. After Stonewall, the movement stormed out of the closet of silence to demand rights through direct action protest and demands for inclusion. Organizations such as the National Committee for Sexual Civil Liberties and local groups worked to change the law to accord with the new narratives. In the 1970s, half the states eliminated sodomy statutes. The very idea that gays might accept the label "mentally ill" in order to escape punishment soon passed into oblivion. In 1974, the American Psychiatric Association declared that homosexuality "does not constitute a psychiatric disorder" and "implies no impairment in judgment, stability, reliability, or general social or vocational capabilities." With the support of medical science, the story of homosexuality as perversion changed; gays were no longer considered mentally ill. The next year the U.S. Civil Service Commission eliminated its ban on hiring gays and lesbians. Coming out became increasingly popular, but a vocal, well-organized resistance continued. Not only did gay liberation challenge the heterosexual basis of pleasure, but gays went further, publicly insisting that their relationships receive endorsement. In doing so, they disputed the assumption that heterosexual marriage and family were the only acceptable lifestyles. Their position went well beyond hidden homosexuality, which most people tolerated or ignored.[31]

Most prosecutors continued to ignore private, consensual homosexual sex, seeing it as nonthreatening. When cases were brought, the response of judges paralleled their approach to prostitutes and their clients. As long as the sex was voluntary, the rule against convictions based on accomplice testimony prohibited either party from testifying against the other. Conviction required the testimony of a third-party observer, which implied the absence of true privacy. Homosexuality did not gain formal legal legitimacy, but gays could engage in private homosexual activity with little fear of criminal prosecution.

Despite the changing climate, racial stories continued to have a major influence when black gays were prosecuted. At a time when adult consensual sex was punished lightly if at all, courts upheld convictions of African Americans for consensual homosexual sex and gave them comparatively heavier sentences. As recipients of anal intercourse or participants in oral sex with another man, gay African Americans defied both gender and racial mores. They challenged the white male's deeply ingrained notions of black male sexuality, which remained psychologically necessary to his own self-definition. In 1961, the Georgia Supreme Court let stand John H. Beckham's conviction for being the receptive partner in anal intercourse and ordered him to serve two to five years in the penitentiary. In another case, the Virginia Supreme Court upheld the sentencing of thirty-year-old Alfred W. Howard to eighteen months for performing oral sex on Russell Farrar, a white man.

Farrar was charged, but was acquitted because newspaper reports of Howard's conviction named him as a participant before his trial. Farrar's release reflected the notion that he was simply enjoying the services of Howard, who was considered a pervert for performing oral sex on a man. However, a dissenting judge pointed out that the acquittal was ridiculous. There was no evidence that the jurors even read the newspaper account; they had not even been asked whether they were "biased or prejudiced from any source or in any manner." Racial stories influenced the verdict.[32]

The changing narratives of the gay liberation movement did not immediately lead courts to accept gay relationships. However, the changed narrative's emphasis on more civil liberties protection accelerated a general reluctance to punish gay sex among white males. This reluctance reached its height after a landmark 1971 Florida case arising from the convictions of Alva Gene Franklin and Stephen Joyce. The law they violated had been on the books since 1866. It punished the "abominable and detestable crime against nature, either with mankind or with beast," with imprisonment in state prison for not more than twenty years. A police lieutenant arrested Franklin and Joyce after seeing them leave a public restroom on the Municipal Pier in St. Petersburg, Florida, at approximately 2:45 a.m. He shined his flashlight inside a car and saw them committing "a crime against nature."[33]

The state supreme court sidestepped both a new narrative of acceptance and the old narrative of sin and perversion, instead holding that the law was "void on its face as unconstitutional for vagueness and uncertainty." They thought it "a very serious question" whether the "average person of common intelligence" would know what was prohibited; this law and "others relating to a variety of sex offenses" needed immediate legislative attention. The court had upheld the law previously but thought it high time for reconsideration; after all, the U.S. Supreme Court had affirmed the right to privacy in *Griswold v. Connecticut* (1965) in the interim. The climate was clearly changing, and so was the story of what was permissible. The court emphasized the law's archaic language, claiming that "people's understandings of subjects, expressions and experiences are different than they were even a decade ago. The fact of these changes in the land must be taken into account and appraised." The law "could entrap unsuspecting citizens and subject them to 20-year sentences."[34]

Wanting it clearly understood that the changed narrative they endorsed was civil libertarian, not a new view of homosexuality, the judges hastened to explain that their interest was based only on a due process story: "We do not, of course, here sanction historically forbidden sexual acts, homosexuality or bestiality." They only wanted the "forbidden conduct" stated in terms that could be understood by the "average man of common intelligence." Until the legislature acted, "this sort of reprehensible act" could be punished by a fine not exceeding $500, or imprisonment not exceeding six months. The crime was described as committing "any unnatural and lascivious act with another person." They sent the case back to the trial judge to impose a lesser sentence.[35]

By the 1980s, the regulation of gay sex consisted largely of a few cases punishing homosexuals under laws outlawing sodomy or "the crime against nature." Nationally, the gay liberation movement and greater tolerance made prosecutions infrequent. In New York, where feminists joined libertarians in favoring decriminalization, a constitutional right to engage in private, consensual sodomy soon emerged. Civil liberties and gay rights organizations pursued legal challenges to enforcement. In 1980, the New York Court of Appeals held unconstitutional the state's punishment of consensual homosexual relations as a violation of the state constitution. In 1983 the New York Court of Appeals decided that to prosecute a gay man for loitering in a public place to invite someone home for "deviate" sex was also impermissible. With these decisions, New York affirmed for homosexuals the new sexual liberalism developed during the 1960s and after.[36]

However, this liberalization had its limits. Neither law nor society eagerly punished gays for sexual intercourse. But when gays pushed for affirmation instead of toleration they were rebuffed. The old story that gay sex posed no threat to heterosexual marriage permitted society to turn a blind eye to homosexuals' "perversion," but approval was too much to ask. The situation resembled the *Turner* case, in which the court could tolerate concubine Sally but any implication that his wife should accept her was intolerable. The U.S. Supreme Court's advancement of privacy rights in *Roe v. Wade* (1973) encouraged some gays to believe the court would outlaw prosecutions of homosexual sex. They were wrong. The Court made clear in *Bowers v. Hardwick* in 1986 that federal privacy rights did not extend to homosexual consensual sex. Gay sex was neither "implicit in the concept of ordered liberty" nor "deeply rooted in this Nation's history and tradition." The Court had extended a right of privacy to a woman and her physician in making an abortion decision, but the homosexual story had not changed sufficiently. Gays were still marginalized and had no political standing as gays in the collective memory of the nation.[37]

The Georgia court was relieved of the need to discuss the criminality of homosexual sex in Michael Hardwick's case only because the prosecutor did not bother to bring charges after he was arrested. While Hardwick was in his bedroom having sex with a man, he was interrupted by a police officer who had come to his house ostensibly to serve him with a summons for a parking violation. The police officer was unwittingly let into the house by Hardwick's roommate. Upon being discovered, Hardwick and his lover were arrested for sodomy, a felony punishable by a term of one to twenty years, and jailed for ten hours before their release without formal charges. If Michael Hardwick had not sued Georgia officials in the civil case that led to the Supreme Court decision, the episode would have been just another example of the toleration of gay sex. However, Hardwick, like other homosexuals by the late twentieth century, wanted his case brought within the purview of the law; he was hoping for the influence of a more positive narrative. In 1916 or even 1940, Hardwick would have been unlikely to have made such an appeal: he would have had no story to tell. However, by the 1980s, the gay liberation movement, gay and lesbian studies in the academy, gays in movies and journalism, and queer theory all purveyed a new story, which gained partial acceptance. Hardwick failed in his objective, but his failure was headline news.

Although the Georgia statute challenged by Michael Hardwick was directed at both homosexual and heterosexual sodomy, Justice Byron White framed the issue as the right to engage in homosexual sodomy. He thus distinguished it from *Roe v. Wade* and other cases on privacy rights, including one that had affirmed the distinct right to not have one's bedroom invaded by the government. Opponents of the Supreme Court decision criticized it as "the voice of a man fearing the sexual interest of another man as the ultimate assault on masculinity, identity, and power." *Bowers* left states free to enforce their fornication statutes against gays and lesbians. Heterosexuals, but not gays, had privacy rights to engage in sexual behavior at home. The Court "expressed no opinion on the constitutionality of the Georgia statute as applied to other acts of sodomy." A total of twenty-five states still outlawed sodomy in 1994, and there was no privacy protection for gays, according to the Supreme Court decision in *Bowers*. The *Bowers* case relied on the old narrative of homosexuality as sin and perversion.[38]

Michael Hardwick's case was decided at a time when old and new stories concerning homosexual relationships competed. In 1980, the Democratic party put a gay rights plank in its platform for the first time. The Centers for Disease Control's 1981 report, the first on the incidence of AIDS, stimulated debate about gays coming out of the closet. However, the prosecutor's decision not to pursue Hardwick and his lover accorded with nationwide reality. In the 1980s there were practically no criminal cases involving homosexual sex—no old-fashioned sting operations or appeals from convictions for engaging in consensual sex. However, gay-bashing, bias crimes, and the fact that 67 percent of the victims interviewed in one survey had either experienced or perceived police as being antigay when they reported assaults, gave evidence of continued hostility in some quarters.[39]

Despite the unfriendly *Bowers* decision, ten years later the right of homosexuals to lobby for legislation to protect their rights was affirmed by the Supreme Court in the Colorado referendum case. The Colorado Court outlawed Amendment 2, which precluded legal action at the state and local level to prohibit discrimination on the basis of sexual orientation. At the same time, however, the President and Congress in the debates over same-sex marriages made clear that the story of homosexuality as unacceptable, legally and morally, was still imprinted in the public mind. Homosexual fornication, like interracial fornication involving white men and black women before the civil rights era, was illegal though not much punished. The idea of homosexual marriage, however, remained taboo, much like interracial marriage before the *Loving* case in 1965.[40]

When lesbians and gay men began to disclose their relationships in child custody, contract, and property disputes, they asked the public and the courts to adopt the new stories of acceptance to displace the old stories of sickness and sin. They wanted not only to redefine sex, as Michael Hardwick tried to do, but also to redefine the family—the gateway to acceptance in civil society—to gradually include homosexual relationships. The courts recognized that a redefinition of acceptable sex involved a redefinition of the family. Judges interpreted standard legal doctrines and chose between the old and evolving stories in deciding the issues.

In child custody cases, early gay claimants were summarily rejected. In 1952, the same year in which the Pennsylvania legislature made homosexuality eligible for psychiatric treatment as an alternative to incarceration, a gay father's suit to remove conditions on his joint custody of his children came before the state supreme court. Luther Bachman and Catherine Bachman, of Lehigh County, divorced in 1946 after nine years of marriage and the birth of two children. Catherine and the children continued to live in the same house where she and Bachman had resided; he paid child support. Bachman was a businessman and active in community affairs. She was "a devoted mother," but Luther received shared custody after the divorce, which continued during Catherine's remarriage. Three years after the divorce, Bachman tried to eliminate a restriction on his custody that forbade anyone except his mother from being present with him and the children. He claimed the condition was "impractical," "embarrassing" to him, and "perplexing" to the children. At the hearing concerning his request, Catherine told the judge that she objected to the children staying with Bachman overnight because they were "too young" and because, since he "admitted his homosexual tendencies," she did not want the children exposed to his gay acquaintances.[41]

At trial, Bachman admitted only that he was "bi-erotic" and he was "as much attracted to male friendships" as to "female friendships." The trial court found that he lived in a newly built, "pretentious" house with his mother and a male friend. The friend could have afforded his own apartment but, after moving from New York City, had lived with Bachman since about six months before the hearing. The friend also appeared "qualified and capable," but had no job, other than employment by Bachman. The court thought Bachman's "propensities were abnormal and his conduct immoral." Furthermore, a "convicted sodomist" formerly in Bachman's employ "testified that he had had relations with him on four occasions." Bachman had not remarried and displayed his gay lifestyle openly.[42]

The trial court left the shared custody arrangements intact. However, the state supreme court decided to make a change in "the best interests and permanent welfare of the children." Although no "untoward incidents involving the children [had] occurred," the judges thought "harmful influences" might be met with. Because of Bachman's homosexuality, the justices awarded full custody to their mother. She could grant him "such limited visitation" as she thought in the best interests of the children. Bachman essentially lost even shared custody because, in the view of the court, he wanted more than toleration; he wanted acceptance of his homosexual lifestyle.[43]

Judges in *Bachman* and other child custody disputes involving gays reflected the public's adherence to the old story of appropriate family behavior. In this old story, homosexuality remained a perversion. In 1980, the Kentucky appellate court, finding a homosexual parent's behavior too open and threatening, agreed to consider a father's suit to void a custody order granted to his wife when they divorced. The court noted that the couple's daughter was less than a year old at the time of the divorce. Soon the father learned that the mother had begun a lesbian relationship and worked at a lesbian bar. Her lover lived with her and the child, and the two women had exchanged vows and rings in a commitment ceremony. The court agreed that the mother's new lifestyle could harm the infant. The evidence included a court-appointed psychologist's opinion that "there is social stigma attached to homosexuality," so the child would "have additional burdens to bear in terms of teasing, possible embarrassment and internal conflicts." Also, research on the effects of parental modeling on children indicated that she might "have difficulties in achieving a fulfilling heterosexual identity of her own in the future." The court, still enmeshed in the old story, perceived the possibility of positive attitudes toward homosexual relationships as too far removed to counter any negative effects on children.[44]

In the same year, however, a Massachusetts court decided to develop a new legal narrative about sexual orientation. The new story treated homosexual and heterosexual families as similar: both faced difficulties, but could function equally well.

Brenda King Bezio was a lesbian who, admittedly, had led an unstable life and had suffered long-standing financial and physical problems. A trial court decided that a permanent guardian should keep her children, because of her lesbianism and her former inability to care for them. The appellate judges disagreed, finding no evidence that the sexual preference of adults in the home had "any detrimental impact on children," and concluding that her earlier problems were resolved. Furthermore, the record included no proof that children "who are raised with a loving couple of the same sex are any more disturbed, unhealthy, maladjusted than children raised with a loving couple of mixed sex." Therefore, the state could not take children away from their parents "simply because their households fail to meet the ideals approved by the community . . . [or] simply because the parents embrace ideologies or pursue life-styles at odds with the average." Dr. Alexandra Kaplan, a clinical psychologist and professor of psychology at the University of Massachusetts, testified: "There is no evidence at all that sexual preference of adults in the home has any detrimental impact on children." Many factors influence child rearing, and "sexual preference per se is typically not one of them." Dr. Kaplan also testified that a parent's homosexual relationship would not necessarily cause a child to become a homosexual instead of a heterosexual: "Most children raised in a homosexual situation become heterosexual as adults." Furthermore, she explained, the sexual orientation of the parent "is irrelevant to [the child's] mental health." Psychologist David Johnson, a defense witness who had seen the children in play therapy, concurred with Dr. Kaplan. The Massachusetts court accepted the new stories gays and lesbians had been telling for nearly a decade, and also acknowledged the evidence provided for those new stories. The court rejected as unfounded the myths of the past.[45]

However, the work of undermining the stories of danger to children and perversion in a homosexual family was not yet done. Proof of this lay in the decisions of other courts that rejected the *Bezio* decision. The conflicting perspectives in the Kentucky and Massachusetts cases were at issue in Virginia's disposition of Sharon Bottoms's fight for custody of her three-year-old son. One court, adopting the Massachusetts view, found no evidence that the child would be harmed if Bottoms was awarded custody. The Virginia Supreme Court overturned the decision in 1995, preferring the rationale of harm and confused identity used in the Kentucky decision. Professor Nancy Polikoff, of the American University law school, argued that the court had given a "blueprint to any judge who wants to deny custody to a gay or lesbian parent." All such a judge had to do was to selectively quote expert opinion and emphasize the stigma attached to homosexuality.

Homosexual-parent custody disputes remain caught between new and old stories. By 1995, eight states had denied custody to a homosexual parent and five had not. In 1996, the Washington State Supreme Court extended the new positive stories. On the basis of expert testimony, the justices concluded that restrictions on either parent's sexual behavior with partners other than the former spouse were inappropriate: "Problems with adjustment are the normal response to any breakup of a family. But restrictions on a parent's conduct designed to artificially ameliorate changes in a child's life are not permissible. If the problem is adjustment, the remedy is counseling."[46]

Courts in child custody cases could not avoid considering whether an acceptable family meant only a family that practiced heterosexual sex. To decide property and contract disputes between gays, the courts had to acknowledge the reality of a same-sex relationship; however, they could avoid confronting directly whether the relationship constituted a family. Much like courts that relied on due process concerns in deciding sodomy cases, they took refuge in legal stories. They upheld the validity of standard contract and property rules, so important to every enterprise in society, without regard to the parties' sexuality. In Arkansas, Benjamin Selman bought a house in the name of his companion, James Bramlett, with an oral agreement that Bramlett would transfer it to Selman once he obtained his divorce. Selman and Bramlett had been lovers and lived together for about a year. In 1980, the state supreme court concluded that Bramlett knew the title was temporary and must convey it back to Selman. He could not gain a "windfall" by taking advantage of their relationship, "by claiming the stigma of homosexuality." According to this and other decisions, to reinforce standard contract doctrines did not undermine family values.[47]

Similarly, a dispute between tennis champion Martina Navratilova and her lover Judy Nelson was interpreted so as to require no sanction of their lesbian relationship. The matter, the parties agreed, rested solely on the validity of a contract. Nelson, a forty-five-year-old divorced mother of two, began living with Navratilova in July 1984, and traveled with her to tournaments around the world. Nelson and Navratilova signed a "non-marital cohabitation agreement" in 1986. Nelson sued Navratilova upon receiving formal notification from her in April 1991 that their relationship was over. Nelson wanted to enforce the cohabitation agreement, which provided that if they parted they would divide assets accrued since they began living together. Nelson's lawsuit was settled out of court in 1992. However, despite the public awareness of the affair, the legal result avoided sanction of homosexuality and relied solely on contract law.[48]

The law punished homosexual behavior when it became

categorized as homosexuality. As gays sought public recognition they became a threat to gender prescriptions. Judicial opinions mirrored public concern about gender roles and were influenced by race and class narratives. Gay men, lesbians, and African American homosexuals were regarded very differently. Gay males evoked a negative response because they represented the dominant group. Gay male sex was a threat to the image of males as patriarchs and heads of families, who exercised power over women and children. Lesbians were harassed in bars and on the streets, but sex between women was not the target of the sodomy statutes. Further, lesbians did not solicit sex from strangers in public restrooms and other venues, behavior that exposed men to criminal charges. African American men were peripheral to power. However, African American gays faced homophobia within the black community, because of widely accepted fundamentalist religious stories. They also were harassed by the legal system because they defied the image of the sexually consumed African American man. This image was important to white men who defined themselves as the opposite, a civilized other.[49]

Homosexuality in the courts traveled a long and convoluted route, from being an outlawed offense with no story to tell, to being an outlawed offense enveloped in medical stories of sin and illness, to become a story in itself, one of affirming relationships and positive values. Gays and lesbians are still elaborating newer stories in an attempt to gain societal acceptance and displace the old ones that linger in the public mind. Because the old stories change, homosexuals' experiences and self-images change, and hence so do the stories they tell. Languages, stories, and identities are protean dynamic forces, just like the society they reflect or tell about. Indeed, the story about gay men and lesbians has changed enough for a federal Employer Non-Discrimination Act to receive serious consideration. It has also changed sufficiently for domestic partnerships to gain recognition from a few employers. The old story still protects the definition of marriage as a union of one man and one woman, and still appears in child custody arrangements. The work of imprinting new stories has yet to be fully accomplished. Until the work is done, gay and lesbian relationships will be regarded as a major challenge to gender roles—just as interracial marriage was considered a major challenge to racial subordination before the 1960s.

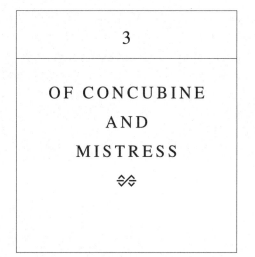

3

OF CONCUBINE
AND
MISTRESS

Inheritance disputes exposed long-term extramarital relationships to public view. Some were mixed-race and others same-race. Those between white men and African American women, in the years of slavery and segregation, were sometimes romantic but often simply exploitative. African Americans and poor whites could be punished for heterosexual and homosexual fornication; however, narratives of race and class privilege permitted wealthy white men to maintain a relationship approximating marriage with little worry about their reputation or the possibility of prosecution. The story left room for such a man to provide for his mistress and children, white or black, without violation—and, indeed, in perpetuation—of white male power and control. Plaintiffs in inheritance cases include African American concubines who sought to secure inheritances left to them and their children, and white mistresses who sued to inherit from their lovers. Judges let African American mistresses and their children inherit according to the provisions of a white patriarch's will because their claims reinforced rather than threatened male domination and race relations. The judge was implementing the will of the wealthy white testator and affirming his power to sexually exploit African American women without retribution. After bans on interracial marriage were declared illegal in 1966, most disputes involved the inheritances of white men and women in live-in arrangements. As with child custody, property, and contract disputes involving gays, the law took no notice of the parties until the courts were forced to address the consequences of the relationships.

Southey Satchell's death, in 1876, brought one African American concubine and her children into court. Satchell was a lecher, who tried to extend his particular brand of lechery beyond the grave. After a long, successful career as a medical doctor, he retired to his farm in Accomac County, Virginia, where he lived happily among a number of retainers and white mistresses until his death. Although never married, Satchell had a close-knit family network. He frequently visited two "spinsters," Mary C. Rew, who lived on some of his lands, and Eliza Scott Sr., who bore him two children. A third white mistress, Ailsie East, bore him a son, Edward East, in 1841.[1]

Edward East followed his father's example in choosing an unconventional love life. However, he crossed racial lines. In 1872, thirty-one-year-old East was living on his father's lands with a "colored woman as his mistress." They had two children, who were "recognized" by the community as East's children. Because of his social status as the son of Southey Satchell, East could violate the laws against miscegenation with no thought of possible punishment. By the time Satchell died in 1876, Ailsie East was long dead. Satchell's will distributed "considerable" largesse among his servants and family. He provided bequests for three "favorite slaves" who stayed with him after emancipation. One of these was seventy-two-year-old Isaac Satchell, who received the land on which he lived, worth $2,500, for life. Isaac also received a cart, harness, livestock, and farming implements plus ten barrels of corn and three stacks of fodder. To Lucy Ewell, Southey Satchell left $100, and to Caleb Satchell his small dairy, a cow, a calf, and $500.[2]

Satchell also provided for his mistresses. Mary Rew inherited life tenure in the land on which she lived. He also gave her $1,000, plus his large dairy, his "best milch cow and calf," and the same amount of fodder as he left Isaac. He left his son Edward East, and legitimate children he might have, a farm he had purchased worth $2,500. However, East could receive the gift only if he paid $130 a month for life to sixty-five-year-old Eliza Scott Sr. He also had to repay a debt he owed his father. Finally, Southey Satchell gave to his twenty-five-year-old daughter, Eliza Scott Jr., and her children a large tract of his farmland worth $9,000 and any residue remaining in his estate. Edward East's inheritance would revert to his sister if he left no legitimate children at his death.[3]

After Satchell died, East lived on the tract of land, paid his father's executors the debt he owed, and paid the senior Eliza Scott her required annuity each year. When East died accidentally on March 30, 1885, his half-sister, the younger Eliza Scott, took immediate possession of the lands and other property. She insisted that East had no other legitimate heirs. Not only did the African American children and their mother have no claim on Southey Satchell's estate but in the absence of a will, they had no legal right to East's property, consisting of some farming implements and household goods.[4]

The state supreme court let Satchell extend his reign from the grave. They upheld the award of the property to Eliza Scott, finding that Southey Satchell deliberately limited inheritance rights to his son and the son's *legitimate* children. He disapproved of the son's "living in open shame with a negro mistress" and thus held Edward in less regard than his daughter, Eliza. The promiscuous life led by the testator himself was irrelevant. The white women in Satchell's entourage were by definition disreputable, but they were white. As a wealthy white man he was permitted to perpetuate such unconventional relationships. They did not threaten a social order based on racial polarities. According to the court, Satchell's children, though "unlawfully begotten, were born of women of his own race." His son was "less fastidious in his tastes."[5]

In affirming Satchell's disapproval of his son's relationship with an African American woman and his disinheritance of his mulatto grandchildren as illegitimate members of society and the family, the court held that East's interracial liaison was offensive to the father and sustained Satchell's bequests. To do otherwise, according to the court, would "falsify all experience and fix upon the white race a stigma not deserved by the great majority of that race," because the mulatto children would be accepted as if they were equal to the white children in the family. Satchell wanted his son to behave in accordance with the accepted racial story. He wanted him to marry a white woman and produce legitimate heirs. An affair with a black woman constituted an acceptable unacknowledged subplot, but it could not take over the story. Because the estate left at East's death was still controlled by his father, East could leave his African American children nothing. Satchell's will controlled the property.[6]

Mulatto offspring of white fathers presented a difficult problem for the courts in the years when interracial marriage was illegal. They had no lawful standing as their father's children, but they, and their mothers, required support. The courts decided to base their decisions on the formal legal rule that the law would implement the proven will of the testator. They chose as a primary value the upholding of the privileges of white male patriarchy, which included the power to direct the disposition of property, as we have just seen, after death. The Virginia judges in the *Satchell* case sought to accomplish his desires—in this case, to support his white mistresses and express disapproval of interracial concubinage. They upheld Satchell's wishes in distributing his property. Because their grandfather, the patriarch, decided to exclude them, East's African American children and their mother were left with fewer property rights than Edward East. Reliance on the will of the testator, however, meant that in Virginia, which had a large mulatto population, court decisions could also permit mulatto heirs to inherit. The outcome depended on the will of the deceased patriarch. The racial story echoed the story of paternalism and patriarchy. If he was wealthy enough, the white male patriarch could override racist legislation.

The court worked within the patriarchal narrative as played out in the *Satchell* case when it let John Johnson, a widely respected lawyer from Appomattox County, bequeath property to his mulatto children. He had "several colored people about, formerly his slaves." He willed some land to certain "persons of color," who were also reported to be his children, and left the residue of his estate to his lawyer with the understanding that the lawyer would defend the children's holdings against his white relatives. Also in 1889, the court upheld the intent of William Thomas, a white man who died intestate, to give his property to his African American daughter. His estate was worth about $200,000. Lewis lived with an African American woman—his former slave—and their two daughters. After the death of his mistress and one of their daughters, he and his surviving daughter, Bettie Thomas Lewis, shared a household near Richmond. Thomas provided her with a companion. He had taken both children to Saratoga Springs, "where all had eaten at the same table." Bettie Thomas Lewis was "the only light of his long life." His legal relatives did not visit him and wrote letters only to ask for money. Bettie cared for him through his final illness. A local newspaper noted that the gift to Bettie Thomas Lewis reportedly made her the richest person of color in Virginia.

In 1890, the Virginia Supreme Court also let Alice Strange inherit real estate from her white father, Thomas Strange, of Lynchburg. Alice was Strange's "natural daughter" by "Belle," an African American woman. She lived with the white family headed by her father and was accepted by his wife as equal to their own daughter until she was old enough to "leave the paternal roof" and attend boarding school in Washington, D.C., where she remained until graduation. The letters exchanged between Alice and Mr. and Mrs. Strange showed "the deepest parental affection and the most anxious and tender solicitude . . . for her as his favorite child." The judges thought it important to detail the warmth and closeness of their relationship to support the decision "however revolting to the moral sense and offensive against public policy." Strange also left Belle, who lived elsewhere, a legacy of $150.00 per year, payable unless she remarried.[7]

In inheritance case after inheritance case Southern state supreme courts between 1868 and 1900 upheld the power of propertied white men to leave estates to their African American mistresses and their children. Cases in which African American children inherited from their fathers have been discovered in every Southern state except North Carolina and Alabama. On those few occasions when African American claimants did lose, only small amounts of property were involved and in most of these cases they had already inherited substantial property from their fathers before the adjudication at issue. Courts insisted on affirming the power of wealthy white male patriarchs.[8]

White fathers provided for their children whether they acknowledged them or not. The judges routinely upheld the father's will, with only a very occasional rhetorical outburst to show that some understood that these relationships were disapproved, though they might be tolerated. One justice, in an 1874 Louisiana case, voiced a typical objection: the father "knew when he was begetting these children what the consequences would be to them. If they suffer, it is from his fault, and not the laws civil and moral which he defied." Judges expressed the tension between support for male power and a need to chastise the father in making these decisions; they essentially chose between narratives of racial subordination and white patriarchy.[9]

The fact that African American women and their children won inheritance claims does not disprove the evidence of increasing racial hostility in the South after the war. The judges balanced a complex array of themes. They enforced the reigning assumptions of propertied white male power in their decisions, and the exercise of that power included the sexual exploitation of African American women. The courts also adhered to the antebellum understanding that the men must provide for their white families; judges insisted that the intention of the testator to leave the property in question to his African American family must be unequivocal.

When the white father left no will, his African American and mulatto family had to negotiate a difficult legal terrain. The law for distributing the estates of those who died intestate generally restricted the inheritance of "bastards." This meant that Edward East's children received nothing, not only because of their grandfather's rejection but also because their father had neglected to provide for them by will. As "bastards," they had no automatic right to inherit. Only legitimate children could register that claim.[10]

African American mothers and mulatto children left out of a man's will had to prove that he intended to include them. Alternatively, they could attempt to persuade the court that their parents had a common-law marriage and that, therefore, they inherited as legal heirs. Black women and their children actively pressed their own interests despite confrontations with white relatives, who would argue that the testator intended no inheritance and that racial proscriptions ruled out the possibility of common-law marriage. African American women who claimed the estates of white men had an exceptional problem in Louisiana: under the Napoleonic Code, donations of "immovables"—real estate—to a concubine were illegal. To circumvent this provision, women tried to show either that they believed in good faith that they were married, or that they did not fit the definition of a concubine. They also tried to avoid asserting directly that their child had a white father; otherwise, the court might define the mother as a concubine and reject the child's inheritance as an indirect attempt to make a donation to the mother. Pelagie Hibard had additional problems when she sought the inheritance left to her son Philippe by Alexander Marionneau, a wealthy white man who raised and educated him because he was "intensely attached" to the boy. Pelagie was a slave when Philippe was born, and Marionneau had him legitimated without recording her status as the mother. Marionneau willed Philippe his entire estate, but the executor refused to follow the terms of the will, keeping the property for his own use. The executor, and then his widow, challenged the propriety and validity of the will, preventing the transfer of the property for over ten years. Pelagie Hibard ultimately prevailed, but unfortunately her son had died of consumption in the interim. The court refused to use the formal legal rules requiring acknowledgment of illegitimate children to void the inheritance. In the end, the court affirmed the story of white patriarchy. Marionneau, the court decided, had obviously intended the boy to inherit.[11]

Disputes over interracial inheritances from the estates of wealthy white men enacted complex narratives of the powerlessness of white families to preclude such relationships and the law's indulgence of wealthy white men's power to negotiate racial barriers. Philip May and other scholars have described the black mothers and various children of Florida's Zephaniah Kingsley, a polygamous miscegenator and ex–slave trader. Kingsley's African American families had to fight for their inheritance against various white claimants. The African American heirs won everything except one small piece of property, which they lost because of the timing of a deed Kingsley made.[12]

Historian Jonathan Bryant has detailed the interracial relationship of prominent Georgian David Dickson, who in the 1840s took one of his slaves, Julie, as his mistress. Eventually, Dickson became Hancock County's wealthiest planter. He and Julie had one daughter, Amanda, whom they "pampered." Dickson's will gave Amanda's sons, Julian and Charles, two tracts of land but left the remainder of his estate, valued at $1 million, to Amanda.[13]

Dickson's white relatives hired high-powered attorneys and filed objections to his will. A local jury upheld the will against the plaintiffs' claim that Dickson was mentally incompetent, and in 1887 the state supreme court upheld the lower court's decision. Bryant believes the judges upheld the will because they were interested in protecting property rights and knew their decision would not undermine race prescriptions, such as the segregation and subordination of blacks. Involved as well may have been the principle that the law should encourage fathers to provide for illegitimate children whatever race they were assigned to. The court acted to indulge the power of wealthy white males to have interracial sex and to allocate property to their African American mistresses and their children.[14]

Some African American women who lived comfortably with propertied white men exercised a great deal of power in the relationship. They ran households in which their white "spouses" not only acknowledged their children but also displayed affection and concern. More than once a father "requested a friend to be present and stand as godfather" to his children. In other families, both mother and father "openly called the children their own." The father "instructed them to be educated as such and as his children employed physicians to attend them in sickness." African American women did not project themselves as victims in the inheritance cases but as women empowered to pursue their interests in collecting from their white lover's estate.[15]

The most protracted struggle in the Texas courts required years of dedication, through four lawsuits, by a strong-minded African American woman, Betsy Webster. The story of Betsy and David Webster, a wealthy white citizen of Galveston, was in fact as romantic as the story of Alex Haley's paternal grandmother Queen. They lived for many years in a home of "comfort and taste," described by the Texas courts as "a white cottage embowered amid flowers and orange trees." At his death in 1856, Webster emancipated Betsy and bequeathed her his real and personal property in Galveston. Included were twenty-one town lots, horses, and household goods, to be held in trust for her use. One of Webster's cousins contested the will. Although Betsy Webster was already elderly, she actively pursued her inheritance rights. She hired Potter and Ballinger, a prestigious law firm, which successfully defended her manumission and legacy under the will. However, in payment for their services, in 1857, the lawyers executed a conveyance giving them one-third of the estate, consisting of seven lots in Galveston.[16]

There was no evidence that Mrs. Webster had ever agreed to this transfer. Feeling abused by the outcome, in 1866, when she discovered the transaction, she sued for the return of the property, which Ballinger and Potter had meanwhile sold. At the time, the state supreme court noted that "she was shown to be a very intelligent, careful and resolute old woman but she was going on eighty years of age when this suit was brought." Texas Supreme Court Justice Amos Morrill, a Unionist and longtime Texas lawyer, affirmed the trial judge's verdict against Mrs. Webster's claim. In deciding the case, Morrill found William Ballinger's reputation decidedly more impressive than an ex-slave's claims. Mrs. Webster's "charges of fraud against her attorneys . . . have little foundation to stand upon in the minds of those well acquainted with them."[17]

Given the legality of slavery in 1856, Justice Morrill thought Mrs. Webster should be grateful for her manumission: no lawyers with "less legal, political and moral standing in the community than her counsel, could have saved for her either the property or freedom devised." He agreed with Ballinger that Mrs. Webster should have spent her money on "erecting a monument over the grave" of her counsel rather than showing "avarice" instead of "gratitude" by suing.[18]

This was not, however, the end of Mrs. Webster's efforts to gain legal redress. Another fraudulent transfer of property came to her attention when the supposed new owner tried to oust her. The challenger won at jury trial. When Mrs. Webster used the same lawyers who had represented her in the earlier case against the law firm, her opponent probably thought he would surely win based on the earlier decision. However, Republicans had appointed new justices. Moses B. Walker, the only carpetbagger on the strongly Unionist Supreme Court, wrote the opinion which voided the deed. The court simply found the law was misunderstood in the earlier case.[19]

Walker acted within the meaning of the Reconstruction freedom story rather than the old story of Mrs. Webster's slave status. He was not deterred by the status of William Ballinger's law firm or by the fact that it had achieved Mrs. Webster's emancipation. He thought she had been ill served by the lawyers and the trustee under the will. Even if she could not have acted for herself before the war, upon emancipation she had citizenship and a legal voice—the right to have her story vindicated. The appropriation and sale, by the lawyers and trustee, of the property left to her was unconscionable. A trustee was required to use the income for the beneficiary but could not sell the assets without the approval of a court of competent jurisdiction. The case must be retried, with the trustee as a party.[20]

Mrs. Webster was also a party in two property disputes involving persons hired to care for her on the understanding that they would receive property upon her death. In the first instance, a deed executed by one lawyer was denounced as a forgery. In 1880, at almost one hundred years of age, Betsy Webster resolved her last case. At the time, according to her lawyer, she was still "of good mind, and rather smart for her age." Only grit and determination had made it possible for Mrs. Webster to defend her interests over the years. In the first two lawsuits, the courts carefully considered whether David Webster had really intended to contract a "marital relationship" with her. The style and continuity of their living arrangements, and Betsy's deep attachment to their home, in which she remained during the war, denoted serious intentions. The courts' approval of her inheritance implemented the will of the testator and indulged wealthy white male power, in this case that of David Webster.[21]

Well into the twentieth century, inheritance cases reaching far back into the nineteenth century or arising from interracial relationships begun during the Jim Crow era, were still coming before the courts. Judges continued to affirm the old story of propertied white male privilege and racial subordination. They saw that inheritance by African American mistresses and their children under a white testator's will affirmed the white patriarch's power and a social order based on class, gender, and racial subordination.

In Louisiana, Amanda Kyle, an African American woman, claimed an inheritance from her lover, James Walter Jones of Dunn in Richland Parish, when he died in 1926. Their relationship had begun shortly after 1900, and they lived together for more than twenty years. Neighbors described Kyle as Jones's cook and housekeeper. She also attended to customers who came to his general merchandise store, and she had access to the store's cash drawer. From 1904 to 1908, she slept in his house, occupying a separate bedroom. Sometime thereafter, he built her another house on his land, where she lived with her two nieces.[22] When Jones died on April 22, 1926, he left Kyle his entire estate, valued at $40,000, including $15,000 in real estate.

Jones's nephews and nieces sued to revoke the will. They claimed that Kyle had moved into the separate house because the concubinage in which the couple had lived became a felony under the 1908 revision of the law on the subject. Jones's white relatives cited the provision of state law that Pelagie Hibard had avoided which forbade donations of real estate between those who lived in open concubinage and limited a donation of personal property to one tenth of an estate. So rather than claiming that Jones could not have had a love relationship with an African American woman, relatives insisted that Kyle and Jones were lovers and she was not his employee.[23]

The state supreme court reversed a trial court decision in the relatives' favor and awarded the estate to Kyle. The court found that both parties' discretion and her insistence that she was only an employee made it possible for her to inherit. Louisiana law prohibited Jones and Kyle from legalizing their relationship. However, the court wanted to uphold Jones's desire to leave his estate to his concubine, and it did so. Kyle, by all accounts, was entirely loving and kind and there was no reason to doubt Jones's desire to provide for her.

All of these decisions must be seen in terms of an assumption made by courts throughout the South, that implementing the will of the testator reinforced racial subordination by recognizing white patriarchal authority. White gentlemen, whether judges or testators, had common bonds and interests. The fact that African Americans benefited from these gentlemen's agreements to condone white male–black female relationships was incidental to the reaffirmation of white male desire.[24]

In a 1944 case upholding an African American woman's inheritance, the Alabama Supreme Court again affirmed the patriarchal story, with rhetoric that, like the story, had changed little from the previous century. The judges were well aware that the state outlawed "race amalgamation" so as "to safeguard the racial integrity of white peoples as well as the racial integrity of Negro peoples."

"A universal public opinion prevalent in both races" found that "it is reprehensible enough for a white man to live in adultery with a white woman, thus defying the laws of both God and man, but it is more so, and a much lower grade of depravity, for a white man to live in adultery with a Negro woman. Fortunately, the cases of such depravity are very rare."[25]

Having issued this disclaimer, the court acknowledged the right of a well-to-do white man to freely establish an illicit relationship with an African American woman. Watts "was a bachelor and preferred to live this life of shame and face the criticism, or perhaps ostracism that would naturally follow." Because he had no white wife, his actions did not sully the institutions of marriage and white supremacy. Among the businessmen with whom Watts consorted over the years, "he was not ostracized, but continued to enjoy their confidence and continued to carry on business with them as usual." Consequently, "however boldly he may have defied the laws of our State and its public policy, and the recognized traditional racial distinctions, organized society took no steps to interfere." This case represented a slowly disappearing old story. Social and political change would soon lead to the *Brown* decision. The ban on interracial marriage would finally be declared unconstitutional by the U.S. Supreme Court in 1967.[26]

State supreme court justices treated the inheritance claims of white mistresses in same-race relationships very differently from those of African American mistresses and mixed-race children of well-to-do white men. The protection of racial paternalism was not an issue, nor was white male lust for interracial sex. White mistresses were regarded as if they had been selling sexual favors—as if they were prostitutes claiming payment from the dead. The mistresses sought to project a story of respectable white female behavior, but the justices regarded their stories with skepticism, and they usually lost. They were consigned to the status of the immoral white woman who deserved disrespect.

Their white lovers were just as emphatically complicit in

disreputable behavior. No racial proscriptions or other legal bans prohibited marriage. If the man had a legal wife, he and the mistress were insulting his spouse and the institution of marriage. If he had no legal wife, the justices assumed he would have married the mistress if he had sufficiently valued the relationship. Furthermore, both parties showed disdain for the institution of marriage by living together without benefit of the law or religion. When a will existed, the courts obscured the intent of the testator by invoking other legal principles to draw conclusions from the drama they saw.

Clara Carter faced the typical judicial skepticism when she advanced her claims. A white woman, she lived for a number of years on a small part of Lewis Bivens's land in Rutherford County, Tennessee, while he resided nearby with his wife, Nancy Ann, and their children. During the last two years of his life, Bivens moved into Clara's house, where she cared for him. (He suffered from a disease "of an offensive and loathsome character.") Although Bivens deeded to Clara only the house and land where she lived, his relatives successfully claimed it. In 1873, the state supreme court decided that she "had been fully compensated for all lawful and proper services rendered [Bivens]" and concluded that he had prepared the deed under the stress of his illness.[27]

The cases of white mistresses turned on the courts' strong desire to protect the institution of marriage and on their suspicion of immoral white mistresses. In inheritance cases involving African American mistresses, the courts usually avoided moral strictures concerning the behavior of the parties. White males could indulge their desire for a relationship with a black woman without suffering sanctions for inappropriate gender role behavior. In fact, the courts held, they acted appropriately within the prerogatives of their station as gentlemen. Wealthy white men could freely indulge their desire for sex with black females, who were considered rather less than human and incapable of sexual purity. Thus neither party was deemed immoral for conducting an illicit relationship. The white man and black woman did not threaten social order, and the relationship simply exemplified the story that gentlemen will be gentlemen. However, if the mistress was white, the courts were particularly sensitive to any arrangements that impugned the sanctity of marriage or interfered with a legal family's resources. The Tennessee judges faulted Lewis Bivens because he insulted the institution of marriage.[28]

Narratives of different moral standards for poor white females and of class and religious distinctions played a major role in a Mississippi inheritance dispute. George Calvert and Kitty Denny of Vicksburg, Mississippi, established a boardinghouse and construction business over the ten years that they lived together. When Calvert died, he and Denny had a nine-year-old child. Denny sued asking for dower (the widow's legally mandated share of her husband's estate) and support for her daughter for one year, as allowed under state law, until the estate was settled. She claimed that by mutual consent and by their manner of living together she and Calvert had established a common-law marriage.

Denny won in the lower court but lost on appeal. Their living arrangements and interaction with each other convinced the court that Calvert had never intended a marital relation. First, although both were Irish, she embraced Catholicism, while he exhibited "that strong antipathy to it often found among Irish Protestants." Also, Calvert had once attributed his refusal to marry Denny to the fear that "his relations would come from Ireland and from the North and kill him if he did so."[29]

Second, witnesses testified that Calvert represented Denny to neighbors as no more than a housekeeper. She was not "called upon or visited by any lady whatever save one"; she did not sit at the table with Calvert when guests were present; and no one saw them out together in public places. The court refused to infer a marital relationship. Calvert could have married Denny and evidently chose not to. She and her child inherited nothing. From the court's perspective, Denny carried on an illicit relationship with her employer, who was simply cohabitating with a servant. Calvert, the court decided, had treated her as little more than a convenience and had not intended that Denny inherit.[30]

After the turn of the century, political and social change stimulated a new story about gender roles that had consequences for white mistresses in the courts. Middle-class and working women went boldly about, unchaperoned, on city streets and bobbed their hair. Single women worked in offices and shops and started working as salesclerks in those new "temples of commerce," department stores. Affluent women wandered about the stores alone or with friends of either sex, utilizing the refreshment rooms, cloakrooms, and reading rooms, and places that unaccompanied women formerly could not visit without damage to their reputations.

The New York Court of Appeals, influenced by the changed approach to gender and female respectability, began to allow mistresses to inherit under certain circumstances, especially if there was evidence that the testator had so intended. The court viewed favorably a poor (but good) girl who tried to save a dissolute, unmarried man from a life of ruin. The court approved H. M. Levengston Jr.'s bequest to his mistress, Caroline Finlay, despite his father's objections. Levengston had died unmarried in March 1912, about five months after the execution of his will. Levengston's father, as the son's sole legal heir and next of kin, unsuccessfully claimed that his son was not of "sound mind and memory and capable of making a will; and that its execution was obtained by fraud and undue influence." The court brushed away these objections and implemented the testator's intent. For about four years before his death Levengston had "practically maintained a house at Saratoga" where he lived with Finlay, an unmarried dressmaker. The court admitted that the details of their "illicit relations" were unclear. It observed, however, that "her influence seems to have been to restrain him from drinking," and that aside from "her relations" with Levengston the evidence "discloses nothing against her character." The court carefully circumscribed its ruling by emphasizing Finlay's moral influence on Levengston as a basis for the decision.[31]

In another New York case, in 1932, the court found the claim of Charlotte Fixel, known professionally as Charlotte Lesley, irrefutable. She fit perfectly the story of the "New Woman," being a single, highly educated professional. The court described her as belonging to a prominent family, which included an uncle who had served on the New York State Supreme Court, David Leventritt. She had studied "voice culture" and later went on the stage, "appearing in many well-known productions."

In 1920, Lesley began dating Abraham Lincoln Erlanger, a "monarch of the theatrical world." Erlanger's wife had divorced him in 1912, claiming adultery, and the divorce decree forbade Erlanger from remarrying during his ex-wife's life, a permissible practice at that time. Erlanger had prospered since a New York theater owner and producer, Henry Greenwall of the American Theater Stock Company, had loaned him $500 and given him free office space to start a business. Erlanger, however, had repaid Greenwall by becoming a major competitive booking agent and theater owner. Erlanger and his partner, Marc Klaw, went on to build theaters in major cities throughout the nation. Major theatrical productions and stars of the day, such as Ethel Barrymore, appeared on their stages. Klaw and Erlanger prospered until Erlanger had a stroke in 1928.[32]

Erlanger and Lesley shared a house on West End Avenue in Manhattan from the early 1920s on, and Lesley continued her acting career until Erlanger fell ill. Soon afterward, they moved to Atlantic City, where they lived in a hotel while developing plans for the construction of a "lavish" estate. After Erlanger's death in

1929, Lesley discovered that he had left her nothing in his will. The multimillion-dollar estate went to his brother, Mitchell Erlanger, who had recently retired as a New York Supreme Court judge, and other relatives. She sued to contest the will, insisting that as Erlanger's common-law spouse she deserved a widow's third. The trial lasted over a year; the probate court heard 240 witnesses and produced 9,200 pages of trial transcript. Lesley argued that their residence in New Jersey during the last years of Erlanger's life revoked the New York decree, which had ordered him not to remarry. Witnesses testified that Erlanger introduced Lesley as his wife in every setting imaginable.[33]

The actor Eddie Cantor, who had known Erlanger since 1915, testified to being introduced to Lesley as Mrs. Erlanger in London in 1925. Producers, actors, physicians, dentists, hotel clerks, and household servants all recalled Erlanger introducing Lesley as his wife. Friends testified that Erlanger gave Lesley a ring after their move to New Jersey, and that he announced they were now doubly married. Thus, Lesley argued, she and Erlanger had established common-law marital status.[34]

Erlanger's relatives insisted that if the court recognized this as a common-law marriage Erlanger had been a bigamist. They also argued that he had transported Lesley across state lines for immoral purposes and thus should have been prosecuted under the federal Mann Act outlawing "white slavery." They also showed that Erlanger's will stated he was unmarried, as did his tax returns. Lesley maintained preexisting checking and savings accounts in both her stage name and her birth name. When Erlanger deeded property to Lesley, he used her birth name.[35]

Lesley emerged victorious. The justices pointed out that "the habit is growing on the part of married women to retain their maiden names, especially where they have been, or are, members of the theatrical profession." The court declared that Erlanger's relatives behaved outrageously in their attempt to draw "a sordid picture of continuing breach of the moral law" by the conduct of Lesley and Erlanger. The couple were the perfect picture of "a husband and wife in constant quest of social contact and companionship with decent and respectable people," not a man and a woman "with hearts defiled and minds obsessed with lust." Lesley's care and concern for Erlanger were "a persuasive symbol of the sincerity of their relationship." The court granted her a widow's share of the estate—which, ironically, proved to be so encumbered with debt that it was worth much less than she had thought.

Lesley won because the New York court no longer accepted the old story of "true Womanhood." Gender and sexual boundaries were less tight. In addition, although members of New York's elites testified on both sides, Lesley's class connections were the more powerful. That such a highly visible socialite would carry on a sordid affair appeared decidedly implausible to the court.[36]

Despite Lesley's success, white mistresses who had no class connections to speak of continued to have difficulty inheriting in other venues. In a 1935 Colorado case, Rena Lamborn's inheritance from her paramour disappeared, thanks to the usual stories of "undue influence" and "immorality." The sister of Samuel Braden, a childless sixty-year-old widower, succeeded in overturning his will, under which Lamborn was given one half of the estate while a nephew was "cut off" with a legacy of $1.

The court explained that in Colorado a mistress had to demonstrate that a will or deed to her was "uninfluenced by her relationship" with her lover. The court approved of attaching "to illicit cohabitation this stringent rule." When the deceased left his bounty to someone unrelated "to him by blood or marriage," the "clandestine" nature of the relationship made it too difficult for family claimants to prove the existence of "undue" influence. The court's view made it practically impossible for a mistress to inherit when challenged.[37]

The struggle of the women's movement in the 1960s and 1970s to rewrite the gender story changed the legal treatment of white mistresses, as did new attitudes in sexual matters. In 1960 the FDA approved the birth control pill. Growing popular acceptance of premarital sex and live-in relationships aided the process of change. The courts gradually accepted a new sexual story, that of women's sexual freedom. In a 1974 case, for example, Arizona's Supreme Court expressed impatience with the old arguments that barred white mistresses from inheriting because they had violated the codes regulating white women's sexual behavior. Gus Fotopulos was a "rollicking, roistering, heavy-drinking woman chaser." Divorced, with no children, he lived in Phoenix from 1941 until his death in May 1970. Even when he lived with his parents, he maintained an apartment "where he entertained girls, most of whom were considerably younger than he." He began a relationship with Irene Parrisella, who worked at the "profitable bar" he owned. She moved in with him. He gave her an engagement ring and announced he planned to marry her. When he died, he left his entire estate to her. His two brothers, Chris and George, sued to void the will, citing the "undue influence" Parrisella had had on its making. The appellate courts rejected their claim. By the 1970s, the old story of immorality that precluded inheritance by white mistresses had been displaced. Popular approval of premarital sexual relationships freed the courts to apply the rule that called for implementing the will of the testator.[38]

In the 1970s the new story of premarital relationships and live-in arrangements led courts to manipulate the law of contracts to recognize the claims of mistresses. Some claims were filed in inheritance cases, others when a separation was sought. The judges, responding to society's acceptance of premarital sex, placed live-in lovers' contracts on a par with marriage. However, while honoring contracts, courts were loath to condone the selling of sexual favors. To exclude prostitution, the courts emphasized the lack of evidence that the contracts mistresses sought to enforce depended on an exchange of money for sex.

In 1976, a landmark California Supreme Court decision broke new ground by extending the rule that recognized mistresses' rights to inherit: the court gave legal recognition to the rights of a live-in partner. In a suit against the movie actor Lee Marvin, Michelle Marvin asked for the enforcement of a contract to pay her "palimony" after he terminated their seven-year relationship. The California Supreme Court upheld her claim.[39]

Michelle and Lee Marvin's oral agreement had all the attributes of marriage. It provided that while they lived together they would combine their earnings and share equally any property accumulated as a result of their efforts. Michelle Marvin claimed that she gave up her "lucrative career as an entertainer [and] singer" to "devote her full time to Marvin." They lived together from October 1964 through May 1970, presenting themselves publicly as husband and wife although Lee was still married to Betty Marvin until their divorce became final in 1967. The property accumulated during Lee's cohabitation with Michelle, including film royalties, was worth over $1 million. Furthermore, she claimed Lee Marvin had agreed to support Michelle for life.[40]

The court, ignoring arguments that any agreement was unenforceable because cohabitation without marriage was immoral, found Michelle Marvin's complaint valid. The judges would refuse to enforce such a contract only if it was "explicitly and inseparably based upon services as a paramour." Otherwise, adults who voluntarily lived together and engaged in sexual relations were as competent as any other persons to make contracts respecting their earnings and property rights. No state interest prevented the enforcement of such agreements. The court observed that "during the past 15 years, there has been a substantial increase in the number of couples living together without marrying."[41] Furthermore, "many young couples live together without the solemnization of marriage, in order to make sure that they can successfully later undertake marriage."

The justices were not seeking "to resurrect the doctrine of common-law marriage," which had been abolished in California in 1895. They did not hold that Lee and Michelle were "married," nor did they grant Michelle rights under the Family Law Act, which required an equal division of property in a marriage. They merely upheld the agreement Michelle insisted she and Lee had made; she had "the same rights to enforce contracts and to assert her equitable interest in property acquired through her effort as does any other unmarried person." However, the court defined the issues narrowly in order to preserve intact the story of the centrality and importance of marriage. Living together, according to the court, was a trial run for marriage and not marriage.[42]

Michelle Marvin claimed more than the standing of an ordinary mistress: she and Lee lived together and had an oral contractual agreement. Without a contract, written or oral, neither she nor any other mistress had a right to palimony. The court awarded her $1,000 per week in "severance pay" for a two-year period to enable her to reestablish herself in a career.

After the *Marvin* case, mistresses tried to apply the result in inheritance disputes. However, the courts generally required a written agreement in such cases.[43]

The mistress cases showed clearly that the law is never static but responds to the emergence of new stories. Decisions in mistress cases were consistent with the narratives of race, class, gender, and appropriate sexual behavior that society embraced. Inheritances for African American mistresses in the days of Jim Crow upset neither patriarchy nor racial subordination. Rather, they enforced the racial and sexual status quo. The sexual desirability and availability of black women were part of that tradition. Well-to-do white men who took African American mistresses were not violating the taboo on interracial marriage; in fact, the black woman's availability confirmed that taboo. Respecting men's desires in inheritance matters concerning their families black and white, the courts affirmed racial mores rather than challenging them. The state supreme courts consistently showed respect for patriarchy, upholding the intentions of white male testators but not the claims of disreputable white women who, without benefit of a will, sued for inheritances from married men. When public attitudes changed and live-in arrangements became socially acceptable, judges embraced a new story. In affirming the inheritances of live-in lovers when the intentions of the deceased were proved, they represented these relationships as forerunners of marriage and therefore as acceptable. Men and women who lived in informal, consensual arrangements were no longer immoral. The courts' position on white mistresses' claims moved from rejection to acceptance. Race, class, and sexuality still figured in disputes when someone tried to leave property to a non-relative or other unusual beneficiary. However, because objections overtly based on race, class, gender, or sex were no longer acceptable to courts, they had to masquerade as claims of fraud or duress. Courts manipulated the legal rules to permit or disallow the inheritances, depending on how well the narrative fit prevailing assumptions of appropriate behavior.

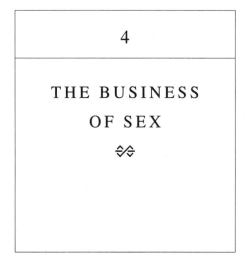

4

THE BUSINESS
OF SEX

Prostitution may be the oldest story ever told. Sporadic efforts to punish it have brought into court narratives of gender and sex, of male desire and disreputable women of easy virtue, and of tension between the punishment for evil and toleration of sin. Protection of prostitutes—if not of prostitution—was usually the result.

Racial stories could complicate courts' decisions, as they did in the case of James B. Shillcutt. Melody Plante, of Milwaukee, first met Shillcutt in 1979, when she was seventeen years old. He asked her if she wanted to become an "exotic" dancer. She agreed and began accepting the dancing engagements he arranged in local bars, giving him the money she earned. He soon began encouraging her to "talk to guys in the bar and see if any of them want to go to bed." According to Plante, when she refused, he "slapped [her] around" until she complied. She subsequently performed "approximately ninety to one hundred acts of prostitution," for which Shillcutt took the money and paid the bills. Whenever she resisted he abused her physically. He also acted as booking agent for several other dancers.[1]

The police arrested Shillcutt for soliciting prostitutes and keeping a place of prostitution. Although they also arrested Plante, they filed no charges, because she agreed to testify against Shillcutt. On the basis of her testimony, the jury convicted Shillcutt and the judge sentenced him to two consecutive five-year prison terms.

But after the trial, one juror, a Mrs. Curran, came forward to report that racial bias had swayed the deliberations. The record does not disclose whether there were blacks on the jury; however, the case was tried in Winnebago County, where only 380 of 132,000 residents were African American. According to Curran's affidavit, the jurors had been deliberating for nearly six hours when one male juror remarked, in the presence of all the other jurors, "Let's be logical, he's a black, and he sees a seventeen-year-old white girl—I know the type." Curran testified that a second juror responded, "A man like that isn't capable of loving anybody." Another juror agreed. Twenty minutes later the jury announced a guilty verdict. The injection of a racial story had influenced the outcome, and Shillcutt's lawyer asked for a new trial.[2]

The trial judge held a hearing on the subject. He concluded that Curran was "a credible witness, and that the statement in fact did take place," but that it did not warrant a new trial. "Although [the statement] could be categorized as a racial slur," the court did not believe it had necessarily prejudiced the jury.

The state supreme court upheld an intermediate appellate decision approving the trial court's verdict and rulings.[3] Likewise, it discounted the meaning of the statement, which invoked stories of race imprinted in the minds of the jurors. The court preferred to downplay the issue of racial bias; its decision advanced the story that legal rules gave them no alternative but to protect the privacy of jury deliberations. Ignoring other permissible interpretations, they declared that the law protected a juror from testifying "to the effect of anything upon his or any other juror's mind or emotions" in reaching a verdict. In holding to a narrow interpretation of the principle of juror privacy, the justices asserted that no court should attempt to discover what influenced the jurors' votes. "Generally, it seems better to draw [the line] in favor of juror privacy; in the heat of juror debate all kinds of statements may be made which have little effect on the outcome, though taken out of context they seem damning and absurd."[4]

Justice Shirley Abrahamson, the first woman on the Wisconsin Supreme Court, took an entirely different view of the case. She believed the influence of the racial story made a retrial necessary: the "gratuitous reference to the race of the defendant and the race of the victim can be taken as a deliberate attempt by a juror to employ racial stereotypes to bolster the state's case, which depended on the jury believing the state's witness rather than the defendant's testimony."[5]

Abrahamson wanted the court to require the trial judge to take testimony from all the available jurors concerning the discussion in the jury room; so as to explore the views of the jurors and the impact of the story. She recalled a 1982 case in which a juror referred to one of the participants in the trial as "a cheap Jew." In that case, the appeals court broadly interpreted the legal rules and reversed the trial court, saying that "trial courts should do all within their means to ensure that verdicts have not been compromised by jurors who harbor prejudice towards any minority. . . . Prejudices should not be allowed to creep into the jury room by extraneous information that the jury determines would have affected an average hypothetical jury." Stories of race involving African Americans or interracial relationships were just as pernicious, Abrahamson argued, as stories that were anti-Semitic.[6]

Shillcutt's case provides another example of how race, class, and gender stories convey what society and law will tolerate in sexual matters. Pimping and pandering were offensive enough, but a black man's sexual exploitation of a white woman was totally unacceptable. When African Americans engaged in same-race prostitution it only confirmed the immorality of the race. A white prostitute's complaint that a white client had physically abused her would be rejected, because of his privileged position and her lack of status. Only the prostitution and abuse of a white woman by a black man was truly unacceptable. Shillcutt's case also shows how courts advance a "rigidity of legal rules" story to pretend that the race and gender stories they share with the jurors are inconsequential. The frames of reference concerning prostitution that were on display in Shillcutt's case had not changed much since the nineteenth century. State courts consistently validated the story that prostitution was acceptable because it permitted the expression of male desire with lower-class, immoral women and did not threaten hierarchies of race, gender, and class subordination. The judges were more likely to punish interracial prostitution and less willing to uphold intraracial convictions. These attitudes can be seen in the 1879 case of Mollie McCoy, who plied her trade in Pensacola, Florida's red-light district. The case exposes stories about the indulgence of white men, racial conventions, and the prerogatives of class that postbellum Southern culture deemed tolerable.[7]

McCoy's bawdy house, at 15 West Zaragosa Street, fit the bill of the high-class den of prostitution. It was a twenty-room brick edifice, with "Mollie's name in gilt letters on the door," and it boasted gold wallpaper and crystal ornaments. Set back among oaks and magnolias, the house had a high ceiling and floor-length windows "masked by curtains of cherry colored stain." The only African Americans allowed in were servants, including a black maid who ushered visitors into the main parlor with an air of gracious hospitality. Mollie, "an impressively stout woman . . . with the command of a first sergeant," dressed her girls in a "grand and showy manner" and forbade them to drink, smoke, or "act indecently." Mollie's place was frequented by a tony clientele, including judges from Alabama and Mississippi. It rivaled in reputation New Orleans's most select bordellos.[8]

Pensacola did not license brothels. However, the police permitted the houses to operate with the understanding that they would conduct raids from time to time. It was agreed that the madams would pay fines, thus enriching the city's treasury, then continue their operations. Occasionally, when they felt they had been raided and fined too often, they appealed, as McCoy did in 1879, instead of paying. On appeal, the state supreme court gave a legal reason to reverse the charges; the hours during which she kept the bawdy house, an essential element of the crime, was not proven by the prosecution. The judges did not want to punish Mollie McCoy. They accepted the story that prostitution did not threaten moral values or the racial and gender status quo. Indeed, favorable treatment of white prostitutes and madams, in their view, reinforced existing hierarchies and gender roles.[9]

Behavior that conflicted with this story line or with prevailing views concerning gender roles was punished by the courts. For example, a Georgia court upheld an 1872 conviction for keeping a "lewd" house against Malta Scarborough of Sumter County. Scarborough, his wife, and their three grown daughters lived together. Witnesses had seen the girls with young men "going into the bushes together" to have sex. They had also seen them in bed with men while their father was in the same room. The wife had also been seen "going to the bushes with men." Malta's vulnerability to the law resulted from his poverty and lower-class status. A laborer, he tried to escape liability by explaining that he often worked away from home. The jury found him guilty, on the trial judge's instructions that if the women carried on lewdness with "his connivance or permission" and in his presence, he was responsible.

The appellate court rejected an argument that Scarborough was "a mere tool in the hands of others." They announced that the husband and father "is the head of the family, and can control what is done there." By not exercising control, he submitted to the degraded behavior of his wife and daughters. He contradicted the manhood story. A father and husband had to exercise discipline and to manage his household in accord with gender prescriptions. Therefore, the jury was right to convict him.[10]

Across the nation, in the 1860s and 1870s, feminists and moral reformers tried to imprint different stories that they hoped would contain prostitution. Their story was that male economic exploitation led to sexual exploitation. The women were innocent and the men were vultures. The reformers worked hard to prevent cities from establishing red-light districts and fought attempts to regulate prostitution rather than eradicating it. Regulation, they believed, amounted to legalization. Out of the reform movements grew social purity campaigns, concerned with adolescent sexuality and ready to use the state to enforce a repressive sexual code. Making prostitution illegal put the public and the law clearly against vice. The public health movement emphasized a medical story: prostitutes polluted young men. In punishing prostitutes, post–Civil War Southern justices took note of stories of disease and sin. However, male access to prostitutes, they knew, was recognized as a legitimate feature of male-dominated society. After all, judges frequented houses of prostitution, including Mollie McCoy's.[11]

The legal system tolerated prostitution in the Victorian era because it fit the narrative that men needed a sexual outlet. Prostitutes thrived mainly in poorer neighborhoods; so long as they remained there, more respectable communities need not worry about them. Further, the public believed that men possessed superabundant sexual energies that required frequent release for the sake of men's mental and physical health. As one medical expert put it, men had "to exert heroic self-control; if they failed in these efforts, they could still protect women in their own milieu by going to prostitutes." Reformers had limited success in urging their story that continence was a remedy for sexual excess that destroyed men's bodies and minds. Finally, the story that prostitution protected the respectable woman, the "angel of the house," from male sexual desire played a role in blunting reform. It would have been cruel to impose sexual lusts upon such rarefied, naturally innocent, gentle creatures. So the overriding story was toleration. The public wanted prostitution to remain illegal while, in reality, men continued to buy sexual favors.[12]

Local people continued to push the boundary between toleration and punishment. They showed their contempt for prostitutes in jury convictions after the occasional arrests, and in other ways. The *Roanoke* (Virginia) *Times* of May 15, 1873, for example, reported that "a lewd white woman was tarred a few nights ago by some of our young men" in Salem, Virginia, and concluded: "Served her right." The incident may have reflected sexual sadism or lower-class resentment of upper-class males, rather than a concern for propriety.[13]

However, local objections could not prevent prostitution from thriving, even though it remained illegal in every state. Illegality alongside permissibility would continue so long as the tension between male desire and female respectability remained unresolved. Payoffs and protection, which largely insulated the prostitutes from jail, also remained part of the story. Cities gained revenue from occasional police crackdowns on brothel owners for operating a bawdy house. Cities also licensed brothels. Urban law enforcement officials allowed prostitution to go on if it confined itself to the red-light district. Any white woman there was presumably a working girl; no respectable white woman would enter, and the only African Americans permitted were servants and entertainers. With these regulations in place, prostitution was contained within the red-light district, where it posed no threat and helped to enforce white male supremacy.[14]

However, toleration did not extend to open interracial sex. In the 1890s, three African American prostitutes, Mamie Peabody, Belle Johnson, and Tinie Walker, lived in Vicksburg, Mississippi. They "did no work and had no property." But they rented a house and were in the habit of "idling their time away during the day, and of dressing up in the evening and sitting on the front steps of the house, or strolling on the street." With "fair speech," they would solicit men to enter the house with them. Also, witnesses reported that white men frequented the house. One defendant was "seen in bed with a white man."[15]

The prosecutor presented no eyewitnesses to intercourse, but the trial court concluded that the defendants behaved like prostitutes. In judging Peabody, Johnson, and Walker, the appellate court embraced a "biblical authority" story rather than legal proscriptions. They reflected on the "loud and stubborn" harlot in Proverbs 7:6–23, who attracted a young man in the streets. The justices concluded that the actions of Peabody, Johnson, and Walker matched the biblical profile, whose colors had lost "none of their vividness in the lapse of centuries." The Bible, "reflected in all the text-books and decisions," supported the women's convictions.[16]

The risk of arrest was part of the business for Peabody and her colleagues, as for other women whose vocation was prostitution. Peabody, at least, continued to ply her trade although the three women owed a fine after losing the appeal. In 1900, she was running what appeared to be a brothel in Vicksburg, although it was described by the census enumerator as a "Boarding House." She was twenty-seven then, and her eleven-year-old daughter and six-month-old son were living with her. A twenty-two-year-old black woman, described as a chambermaid, also lived in the house.[17]

A woman's status as a prostitute could influence a decision

against her in other disputes. Cornelia Fullilove, a young Mississippi woman, left her child for several months with Rachel Banks, the child's paternal grandmother. When Fullilove returned to claim the child, Banks declined, claiming that Fullilove was an unfit mother. Fullilove conceded that she had been "a common prostitute," but insisted that she had reformed "morally." She had "joined the church" and now earned "a livelihood by taking in washing." In 1884, the court found little "evidence of her reformation and honest occupation." The best interests of the child lay in remaining with Banks. The court concluded that Fullilove had essentially given the child away.[18]

At the turn of the century, as immigration from southern and eastern Europe increased, the prostitution narrative developed another theme. Middle-class moralists began to emphasize a connection between immigration and prostitution. Public discourse blamed some combination of genetics and poverty for driving immigrants, along with African American women and other unfortunates, into prostitution. At least thirty-five vice commission reports published between 1910 and 1915 agreed about the dimensions of the problem and its solutions. The Chicago Vice Commission's 1911 report, "The Social Evil in Chicago," concluded that prostitution "is a man and not a woman problem . . . commercialized by men. . . . So long as there is lust in the hearts of men [the Social Evil] will seek out some method of expression. Until the hearts of men are changed we can hope for no absolute annihilation of the Social Evil." Reformers pushed again for complete eradication. They believed prostitution should be neither regulated nor condoned. They knew, however, that some women in distressed circumstances saw selling sexual favors as an easier life than more "respectable" occupations.[19]

To protect women's virtue, the reformers tried to hold the line against vice. They instituted boardinghouses for poor working-women and established moral suasion societies. They exaggerated the existence of highly organized local vice operations into inter-state and international rings that kidnapped young women and forced them into "white slavery," or prostitution. Novels, movies, and plays capitalized on the "white slave trade" theme. The cru-sade led to passage of the federal Mann Act (1910), which out-lawed the transportation of women across state lines for immoral purposes, and to similar state legislation. "Immoral purposes" included both prostitution and consensual noncommercial sex. The Mann Act also provided for the deportation of immigrants involved in prostitution.[20]

After the turn of the century, brothel closing took center stage. Starting in Iowa in 1909, thirty-one states permanently closed buildings found to house prostitutes. During World War I, purity crusaders educated soldiers about avoiding illicit sex so they would remain "Fit to Fight." Crusaders also closed brothels and rounded up prostitutes who catered to the military. By 1915, nearly every state had outlawed brothels and the solicitation of sex. By 1920, the last official red-light district in the United States had been closed. Stories of fear, of immigrants who spread dis-ease, and then of the need for a public health movement (the latter story arising as a result of endemic syphilis found in World War I recruits) had combined to fuel the brothel closings.[21]

While the brothels closed, men still enjoyed the sexual favors of the New Woman, in an era of more sexual freedom for both respectable women and old-style prostitutes. The shift only extended gender and racial subordination. Where prostitutes had once resided in brothels and been employed by madams, now con-trol of the profession passed to men. Prostitutes became either streetwalkers or call girls controlled by male pimps. After the red-light districts closed down, African American women were less likely to gain work as call girls, a lucrative occupation reserved for white women. Their work required call girls to enter hotels and restaurants, which black women could not do without raising suspicions. As a result, black women were more likely to work on the streets, where they were exposed to local police sweeps and more easily identified as prostitutes. Streetwalking served, conveniently, to reinforce negative stories about black women's sexual behavior.[22]

Under this new system, prostitutes and pimps were found blameworthy, but the men who purchased sex from them remained immune from punishment. In 1918, the Louisiana Supreme Court expressed attitudes commonly held in the Progressive period. In its review of the prostitution convictions of Bessie Price, Dollie Maxwell, and their male client, S. L. Ferguson, of Shreveport, the justices upheld the women's convictions while reversing Ferguson's. The women's solicitation of him had led to their arrest. First, the court rewrote the historical record, emphasizing that "in this country prostitution has been looked upon at all times and everywhere as a great evil which it is the duty of every well-ordered community to try to get rid of by every means in its power." However, Ferguson had been wrongly convicted. His fornication, committed secretly in the privacy of a room, did not "offend against morality." In the absence of specific legislation on the subject, "isolated acts of adultery or fornication in the privacy of a chamber do not constitute public prostitution." The court extended the narrative of toleration for male behavior while punishing the women who were the objects of desire.[23]

An occasional ruling challenged the narrative of male indulgence. In 1920, a New York appellate court reversed the conviction of Beatrice Edwards for prostitution because the police failed to arrest the man to whom she allegedly was selling sex. The language of the statute was gender neutral and, the court said, "a man who induces, entices, or procures a woman to commit prostitution, either with himself or with another, is a vagrant, and the man who aids or abets or participates in the commission of prostitution by a woman is a vagrant, and in either case is equally guilty as the woman." The judge was aware that the "custom" was not to charge the men, but "the time has come when the custom cannot longer be permitted to continue. Men caught with women in an act of prostitution are equally guilty, and should be arrested and held for trial with the women." Otherwise, enforcement of the law amounted to "unjust discrimination against women," when the offense required the "participation of men." The court's view did not gain acceptance.[24]

In 1936, for example, a city court in Brooklyn decided to release a man who had been charged anonymously to protect his identity. The woman was arrested and pleaded guilty. The court said that given the "ever-changing conception of morality, and certainly in the interest of the public health, it would have been wiser to bring the male participant, as well, under some sort of governmental supervision." But even though the fact might not be "just or fair," these laws were understood to be "directed against the female, not the male." The court was aware that some reformers wanted to decriminalize prostitution: "In this more enlightened day and age, when there is strong support for the movement toward lifting the stigma of criminality from the woman, I am loath to place that stamp upon the man."[25]

When prostitution and patriarchy came into conflict, the courts insisted on men's adherence to the gender roles that underlay male domination. In 1905, the Washington State Supreme Court let stand Anton Michael Ilomaki's conviction under a 1903 law for "placing and leaving his wife in a house of prostitution, knowing the house to be such." The husband, and everyone else, knew that the residence where Sofia Ilomaki lived was a house of prostitution. Ilomaki had a duty to remove his wife from the premises. C. E. Southwick of Hot Springs, Arkansas, charged with pimping his wife to other men, escaped punishment only because she "was a prostitute before appellant married her." Men needed prostitutes, but society needed husbands to control their wives, which ruled out selling their sexual favors.[26]

The "responsibility of husbands" story led the Pennsylvania

Supreme Court in a 1934 case to uphold the conviction of Owen Shultz for keeping a bawdy house. His wife, Elizabeth Shultz, leased two rooms in their house to William A. Moore, who in turn moved Alice Fonner into the house. Fonner had sex with Shultz and also with other men there over a period of about six months. Mrs. Shultz also took some of the men to her room. Access to the room was through the Shultzes' dining room. The commonwealth charged that Shultz had a duty as "head of the household to see that those rooms were not leased even by his wife for that purpose," even when he was not at home. Shultz's attorney objected that "the management and conduct of a household in the absence of the husband is primarily the part of the wife." The jury should not presume his client's guilt because he owned the house. The court agreed that the expression "head of the house" did not presume he knew of every action of his wife. However, because he knew about the prostitution he was responsible.[27]

In a different twist on the "husband's responsibility" story, a Washington state procurer, William P. McGinty, alias Bill O'Hara, succeeded in overturning his conviction for living with a prostitute, on the grounds that she was his common-law wife. In the 1942 case, police testified that they had arrested Patricia O'Hara in a hotel that "had the reputation of being a house of prostitution." Her pocketbook contained a record that two days before, a physician had examined her and found her to be free of "any venereal disease"; such examinations, the police testified, were a "usual procedure" for prostitutes. They also arrested O'Hara, who had rented the hotel apartment. He claimed innocence: she was already "hustling" when he met her in Chicago, and he had not "turn[ed] her out" as a prostitute. Just when it appeared he would be convicted, Patricia O'Hara testified that she and McGinty were married. The prosecutor asked her when they were married, and McGinty's counsel unsuccessfully objected that a wife is not permitted to testify against her husband. The state supreme court reversed McGinty's conviction: once O'Hara said they were married, no questioning could legally go forward unless the husband agreed. It did not matter that O'Hara dated the common-law marriage after the charges were brought.[28]

Courts continued to accept the story of the husband's responsibility in prostitution cases. In 1957 the California Supreme Court affirmed the conviction of Charles Head for permitting "his wife to remain in a house of prostitution." Head owned and operated a shoeshine stand in Barstow, and also worked as a janitor. He and his wife, Clara, who was "colored," lived in a two-room cabin in an area known as River Bottom. The police arrested Head, his wife, and a customer in the cabin after keeping them under surveillance for three or four evenings before the arrest. They saw Charles Head soliciting marines and soldiers on the street.[29]

A certified copy of a marriage certificate showed that Head had married Clara Luzetta Durant, identified as the woman arrested in the cabin. Head claimed that he "did not know of the prostitution activities of Mrs. Head; that he and his wife had been on the outs and that he had stayed in one room of the house, while she stayed in the other."[30]

The court concluded that Head not only knew about the prostitution but "actively participated in maintaining the house involved as a house of prostitution. Furthermore, he procured customers, conducted them to the place, and evidently shared in the proceeds obtained from the illicit business conducted therein." Husbands remained responsible for their wives' behavior. To decide otherwise would undermine gender roles and the need for male control of the family, basic societal values.[31]

Courts also, infrequently, upheld convictions for enticing young women into prostitution. Everyone's story of female respectability included the proviso that no respectable white woman would find herself in a position to attract an enticer. Furthermore, the new sexual freedom offered a basis for the courts to decide that it was not unusual for a single girl to run away from home seeking excitement and a job. With the exception of highly politicized cases like that of African American heavyweight champion Jack Johnson, who was convicted of taking a white prostitute across state lines for immoral purposes, the courts reversed state "white slave" convictions on technicalities. In 1924, the Florida Supreme Court reversed the conviction of Albert E. Lewis of Miami for enticing an eighteen-year-old Atlanta girl to leave her husband for purposes of prostitution. Mrs. Hudson traveled with Lewis, his wife, and a companion, Mr. Fain, to Jacksonville, where they stayed at the same hotel. Fain and Hudson registered as husband and wife and occupied the same room for two weeks. Fain paid their hotel expenses. Then Mrs. Hudson went to Miami with the Lewises and another couple, Mr. and Mrs. Murphy. The Lewises remained there a week and then moved, leaving behind Mrs. Hudson. The appeals court found no evidence that Lewis induced Hudson to leave home "for immoral purposes." She admitted she had already left her home in Georgia, where she met the Lewises and Mr. Fain, and that she came to Florida with Fain "as his wife, and lived with him two weeks in the city of Jacksonville as his concubine." In the view of the court, she had freely decided to become an immoral woman and became fair game when she took up with those who pimped her.[32]

The Missouri Supreme Court shared the Florida court's acceptance of the narrative that runaway girls were independently starting a new life. In a 1930 case it reversed the conviction of August Carroll and Stuhlman for taking sixteen-year-old Viola Fern Barnes, of Lincoln, Missouri, from "the home of her father" for the purpose of prostitution. She left in September 1929, and her family had not heard from her. Witnesses reported seeing her with Carroll and Stuhlman once or twice. They admitted that Viola rode with them to St. Louis but claimed that they had breakfast with her and then left her "on the sidewalk in St. Louis." They had no idea what she did after that. She was looking for work and "spoke of going to Detroit or Memphis." The high court was of the opinion that Viola "voluntarily ran away from home" and was "concealing her whereabouts from her father and earning an honest living for herself." They saw no reason to conclude that "a good and virtuous girl," as described by her father, would become a prostitute.[33]

While the "female freedom and male indulgence" story held sway, regulating prostitution remained a low priority for the public and the legal system. The only aspect of the vice that continued to draw public notice was the possibility that prostitution spread venereal disease. U.S. public health officials emphasized the problem to gain taxpayer support for their programs. In 1937, 92 percent of those asked in a Gallup poll thought Congress should appropriate $25 million to "help control venereal disease." In the same year 87 percent thought they would like, "in strict confidence," to have their physician give them a venereal disease test.[34]

As the war began, the story concerning prostitution and social hygiene changed slightly. As we have seen, during World War I prostitution was seen as an issue of national defense as well as a moral concern. By October 1942, 55 percent of those polled thought prostitutes around army camps should be required to take weekly medical exams and that officials should "quarantine those who were diseased." Furthermore, 45 percent thought police efforts to "drive out all prostitutes" around camps were a good idea. The primacy of the national-defense concern became evident after the war, when a decline in public interest led the polls to drop the question.[35]

During the war the propensity of young "victory girls" to run away from home to consort with soldiers at military camps raised moral questions. But the sex was apparently noncommercial. After the war, concern about juvenile delinquency and teenage runaways intensified. In 1949, the California Supreme Court did not let claims of consent interfere with the punishment of Richard

Coronado and John Monteiro for pimping a sixteen-year-old schoolgirl. Perhaps the fact that they pimped her to Chinese and Filipino workers at a labor camp south of Sacramento presented an unacceptable modification of the runaway story. The girl, who had run away from home, met Coronado who "seduced her and induced her to become a prostitute." In June 1948, he and Monteiro took the girl to the camp, where she was paid $5 for each act of intercourse. She gave the money to Coronado and Monteiro. Coronado was a barber and Monteiro had a job and a veteran's pension; the appellate court rejected the men's defense that the antipimping law was directed only at vagrants who lived off prostitutes. The court said that both "opulent" and "impecunious" pimps harmed good morals; in fact, the opulent ones were "more odious" than the poor ones.[36]

In accordance with the "licentiousness and inferiority" narrative, the law took little notice of same-race prostitution among African Americans, even when blacks ran a rooming house for assignations or prostitution. The rise of cheap hotel chains soon reduced the market for black brothels. Still, in neighborhoods where streetwalkers prowled, the houses could survive as cheap off-the-street venues for quickie sex.

However, the crossing of racial boundaries excited law enforcement interest and led to punishment. Edna Shuford Davis, an African American living in Hickory, North Carolina, in 1955 was punished because she transgressed racial convention. Police kept her house under surveillance and arrested her after they saw white men and women visiting at night. She was charged with "telling fortunes without a license and with abetting prostitution." The judge fined her $600 and sentenced her to two years in jail, suspending the sentence for three years on condition of good behavior.[37]

County police continued to watch Davis's house and reported that the suspension did not seem to limit her activities: many cars continued to visit her home at night and remained there for various periods "ranging from a few minutes until hours." The cars' occupants, seen entering and leaving the house, "were white men and white women, the defendant being a Negro."[38] Police arrested Davis again six months after her trial for violating the conditions of her sentence. The local court concluded that she was back in business, "engaged in fortune telling or aiding in prostitution," and ordered her to prison. The North Carolina Supreme Court agreed: "It is an unusual and peculiar circumstance that her home has continued to be the mecca for so many white men and white women during the hours of darkness."[39]

The judicial interest in Davis stemmed from her blackness and from the concern that whites socialized at her home, whether or not for financial gain. If she had served a same-race black clientele, the police would have ignored her. However, she was a black woman who profited from providing a haven for prostitution even after male procurers took over the business. Edna Davis was no ordinary madam. She was a black woman openly running a profitable, integrated "lewd house" in a state where segregation was the law. She deviated from the accepted stories of gender and race. The white men and women who frequented her place were not at issue: they fit the story of whites pursuing illicit pleasure aided and abetted by African Americans.[40]

Appellate courts' reliance on stories of race and gender routinely led to a double standard in deciding prostitution cases. State appellate judges left madams like Edna Shuford Davis alone, unless their activities violated long-standing taboos against public display of interracial contact. The federal Mann Act was still available and enforced, but applied only to activities that involved transportation across state lines. The state appellate courts usually affirmed convictions of male pimps and procurers, leaving johns untouched in the process. Male pimps took over women's work. Some defendants kept houses; others were bellboys in hotels or ran photography studios and massage parlors.[41] They were not behaving like men.

In the 1970s, women's rights activists tried to modify the prostitution story. They began a major onslaught against the double standard of law enforcement, which let male clients go scot-free. Some feminists insisted that female prostitutes had the same rights as men to engage in sexual conduct voluntarily, even if for pay. Moreover, they wanted to protect prostitutes from control and abuse by male pimps. Radical feminists supported protecting prostitutes from abuse; however, they objected to prostitution because they believed it reinforced women's subordination as objects of male desire. Phyllis Schlafly and other traditionalists opposed prostitution as sinful and insulting to marital relations. The control of prostitution fell within the purview of sexual offense laws, which had remained largely unchanged since the nineteenth century. The purpose of these laws was to prevent venereal disease, curtail out-of-wedlock births, and protect marriage and public morals from illicit sex. In the 1970s, liberal feminists supported decriminalization of prostitution while radical feminists joined conservatives in seeking recriminalization. Little change in the law resulted, in any case, and male clients continued to go unpunished.[42]

The resistance to change in the prostitution story depended on new themes as well as old ones. Opponents of decriminalization worried about ruining neighborhoods by exposing residents to the trade in their day-to-day lives; they also feared the spread of venereal diseases and AIDS. They cited connections among prostitution, loan-sharking, drug dealing, and other criminal activity. After New York's legislature, in 1965, made it a crime to patronize a prostitute, an occasional case was filed against male clients. Several times in New York City in the late 1970s, the police department assigned female undercover officers to catch male customers and then publicized the men's names. Protests over the arrests of upright citizens soon ended that experiment. The story prevailed that men needed the services of prostitutes and that if any punishment was called for it should be directed at the immoral women who sold their favors.[43]

Another theme pressed by supporters of decriminalization was that the large share of law enforcement resources directed at prostitution could be used to suppress more serious crimes. A 1987 study of prostitution enforcement, focusing on sixteen of the nation's largest cities, found that police made as many arrests for prostitution as for all violent offenses, including rape, robbery, homicide, and assault. In Boston, Cleveland, and Houston, perpetrators evaded arrest for 90 percent of violent crimes, while police resources were spent to control prostitution.[44]

Police officers did not welcome complaints about the time and energy spent on prostitution; they liked the work. What could be more in keeping with the male role than appearing to seek sexual services? Besides, prostitutes were less dangerous than other perpetrators engaged in nighttime or violent crimes. Also, the decoy method gave officers a chance to "look like guys with money to burn." Undercover officers had to rent or lease cars to make sure they escaped recognition. They needed time and money to spend on wardrobes, hairstyles, and other means of disguise. They also might need false identification and credit cards, and a hotel room in which to wait for the prostitute to arrive after being called. To appear as out-of-town customers, they would need suitcases and airplane tickets. None of this discussion affected the perpetuation of the story that prostitution should be tolerated but illegal. Police departments continued to use law enforcement resources for the work, which left prostitution largely untouched.[45]

In a few appellate cases decided in the 1970s and 1980s plain-clothes officers followed entrapment procedures to gain successful convictions of prostitutes. However, when police officers did not engage in entrapment and offered payment first, courts would reverse. Claudia Seabrooks's 1980 New York conviction was reversed because the only evidence was that police saw her in a car with a man and noticed "her jeans were unzipped and that she was sitting next to the driver." Even though she was in a high-prostitution zone, the appellate court found no evidence that any money or goods were given or promised to her. Prostitution required payment. "Free love has never been considered prostitution by any society." Prostitution was of so little concern that, if an appeal was pursued, the courts were not eager to punish.[46]

The resurgence of local antivice groups shaped the prostitution story. They demanded crackdowns in cities and small towns. A group in Joplin, Missouri, targeted James Peacock, who ran the Tokyo Sauna. In 1987, the Missouri Supreme Court upheld a nine-month prison term and a $5,000 fine imposed on Peacock for promoting prostitution. An undercover officer went to the building he operated to see what business was conducted there. With $80 given to him by the deputy sheriff "to use if need be," he acted as a customer. He enjoyed a sauna steam bath, a body shampoo, and a complete body rub with oil, after which the masseuse, "a young oriental female," performed fellatio, "followed by regular sexual intercourse" with the woman on top.[47]

The chairman and "two or three ladies" from the local antivice group, the Joplin chapter of Citizens for Decency Through Law, attended Peacock's trial. The group described "itself as the moral watchdog of the community." They gathered evidence, made complaints to the prosecutor, and attended trials in cases involving prostitution, pornography, and any behavior that "the law classifies as crimes affecting the moral climate of the community." Local groups could induce law enforcement to make sweeps but not to engage in a consistent effort to end prostitution. Their efforts, like those of earlier reformers, reflected the tension in the prostitution narrative between toleration and suppression.[48]

In the 1990s police continued to make occasional sweeps

announced as efforts to end prostitution without any serious belief they could end the practice. In New York City in 1996 and 1997, a series of sweeps called Operation Inside, conducted in the borough of Queens, included the unusual practice of arresting clients and parading them before the press. Thirty-eight handcuffed men who had been arrested in a brothel were walked past reporters and television cameras and taken to jail. The police believed that this rare use of the "perp walk," used to embarrass high-profile suspects, might warn others away from the area. The men were charged with patronizing a prostitute, a misdemeanor probably punished by the payment of a fine. However, the police did not expect the arrests and perp walk to end prostitution in the vicinity. One sergeant said he had been in the area for ten years and "it has always been bad," before and after his assignment to the area.[49]

Cases involving homosexual prostitution began to appear in the appellate courts in the 1980s. The gay liberation narrative that gays have civil rights may have encouraged homosexuals arrested on prostitution charges to appeal their convictions, rather than pay their fines and avoid public notice. These defendants did not reckon, however, with the persistence of gender and sex prescriptions that made their punishment likely. As in heterosexual cases, male prostitutes were usually arrested by undercover officers in sting operations. However, gay men were more likely to find their convictions upheld than female prostitutes were. They deviated from the story line. Men needed the services of female prostitutes, but not the services of other men.[50]

The story heterosexual prostitution brought into the courts was of sin as a social good if kept within certain boundaries. The sin must not spread venereal disease, and the sex must remain sub rosa and private. Public acknowledgment of prostitution would threaten marriage and undermine race, class, or gender hierarchies.

The conflict over whether prostitution should be decriminalized continues in legal circles and among feminists. Many agree with Catharine MacKinnon, who sees women as defined by their sexual accessibility to men and argues that prostitution is abuse. Nadine Strossen, president of the American Civil Liberties Union, supports the idea that restraints on sexual expression repress women's efforts to develop their own sexuality and harass women who voluntarily work in the sex industry. The courts continue to reflect the widely accepted traditional narrative that prostitution is immoral and exploitative, while they leave male clients, for the most part, unpunished. The discourse of appellate judges and the decisions they render reflect and reinforce the narrative of not knowing about what everyone knows—the prevalence of prostitution.[51]

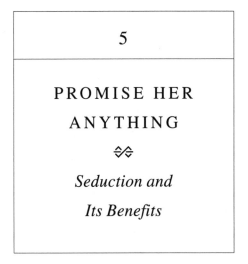

5

PROMISE HER ANYGING

≋

Seduction and
Its Benefits

Seduction cases brought into court such deeply imbedded stories of appropriate male and female behavior that when a legal remedy for seduction became less obtainable it only highlighted the need for its continued availability. When reformers succeeded in changing the legal rules to reflect a new story before the old narrative was no longer fully descriptive, courts manipulated other legal rules to respond to the old story. Seduction actions originally had three primary purposes: to avoid private vengeance, to curb male sexual behavior, and to disgrace or harm the violator as much as a fallen woman. These purposes accorded with the narrative that respectable females needed protection from men who, by promising to marry them, tried to persuade them to have sexual intercourse. Narratives of class and race were part of the definition: "respectable" females only rarely included African American or poor white women. In the late twentieth century, some "respectable" women still brought into the courts stories of vulnerability to male proposals. Judges found reasons to give them the protection they sought.

In March 1872, Emma Chivers opened a drama that displayed the dimensions of the old story when she charged Myron Wood, a Presbyterian minister and teacher, with seducing her into a long affair by means of promises to marry. In the course of the affair she became pregnant. In assessing her complaint the court employed a complex mix of race, gender, and class narratives. The Reverend Mr. Wood arrived in Decatur, Georgia, in 1867 to pastor a church. He also enrolled pupils, including Emma, in his coeducational school. Emma, who was almost sixteen at the time, and her mother, Harriet Chivers, lived next door to Wood, on property owned by Mrs. Chivers's son, who had moved to Montgomery, Alabama, and belonged to Reverend Wood's church. Mrs. Chivers testified that "the war, at its termination, left me penniless." The minister, knowing the family's circumstances, invited Mrs. Chivers to move into his house and "to live as a friend" along with her two daughters. This arrangement allowed Mrs. Wood to help her husband at the school. To pay for Emma's board, Mrs. Chivers cared for the household and Wood's mother.[1]

According to Emma, the minister began walking her home from school occasionally, and had seduced her even before they moved into his house. He told her "his wife did not love him and refused to have anything to do with him." He had married her because "when he became a minister the professors had advised him to marry; that all ministers ought to have wives, he thought he loved her, then . . . he loved her better than any other woman" until he saw Emma. Finally, he explained, his relationship with Emma was entirely proper, based not on "lust" but on "pure and good" feelings.[2]

Wood gave Emma a ring as a bond, telling her that "his wife was sick, she could not live long," and promising to marry her when Mrs. Wood died. Emma trusted him because he was such a "good man, preacher, pastor, teacher," who knew what was right. She claimed she was a virgin when he seduced her and that her newborn infant was obviously his.[3]

Wood's defense counsel relied almost entirely on the "loose morals of the poor" story. He implied that since Emma was already immoral, as was shown by her circumstances, Wood could not have seduced her. Because she was a "bad" girl, she lacked the virtue necessary for seduction. Four young men testified in Wood's defense that they had engaged in lascivious conduct with Emma. Although this was a period when women wore long skirts, one man said "she was not particularly keeping her legs hid." Another classmate said he not only caressed her but saw her with her head in a third young man's lap. Yet another testified that he and a classmate hugged and kissed her.[4]

Wood's defense hinged on the attempt to prove that Emma Chivers, as expected of poor immoral girls, had intercourse with other men. However, the witnesses agreed that no one did more than kiss and embrace her. The evidence pointed to no one who had intercourse with her except Wood. As one of the men put it, he "believed he could go further; [but] did not." On the witness stand Chivers was asked these questions: "Were you in the habit of going into the woods with young men in the night or day time?" "Have you never been blackberry hunting with young men and brought no blackberries back?" She repeatedly denied having sex with anyone except Wood.[5]

Another star defense witness, a "spinster" who lived nearby, injected a racial theme into the narrative. After objecting to being asked her age "because it was rather a delicate question," she insisted that a steady flow of men frequented Mrs. Chivers's house on her son's property day and night. She had observed one of the male visitors there after midnight "on more than one occasion." She admitted spreading a rumor that Mrs. Chivers had once "kept a house of assignation" in Atlanta and claimed that there had been some thought of prosecuting Mrs. Chivers for having "stayed with a negro."[6]

While impugning the Chivers family, Reverend Wood solemnly played the role of the dutiful pastor. He contended that he had visited Emma's family before they moved into his house only in the regular course of his "ministrations" as pastor. He walked Emma home from school to protect her. He refuted claims that he did not love his wife by explaining that he had consented to an abortion to save her life when she suffered complications from pregnancy. Wood insisted he was a loving husband taken advantage of by a loose woman.[7]

The Decatur jury sided with Chivers. The Georgia Supreme Court, however, accepted the story that Wood was a beleaguered clergyman savaged by a poor white temptress, exonerated him, and declared that the lower court's sentence, of not less than two nor more than twenty years, for criminal seduction was too severe. Although the majority believed fornication had occurred, they found that Wood could not have seduced Emma with promises of marriage, since she knew he was already married. A woman who accepted such a promise was "either a fool or she is a bad woman already." Furthermore, the justices ruled, courts should never presume a woman's virtue in a seduction case.[8]

The high court reasoned that a "bad woman at heart," who "may be burning with lust," is not a chaste, virtuous woman; therefore, "a man who by promise or persuasion gets her to have intercourse is blameless of seduction." Emma Chivers was not seducible: she "was ripe for crime already and only needed the chance to fall into it in fact." According to the court, Emma knowingly played "with a viper." A woman "who thus stands upon the brink of the river of vice and indicates her readiness to plunge into its polluted waters, is not the material of which saintly devotees are made."[9]

The majority made clear their belief that virtue in a woman was a function of gender roles and class status. They concluded that the social context in which Emma lived—being poor and having a "bad" mother, who may have consorted with a "negro"— left her already "corrupted and defiled by lustful desires and unchaste wishes." Virtue, therefore, was more a social than "physical condition."[10]

In addition to attributing virtue to social condition, the court was quick to forgive male "indulgences." The gender story accepted by the *Wood* majority included the understanding that males would promise anything to gain sex, and respectable females knew well they submitted at their peril.[11]

African Americans rarely pursued seduction charges or claims. Most were probably unaware that the charge existed. For example, in 1869 an African American father in Georgia purportedly brought suit to seek recompense from the seducer after his daughter died in childbirth. (The suit was unsuccessful.) The state supreme court's opinion implies that the father's white employer actually pressed the suit to recover money he spent on medical care for the daughter.[12]

When African Americans brought same-race criminal seduction charges, the courts assumed the licentiousness of the alleged seducer but were inclined to refuse punishment because they assumed the woman was licentious, too. A Texas appellate court was no more disposed to punish Ben Parks, an African American teacher, for seduction in an 1894 criminal action than the Georgia court in Chivers's case had been inclined to punish Wood. Parks's story was that he had made no promises to marry and that the woman's mother approved of the sexual congress, inviting him to the house and purposely leaving him alone with her daughter.

The appellate court reversed a local jury's conviction of Parks, but not because of evidence concerning the girl's chastity or because there was insufficient evidence of a promise to marry. They found fault in two narratives relied upon by J. J. Swan, the white private counsel hired by the plaintiff, which could have led the all-white jury to decide against Parks. Swan contrasted the girl's family—respectable, hardworking "Negroes"—with Parks, a "scoundrel" who would "not only rob an innocent girl of her virtue, but would go further, and slander her poor old mother." He also invoked the theme of white hostility to educated blacks, reminding the jury that Parks "with his white cravat, white shirt and standing collar, is a professor, and you gentlemen of the jury, are taxed and have to go down in your pockets for your hard-earned money to pay the salary of this professor, to debauch and ruin young girls." The prosecutor continued: "If it had been you or I . . . or any other white man, we would have seized a shotgun, and at the first opportunity filled this defendant with buckshot." After all, if Robert Alexander, the girl's father, "had shot him down on the spot, there is no jury in Falls County that would have harmed or convicted him." Admonishing the jury to do its duty as white men, he concluded: "The reason and cause of the loose morals among the race to which the defendant belongs is that white jurors continue to loose black devils like the defendant." The local jury was impressed with the white counsel's arguments. However, the Texas appellate court had no more concern for the "loose morals" of the race than the *Chivers* court had had about a preacher who took advantage of a young parishioner. Certainly it had not enough concern to impose a four-year prison sentence.[13]

African American women who claimed seduction by a white man were foolhardy. They wanted the court to accept a story that contradicted societal indulgence of white male sexual exploitation of African American women. The courts dealt with these contradictions in disputes from Louisiana and Virginia. In Louisiana, Lilly Carson's 1899 case dramatized the toleration of relationships between African American concubines and the wealthy white men who established households for them, a practice that had been common in Louisiana for years.

Carson went wrong when she tried to add a new line to the story by claiming that her paramour had seduced her with promises to marry. She met Edward L. Slattery in New Orleans in 1898, at a quadroon ball. Carson, disguised behind a domino mask, encountered Slattery, who asked her to dance. When they danced a second time, he asked how he could find her again. From behind her mask, Carson gave him her name and address on North Rampart Street. He courted her assiduously until she agreed to become his concubine. As expected under such arrangements, he supported her and a daughter born of the alliance. But after they had been living together for ten years, Slattery decided to dissolve the relationship, providing no support for Carson or the child. When she decided to sue him to compel payment, her lawyer chose a seduction action. She asked for damages of $50,000—half for herself, and half for the maintenance of their seven-year-old daughter.[14]

Slattery admitted their intimacy but denied he had seduced Carson. He also insisted that Lilly Carson was "not a person of the white race"; therefore, he could not have promised to marry her. At trial, Slattery claimed that he was not the father of the child and that Carson was not her mother. She wanted to "palm off the child on him" because he had decided to leave her. The judge rejected Carson's explanation that she became involved with Slattery originally because he promised to marry her.[15]

The court described Carson as a decidedly disreputable woman who had moved around and assumed a number of different last names—not "the names of respective husbands, because it does not appear that she was ever married." Also, she had lived in various Northern cities, returning to New Orleans shortly before she met Slattery. Having lived with him for years although not married to him, she was at least "an accessory to her own debauchery." Finally, the child's paternity was "veiled in mystery," because in her wanderings she may have engaged in sex with someone else besides Slattery.

The court found Carson's racial background confused at best. She was obviously not legally white: she had attended Straight University, a local black institution, and had been an organist at a Colored Methodist Episcopal Church. Given the state's interracial marriage ban, she could not have thought Slattery would marry her. However, because she was "white in appearance," the court would not formally decide that she was an African American. Lilly Carson, "owing to her weakness and indiscretions," was "already unfortunate enough." The court's reasoning makes clear that her lack of virtue was additional evidence that she was not white and a sufficient basis to reject her claim. Carson fit the narrative of African American women being sexually available to white men, but the story had no place for claims to marriage.[16]

In a Virginia case thirty years later, the court rejected Dorothy Short's seduction claim because she, like Carson, deviated from the expected narrative. The prosecutor for Rockingham County, Virginia, describing Short as "an unmarried female, of previous chaste character," charged Leonard H. Wood with seduction under promise of marriage. At trial, Wood did not deny the sexual intercourse with Short or the promise to marry. Instead, his counsel relied on the story of racial inferiority. Amid a sea of mulattoes, born from the racial mixing that had always been tolerated in the state, Virginia's laws continued to ban interracial marriage and denied the benefits of whiteness to the "spurious offspring" resulting from interracial sex. The legislature passed a new Preservation of Racial Integrity Law in 1924, defining a "white" person as someone with no trace of any other than Caucasian blood except for a maximum of one-sixteenth Native American blood. Under a 1931 law an African American was anyone with any ascertainable "negro" blood.[17]

When Short took the witness stand, Wood's counsel asked "who her grandfather was on her mother's side." After the prosecutor objected, the trial judge asked Wood's counsel the purpose of the question. He responded that he wanted "to elicit from the witness the information that the ancestor whose identity was sought was one William Campbell, a negro and that the witness, if permitted to answer, would have so testified." The court sustained the objection of the attorney for the Commonwealth and Wood was convicted and sentenced to two and a half years in prison.[18]

On Wood's appeal, the state supreme court voiced approval of the "sound and wholesome" policy of "racial integrity" of the state. However, if Wood actually had seduced Short, "his moral turpitude would not be less because there was a legal inhibition of the marriage between them." The issue would resemble cases in which a married man was validly convicted of seduction when the woman did not know he was married. The question was whether Short knew she had "negro ancestry." The court could understand that she might not have known, because "the natural and humane resolve" of her mother "would be to withhold from her the knowledge of what could only humiliate and distress her." This approach was rational because the evidence "amply justifies the conclusion that she was received and accepted socially by white persons as one of them." However, the conviction could not stand; Short should have been required to answer the inquiry about her ancestry. Class and racial aspersions against her mother defeated Emma Chivers. Short and Carson lost because they insisted upon marriage. They tried to rewrite the racial story in ways society would not abide.[19]

These cases arose from "heart-balm" statutes, which, until the 1930s allowed recovery for seduction, breach of promise to marry, alienation of affections, and other interferences related to marriage and usually attached to persuading a female to have sexual intercourse. Heart balm actions brought into court an array of intersecting stories of race, gender, and class: the vulnerable woman, the male libertine, the shyster lawyer, the licentious African American. The common law early recognized the need for reparations when a daughter was seduced and then abandoned. The father could bring a civil suit for damages; the wrong done was characterized as trespass consisting of assault on the father's servant, because he lost his daughter's "services." (Common-law contract theory generally categorized wives and daughters as servants; husbands could also sue for loss of services in adultery cases. This was an old story, at least as old as Locke and, indeed, much older.) After the Civil War, the courts permitted a parent to bring suit without pretending a master-servant relationship. Women's relationship to the law also shifted. Some states permitted women themselves to sue their seducers for damages. Alabama, Tennessee, and Mississippi authorized such suits by statute, and North Carolina's courts allowed them by inference (without a statute, they interpreted common law to permit them). The cases focused on the abuse of the woman and her disgrace.[20]

At common law, although seduction could be the basis for a civil suit, it was not a crime. In the middle of the nineteenth century, however, Edward Livingston's penal code for Louisiana suggested that it be criminalized. Livingston, a prominent New York lawyer who had moved to New Orleans, was asked by the Louisiana legislature to draft some important legal codes. The "ruin of the unsuspecting victim" and "the disgrace and misery of her connections" required punishment, Livingston wrote. Although not enacted by the Louisiana legislature, his code influenced legal reformers.[21]

Criminal seduction statutes originated in the successful efforts of the moral reform movement to make libertines outlaws. In their campaigns, which led to the passage of criminal seduction laws in Pennsylvania, New York, and Massachusetts in the 1840s, they told and retold the story of the innocent female injured by the rakish male. After the Civil War such laws spread across the country. An anonymous lawyer who wrote the first legal article about criminal seduction laws, in 1882, emphasized that their purpose was to control male behavior. The article noted that civil suits had become rare because a respectable parent would shy away from exposing "the frailty and dishonor of his child in the public court-room, and the libertine generally escapes the money penalty that would otherwise be imposed upon him." The belief that money payments were not enough to prevent the offense also influenced legislatures to enact criminal seduction statutes.[22]

These female-oriented laws, according to the anonymous lawyer, were misguided. They "appeal largely to the emotions" and presume that a man brought before a jury is a seducer. These laws portrayed a woman with "heaven-moving pearls, raining the tears of lamentation, the father in attendance with grief-stricken aspect." The man was unfairly cast as a "libertine and a seducer." This inequity called on the court to interpret the law calmly and dispassionately. Despite the anonymous lawyer's concern, the cases showed that courts became more sensitive to men's efforts to resist characterization as seducers. The judges had no problem considering African American and poor women as already soiled. Pre–Civil War Northern cases told tales of women's innocence and male vice. Now, the stories of class and race overrode the older stories, and women depending on their class and race were presumed to be unchaste, not seducible—as we saw with Emma Chivers.[23]

To prove criminal seduction, the prosecution generally had to establish that a man had sexual intercourse with an unmarried woman "by means of temptation, deceptions, arts, flattery, or a promise of marriage." Proof of the marriage promise required cor-roboration; and, as an accomplice, the woman could not testify. In all eight Southern states that criminalized seduction, women had to be chaste to claim redress under the law. (Arkansas and Missis-sippi did not preclude a married woman's complaint. While the Arkansas and Texas statutes did not require previous chastity, the judges in those two states imposed it.) In the post–Civil War years, we find legislators and judges paying lip service to the stories of female innocence. Damages were permissible. However, few appellate courts wanted to punish males for their sexual conduct. Thus, only a woman whose reputation was above even that of Caesar's wife could have her story accepted by the courts, win damages, or secure criminal punishment for her seducer.

Like other cases involving sexual behavior, almost all civil and criminal seduction cases between the 1870s and the 1930s, when the cause of action was abolished, came from rural areas or small towns, where the woman whose reputation was damaged was known to everyone and anonymity was impossible. Accusers were often angry and vengeful. The civil cases often disclosed tawdry stories of females seduced by in-laws or other relatives too distant for the affair to constitute incest. The usual story included the birth of an out-of-wedlock child, which occasioned the action. For example, Elizabeth Ellington sent her sixteen-year-old daughter, who was a virgin, to live with her uncle James Ellington and his wife in rural Mississippi and learn to double-weave. The girl received food and shelter in exchange for helping with the household work. When she became pregnant, Mrs. Ellington discovered that her husband had seduced and defiled his niece. This discovery "created a difficulty." The girl stayed with her uncle's family until two months before her confinement, whereupon her aunt insisted she leave and return home. In the ensuing 1872 action, Elizabeth Ellington recovered $1,000 for the loss of services of her daughter.[24]

Occasionally, the story told by the parties in seduction cases alluded to the use of abortifacients that did not work, or to the use of "condrums," which they had believed would protect them from pregnancy. In an 1886 Tennessee case, a father won a lower-court decision in his suit seeking damages for the seduction and impregnation of his daughter. The appellate court reversed, noting that the girl had testified that her lover used a "condrum" purchased in the next village, and that she had inspected the article. She "willingly trusted to its efficacy and wantonly yielded to its efficacy and the craving of passion."[25]

The courts were suspicious of adult women who brought damage claims, because they should have been more aware than a young girl that a man would promise them anything to have sexual intercourse. Large audiences would sometimes come to court to hear the evidence and poke fun at an adult complainant. In an 1892 criminal seduction trial in Alabama, the judge repeatedly had to restore order. As the witnesses testified, "There was a great titter and suppressed laughter in the courtroom." The judge asked the audience for quiet, saying he did not see anything "that affords merriment." He also noted the presence of a number of boys aged twelve to eighteen and wondered aloud if their parents knew they were in the audience. He went on to say, "Gentlemen, look out, you don't know how soon the lightning may strike your house." The defendant escaped punishment.[26]

Courts were more receptive to the stories told by fathers and mothers who claimed the seduction of a minor daughter. The Virginia Supreme Court in 1891 upheld a judgment granting damages to a woman who had sued the father of a young man who refused to marry her daughter after the girl became pregnant. The seducer made the mistake of writing to suggest that the girl go to a boardinghouse to deliver the infant, who could then be placed in an orphanage. This way the episode would be "no bother to anyone." He could not marry the girl because to do so would "mar" his future. He would have to leave school, forgo his education, and be a common laborer. Although courts were more receptive to parents' complaints than to those of an adult woman claiming seduction, they expected parents to protect the daughter's virtue and take immediate action against any threat. A slow reaction implied complicity or suggested that the daughter was not respectable or was even a harlot.[27]

Sophie Lee Jones's 1937 seduction claim failed because her parents violated the narrative that parents should protect their daughters. The Virginia Supreme Court voided the five-year prison sentence of Sam Bottoms and reversed his conviction for "seducing and having illicit connection" with Sophie Lee Jones, "an unmarried female of previous chaste character," after she delivered a child in May 1936. At the time of the alleged seduction, Jones was seventeen years old and Bottoms was twenty-two. The court noted that both families were "of the humbler and simpler walk of life."[28]

Jones's story seemed problematic. She claimed that intercourse occurred several times in the parlor "of her father's house, when both of the parents were sitting on the porch and the window of the parlor was open." Also, she said that whenever she and Bottoms were in the parlor "her brothers and sisters had access to the parlor, in and out, from time to time."[29]

The high court found the testimony in support of the seduction charge unbelievable. The most damning evidence against Bottoms was that when Sophie's father, Leonard Jones, confronted him, he did not deny paternity. Another piece of evidence came from a mutual friend, Russell Kidd, who testified that after the child's birth he went to Jones "to suggest an adjustment by the marriage of the parties and that he did so at the instence of the accused and his mother and father." Bottoms replied that these incriminating events resulted from anxiety; "he had never been in any trouble of any nature" and "was willing to do anything to avoid or get out of trouble." Besides, Bottoms never really courted Sophie. He "had never been to church with her or to a moving picture show; he had never given her a present or written her a letter." No one suggested that they marry. Overall, the court found no evidence to suggest that the parties were regarded by either one's family, or by anybody else, as "an engaged couple." The court enforced the narrative that fathers and mothers protected the virtue of respectable daughters. Lower-class people might be more likely to have premarital intercourse but Bottoms had achieved his goal, without promising Jones anything and especially not marriage.[30]

The appellate courts were much less likely to affirm criminal convictions than civil damages for seduction. The penalties in seduction cases were more severe than those for fornication—up to ten years' imprisonment in some states. Because they faced jail, convicted criminal defendants were more likely to appeal their sentences.[31]

Every seduction case required the woman's story to include a denial of licentiousness. For lower-class women, winning a lawsuit required overwhelming evidence of their chastity. Likewise, openly intemperate behavior could hurt the man's defense. Justice Judd of Virginia received a two-and-a-half-year prison sentence because he openly displayed his passion and unreasonableness. Judd regularly visited Susan Jones over a period of years. He drove her home from church on Sundays. She wrote him "a most affectionate letter," to which he asked a friend "to reply in his name the next day in the same vein." The friend "thought she was his sweetheart." Judd's jealousy was publicly expressed. Once, seeing her sitting in the backseat of a car with a young man— another couple was in the front seat—he brandished a pistol, and "his attitude was such that the young women began to scream and threatened to jump out." When a young man took her to an oyster supper, Judd appeared to complain; he announced that everyone there should fear him because "he was a bad man from no man's land."[32]

The "illicit relations" between Jones and Judd continued for about three months after she "yielded," until she became visibly pregnant. He then refused to marry her. A "negro woman, fortune teller," testified that Judd visited her, told her "he was in trouble with a woman and asked her to help him to do something to get rid of the baby." Judd confessed to everything except promising marriage.

The court believed Jones needed protection. Her father was a poor farmer; she and her three sisters worked in a factory to help support the family. "She was of limited education, not strong in moral character, and would probably have escaped irretrievable ruin had not her confidence been secured and her apprehensions put at rest by the machinations of the defendant who quit when he got what he wanted." Jones did not fit the story of poor white immorality. Although poor, she was blameless, given Judd's openly reprehensible behavior. He had no appealing story to outweigh the narrative of her victimization. Furthermore, he had publicly violated all expectations of gentlemanly behavior. Therefore, the gentleman's code no longer protected him.[33]

On the contrary, in 1906, Iowa's Supreme Court rejected the story of Frances Kesselring, a white domestic, that Albert Hummer seduced her and fathered her infant. Hummer had engaged in no open behavior that indicated he was pursuing her. His defense successfully presented her as an immoral lower-class female, pleading the common defense that Kesselring had been unchaste. This was based on hearsay evidence that she had engaged in sexual intercourse with another employee in the household where she worked as a domestic. The defense also buttressed its narrative that Kesselring was a liar by "scientific testimony" from a physician who testified that a woman and man of average height and build were "very unlikely" to conceive a child in a buggy. This defense was not unusual. In an 1876 Michigan case, for instance, Walter Clark succeeded in having his conviction for seduction of Alice Morey reversed because of medical evidence that having sex in a buggy was "highly improbable if not impossible."[34]

To escape the narrative of dishonor for herself and her family, a woman might accept her seducer's agreement to marry in exchange for dropping seduction charges. In some states, the bridegroom had to post bond for the wife's support for five years. Such marriages sometimes led to very unhappy results. An Arkansas Jewish congregation persuaded one of its members, a local merchant, to marry a woman who became pregnant after he allegedly promised to marry her. He refused to live with her or to acknowledge the marriage, denounced her publicly, and demeaned her at every opportunity. When she sued for divorce, he replied that the congregation had forced him to marry her; the marriage should be declared invalid because of duress. The state supreme court granted the wife a divorce and ordered the husband to pay support, denouncing his perfidy for refusing to give her his name gracefully after he had "ruined" her. Men and women had to live up to the stories of acceptable female and male conduct to gain favorable legal outcomes. This man violated all expectations of manly behavior, while the woman fit perfectly the narrative of the vulnerable, respectable female.[35]

A Texas man refused to marry a woman he seduced, even after she bore their infant, until she had him arrested on seduction charges. Once they were married, in the clerk's office, he asked the judge where he could get a divorce. When told he could not do so immediately, he appeared "worried." On the way home he killed the woman, cutting her throat from ear to ear. The Court of Appeals upheld his sentence of life imprisonment. His wife's attempt to minimize the disgrace to herself and her family led to her death.[36]

In the twentieth century, as a result of social and political change and the resultant sexual revolution, reformers began to regard the seduction action as a relic of the past. A new narrative of gender developed when women gained the right to vote and became redefined as political actors. Feminists joined previous legal critics in decrying the use of "heart-balm" laws, including those concerning seduction, in an age when disgrace and the protection of virtue evoked little of the fervor they had in the past. Indiana, long known as a divorce mill, was the first to abolish the civil statutes, in 1935. Roberta West Nicholson, the sole female member of the state legislature and a strong advocate of women's rights, led the movement. Her "Act to Promote Public Morals" outlawed seduction suits by women over twenty-one years old. Speaking for the bill, Nicholson declared, "Women do not demand rights, gentlemen, they earn them, and they ask no such privileges as these which are abolished in this bill."[37]

Women led the movement to abolish heart-balm suits in a number of other states. Katherine A. Foley, a widow who was the only woman Democrat in the Massachusetts legislature, described her abolition bill as one designed "to defeat golddiggers and shyster lawyers," who would no longer be able to blackmail men or extract money from them by means of such lawsuits. She had three daughters and believed "no price could be placed on affection." The National Woman's Party argued that heart-balm suits should be equally available to men or should be laughed out of court. Proponents of repeal cited instances of fraud and blackmail, and pointed out constitutional limitations on invading privacy. Although civil damages were abolished in at least two-thirds of the states, seduction remained a crime in many jurisdictions. Nationally, however, women rarely used the remaining criminal and civil statutes. Reformers accepted a new story. Politically empowered women could resist promises to marry and pressure to have sexual intercourse. They no longer needed the law to protect them.[38]

The reformers believed that a heart-balm action contradicted the new narrative of freer sex, and that it reinforced rather than recognized changes in traditional gender roles. A man might promise a woman anything. It was the New Woman's right and responsibility to decide freely whether or not to have sex. Further, in the new narrative, female purity became less precious as premarital and extramarital sex became more common. Concern for the care of out-of-wedlock children was addressed by paternity suits. Even in those states that continued to criminalize seduction, conviction remained difficult. In 1938, Frank Sinatra was arrested after a New Jersey woman claimed she had sex with him based on an unkept promise of marriage. The charge was changed to adultery when it was discovered that the woman was already married, and then dismissed.[39] Despite the new story that allowed women to vote, hold a job, and experience premarital sex, the public and the courts did not abandon the old story; courts remained sensitive to jilted women. Despite the arguments of reformers, female vulnerability was still a concern.

No temptress or "shyster lawyer" was exposed in a 1938 California case, in which the judges sustained the claims of seventeen-year-old Mary Louise Carter, whom they saw as naive and exploited. Her seducer, Jerry Murphy, a married man of thirty-three, was a traveling salesman for Standard Brands of California. Mary Carter lived with her parents in rural Arizona, where she attended school. During summer vacations she visited Mrs. Irene Brooks, a married sister who operated a beauty parlor in Los Angeles. Carter met Jerry Murphy the first time she visited her sister, but initially, nothing of an "amorous character" developed.[40]

Meanwhile, Murphy and Irene Brooks became good friends. Mary stayed with her sister during the summers of 1934 and 1935. She planned to return home after the 1935 visit to enter Arizona State College. Murphy frequently took Brooks and Carter out to dinner and other "places of entertainment." His attentions soon "centered on Mary," whom he phoned and visited during her sister's absence. Murphy and Mary first had intercourse at Mrs. Brooks's apartment in August 1935, after he plied her with wine. Shortly thereafter, Mary returned to Arizona. The court found nothing showing that Mary had "immoral propensities" or was "lacking in moral propriety or refinement, before she was beguiled by the blandishments" of Murphy. The affair continued when Mary returned to visit her sister, until it was discovered by a neighbor who rang the bell at the apartment one evening and found Carter and Murphy disheveled and disoriented. Carter's "deviation from the path of moral rectitude" resulted in the "shame" of illegitimate pregnancy. A seduction action appeared to provide a remedy for her exploitation by Murphy. Mary was seventeen when he met her. Consequently, the prosecution could have charged him with statutory rape. However, the district attorney preferred to force Murphy to provide for Mary and her baby.[41]

Everything about the case underscored the disjunction between the reformers' new story of female empowerment and Mary's predicament. She told of Murphy's "active participation in the effort to relieve her of pregnancy." When the abortifacient he helped her procure did not work, Mary had a surgical abortion, which so impaired her health that she could not work on a job she found at the telephone company. The court concluded that Murphy never intended to leave his wife to marry Mary. He "deliberately planned by sedulous methods the undoing of an unsophisticated schoolgirl in order to satisfy his carnal and lustful passions." The story of Mary Carter and Jerry Murphy was the very same narrative of unregulated male sexuality and female vulnerability that the Female Moral Society had told in support of criminalizing seduction beyond a civil damages remedy in the 1840s and 1850s.[42]

In addition to insisting that Murphy made no promise to marry, his counsel attempted "to impeach [Mary's] previous chaste character." He introduced evidence that she had been a dance hall girl for one night after she left her sister's apartment and was seeking work. The court found that this stint as a "taxi dancer" occurred after she "came under the influence and domination" of Murphy. The court concluded that if Mary "were a woman of years, with that knowledge of the world which age brings with it at the present day, the case might present a different aspect." Her battle with Murphy "would not have been so unequal, and she would have been held to a stricter responsibility." But she was immature, and the wine he gave her on the first occasion "alone may be well termed an artifice that conduced to her downfall."[43]

Murphy's lawyer eagerly armed himself with the new story used by women who led the fight to abolish heart-balm actions. Because the California state legislature had not yet repealed the seduction action, he asked the court to find it unconstitutional. He argued that seduction should not be a cause of action, because women were so politically and socially advanced: "The notion that they belong to the weaker sex is only entertained by the credulous and unsophisticated." Changes such as the "the radio, moving pictures, the widened field of female activities, and widespread dissemination of information with reference to sexual relations had changed expectations between men and women." Most women would simply grieve at what happened to Mary. Only the "unscrupulous would make it a matter of public parade and profit."

The judges were not receptive; they responded that if the lawyer's arguments "rest upon sound moral grounds, they should be addressed to the law-making branch of government rather than to the judicial branch." Until the legislature acted, the court accepted the reality that some women were vulnerable: "There has never been a time in the history of the civilizations which observe a moral code, that the female sex has been in ignorance as to the magnitude of the misery and ruin which unlawful seduction inflicts upon transgressors." Male aggression and female susceptibility had made seduction a concern "since the earliest civilizations and daughters in early girlhood in the ages past have not been ignorant as to its inexorable penalties." The court affirmed the judgment, issued by a Los Angeles judge sitting without a jury, for Carter against Jerry Murphy for $10,000. The reformers' new story of women's agency did not afford a remedy for the abuse some women experienced.[44]

In states that abolished seduction actions in the 1930s and after, judges, like those in Mary Carter's case, often based their decisions on facts that accorded with the old story of vulnerability rather than the new "sexual freedom and responsibility" narrative.

The cases presented men who acknowledged paternity and financial responsibility at first, but failed to support a child, and they focused on the sexual abuse of young girls. Courts interpreted legal rules creatively to judge the seducers, emphasizing as primary not the woman's virtue but her practical financial need. In 1947, New York's Court of Appeals denied Philip Neumann's motion to dismiss a breach-of-contract finding in favor of Katherine Burger, whom he impregnated during their affair. While the court agreed that heart-balm claims violated public policy, they also found that a remediable injury had occurred. Burger worked for Neumann. He "professed his love for her, and also . . . told her it was his intention to marry her."[45]

Neumann took advantage of his class privileges according to the oldest stories of master-servant exploitation and male vice–female innocence. He acknowledged fathering Burger's child and agreed to support both of them until the child turned twenty-one. He subsequently refused, however, to make the requisite payments. Burger wanted him to pay child support, at least. The court noted that under the common law there was no obligation upon the father to support an illegitimate child. However, if he acknowledged the child as his own and asked others to care for it, "the father would then be liable to the party providing such care by reason of his expressed agreement." New York law has since then made a father responsible whether or not he requested care, and also detailed the manner of payments. The court, discomfited by Neumann's expectation that privilege would enable him to use the end of heart-balm actions to avoid his responsibilities, and by the economic plight of the child and Burger, interpreted the legal rules to find a remedy. The problem fit within the very old narrative of male abuse that had troubled nineteenth-century moral reformers. They found that Neumann's agreement was valid despite the repeal of the seduction statute.[46]

In 1950, the New Jersey Supreme Court struggled to find a substitute civil remedy for a mother who claimed damages for the sexual abuse of her daughter. Josephine Blackman wanted to file a civil suit against Alfred John Iles, Charles Cunliffe, and Joseph E. Jadoun, who "carnally knew and debauched her daughter, a child fourteen years of age, at diverse times and places." Blackman's claim was based on the common-law seduction theory of the loss of the child's services. Her question for the high court was whether she could proceed with her suit. The court answered affirmatively. They were unwilling to define Mrs. Blackman's claim narrowly to preclude any remedy. The New York and New Jersey courts expressed an awareness that the new story, used to abolish the seduction claim, had not invalidated the old story. They interpreted legal rules to provide a remedy for the story they knew, which they assumed everyone else would also know and understand: that men could and did abuse young girls. Besides, these women were not the "gold diggers" whose seduction claims reformers sought to prevent.[47]

Changes in gender role assumptions, the women's movement, greater economic opportunities, and more liberal sexual mores had converged, undermining the old narratives that justified seduction remedies. However, even at the close of the twentieth century, the old story line had not been entirely erased. Instead, bits and pieces of it recurred in narratives weaving sex and power and vulnerability together—in discussions of sexual harassment, incest, and other abuse. Because women want equal treatment but are still socialized to remain gullible and submissive to men, they remain at risk.[48]

Even after seduction suits disappeared, other courts, like those in New York and New Jersey, searched for imaginative ways to provide remedies when a marriage promise soured, especially for women with children. Legal scholar Jane Larson observed that in seventeen states anti–heart-balm laws and similar statutes did not bar common-law seduction suits, and she called attention to a few cases decided in the 1980s. In 1985, a common-law seduction case in Missouri presented the sort of factual situation that Larson thought should support a seduction claim. Alice Parker received $25,000 in actual damages and $50,000 in punitive damages for a series of misrepresentations by her lover during a two-year sexual relationship that led to two unwanted pregnancies. The first pregnancy ended in an abortion and the second in the birth of a child. Although the sex occurred under false pretenses, Parker did not use the seduction action to seek support for her child. She based her claim partly on emotional harm.[49]

In January 1995, Sharon Wildey, a Chicago lawyer, sued Richard A. Springs, an Oregon cattle rancher, for calling off their engagement two months before the wedding date. Illinois, like other states, had repealed its heart-balm laws in 1935, citing their potential for blackmail. However, in 1946, the Illinois Supreme Court declared the repeal unconstitutional because the Illinois constitution required a legal remedy for all injuries. Wildey used a law, enacted later, that allowed such actions under very tightly controlled circumstances. After an Illinois jury awarded her $118,000, the appeals court reversed because Wildey had failed to include the date of their engagement when she sent him the required notice of intent to sue. The court said the date might be seen as inconsequential, but given the history of concern about abuse of the seduction action a strict reading of the law was reasonable. Springs said he had changed his mind about marrying Wildey because she had hidden aspects of her past, including psychiatric problems. He allowed her to keep a $10,000 ring and gave her access to his $10,000 bank account in recompense.[50]

Throughout its history, the seduction action was primarily pursued by white women against white men. In the nineteenth century the emphasis in the story was on protecting the virtue of respectable females, the familial reputation, and the woman's prospects for marriage. In the twentieth century the emphasis shifted to the need for financial support for women and out-of-wedlock children, who might otherwise become public charges.

The narrative of race influenced seduction actions, even though African Americans rarely made claims. Intimations of contact with an African American could buttress claims of white female immorality, as in the Chivers case against Reverend Wood. A damage suit would only be productive if the man had resources. A judgment against a man who had little money or property was useless; as for a criminal conviction leading to incarceration, that would preclude the possibility of financial help. Black women who pursued seduction claims against white men fruitlessly challenged the story of African American promiscuity and their availability for white male exploitation.

The evolution of seduction cases demonstrates that the law is not a series of abstract rules but responds at the point where stories converge. Stories that judges and juries believe will be enforced. Gender roles did not change as quickly as the reformers who abolished the seduction action in their states in the 1930s had thought. Some judges and juries applied the new stories of women's empowerment and independence and of women exploiting men for financial gain. But the old story of women still had the power to persuade, especially since the realities of sex and power were too obvious for judges and juries to dismiss when they were confronted with an actual vulnerable woman. The seduction action—perhaps under another name—was still a work in progress.

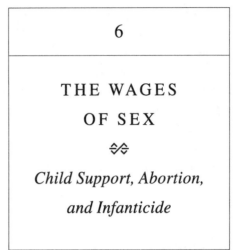

6

THE WAGES

OF SEX

≋

Child Support, Abortion,

and Infanticide

One evening in 1956, Lewis Grubbs drove his girlfriend, Virginia Crowe, to Lexington, Kentucky, to Dr. C. B. Dotye's office, where—without her knowledge—he had arranged for her to have an abortion. Crowe complained that when she learned the purpose of the trip, she refused, but Grubbs insisted that she terminate the pregnancy. She reported that Dr. Dotye "inserted an instrument into her body," causing her to bleed, and that Grubbs paid Dotye $100 for his services. Grubbs and Dotye were charged and indicted separately. Grubbs claimed the privilege against self-incrimination and refused to testify about what transpired in the doctor's office. Dotye admitted that he examined Crowe at her request, because she asked if she was pregnant, and he claimed that upon the examination he found she was already having a spontaneous abortion. The trial jury apparently did not believe his testimony. On the basis of Crowe's testimony, they convicted Dotye, who was described as "a negro doctor," of attempted abortion. The Kentucky state appeals court reversed his $500 fine and one year prison sentence.[1]

The appellate court objected to the prosecutor's repeated attempts to use a racial narrative to gain a conviction. They noted that he tried "to elicit from the appellant (who is a Negro) a statement that it was unusual for a white girl to go to a Negro doctor at night." Dotye's counsel insisted that "by persistent repetition of questions," the prosecutor had "deliberately attempted to inject racial prejudice into the case." Indeed, it was unusual for a white person to visit an African American physician. However, the court was unwilling to convict a physician, even an African American one, for performing an abortion on an unmarried female who survived the procedure. They reversed the conviction deciding that "any undue repetition of questions" on the racial theme was impermissible.[2]

The Dotye case and others involving abortion, infanticide, and child support touched on some of the most sensitive issues of race, gender, and class. The court heard and evaluated sometimes starkly conflicting stories from the participants as they dealt with the consequences of having sex. One story was that of an unmarried woman who wanted to avoid having a tarnished reputation and blighted future prospects. A second story was of the married couple who agreed they could not afford to care for more children after a wife became unexpectedly pregnant. A third story emphasized respect for physicians' judgment and practice and decried nonphysician abortionists who butchered women. Yet again, the courts wanted to indulge men's sexual desire but not their refusal to support their out-of-wedlock children. In the courtroom, discussions of family values and appropriate sexual conduct became intermingled with legal rules and judicial decrees. At issue was patriarchy and power.[3]

The abortion issue, raised in the *Dotye* case, was and remains both sensitive and explosive. As Carroll Smith-Rosenberg and

James Mohr document, abortion, in the early stages of pregnancy, was a readily available remedy until being criminalized in the 1880s. Thereafter, access to safe abortion was problematic until 1973, when the Supreme Court decided *Roe v. Wade*. Decisions in court cases reflected stories of race, gender, class, and sexuality.[4]

In the nineteenth century, white people's fears of "racial suicide" and population decline, and the efforts of American Medical Association physicians to prevent abortions performed by nonphysician practictioners led legislators in state after state to outlaw abortion. Crusades against open sexual expression, and an insistence by the Roman Catholic Church and some Protestant clergy that sex was for reproduction only, triumphed by the late nineteenth century, a victory marked by Anthony Comstock's repressive 1873 legislation. The Comstock Law forbade the mailing not only of obscene materials but also of anything that discussed or aided contraception or abortion.[5]

Class played a major role in the ability to obtain birth control. Despite legal bans, married, well-to-do women increasingly gained access to contraception by the turn of the century, and their physicians regularly prescribed the pessary, an early version of the diaphragm. Husbands informed their wives of protective measures, and women exchanged information among themselves. Middle-class couples worked together to limit pregnancy, practicing the rhythm method and abstinence as well as new forms of contraception. Some well-to-do women also were able to persuade their physicians to perform abortions. Expensive private physicians kept their patients' secrets. By 1890, most women who had abortions were unmarried and poor. Without legal and easy access to the procedure, some women resorted to dubious methods to end their pregnancies—methods that often led to injury and death. Few of their efforts, however, came to the attention of the law. Late-nineteenth-century appellate courts heard very few abortion cases. In the cases that were heard, courts found great appeal in the story of a pregnant woman whose lover did not marry her—a story that led to the woman's acquittal. The pregnancy had already dishonored her.[6]

Margaret Sanger's *Motherhood in Bondage* (1928) underscored the difficulties facing working-class women who sought contraception or abortion. Medical dispensaries and other outpatient clinics for the poor were far less likely than private doctors to prescribe pessaries, because they were expensive. However, poor women gained some access to contraceptives and sometimes aborted successfully with folk remedies. Jesse Rodrique attributes the decline in the growth rate of the black population, which dropped in half from 1880 to 1940, to birth control. The debate over contraception was a heated one among African Americans. Many black women were interested in contraception, participating actively in the birth control debate despite its white-supremacist overtones. Other African Americans thought the race should have as many children as possible. Still others opposed sterilization but saw birth control as politically progressive. Leslie Reagan's study of abortion investigations in Chicago found that all forty-four cases between 1867 and 1940 involved white, working-class women. Half were immigrants or the daughters of immigrants. Because black women were overwhelmingly poor, they were less likely to have physicians and therefore escaped both record-keeping and prosecution. Reagan found only one black woman's death from abortion reported by the coroner, in 1916. There was no record of an investigation.[7]

Criminal justice officials relied on dying declarations, deathbed statements made by the patient, and eagerly punished abortionists when the patient died. They also punished working-class women through public investigations of abortionists that left women who successfully aborted, and whose names were released to the press, open to public scorn. Despite laws that made women codefendants in abortion cases prosecutors rarely charged them. However, when women sought treatment for complications, physicians and hospitals reported them to the police, exposing them to questioning, harassment, and sometimes public exposure.[8]

The toleration the public, juries, and many judges granted abortion shows the power of the "disgraced female" story. Many physicians also sympathized with women who sought to end unplanned pregnancies. State prosecutors concentrated on death cases; otherwise, they found, juries would not convict. But some ambivalence remained concerning physicians who were willing to perform abortions. A Washington State surgeon, Annie K. Russell, was convicted on May 4, 1915, of performing an abortion. The board of state medical examiners revoked her license for an "offense involving moral turpitude," but after the conviction the governor pardoned her. She petitioned the board to reinstate her and was repeatedly refused. Finally she sued, and in 1924 the state supreme court ordered the board to reinstate her as a regularly licensed and practicing physician in the state. Russell was one of many women physicians with respectable practices who performed abortions because they politically believed in women's freedom.[9]

To enforce the gendered notions at the heart of the abortion bans, courts tended to punish nonphysician abortionists, male or female, and to free women accused of self-aborting or those who assisted them. Decisions in nonphysician cases helped physicians in their efforts to monopolize the medical profession. Physicians made war against midwives, homeopaths, and other nonallopathic practitioners, and against quacks like Pasqual Morani, who represented the particularly reprehensible nonphysician abortionist. Morani had been a barber in San Francisco before taking up the abortion business. The testimony showed he paraded as a licensed physician, calling himself "Dr. Morani." The court convicted him of second-degree murder in 1925. Morani played the perfect villain in the story that male M.D.s told of needing to guard the scientific integrity of the medical profession. The story accorded with reigning assumptions of female vulnerability and dishonor.[10] Medical advances in the 1930s enabled doctors to save women who in earlier years would have died of abortion-related infections and injuries. As abortion rates increased, the legal system responded negatively, exercising more control. The story of abuse became more prominent. In the 1940s and 1950s, the "therapeutic abortion committees" of hospitals limited abortion's availability, while police stepped up raids on abortionists' offices. Instead of waiting for deaths and dying declarations, they began raiding suspects and collecting records and medical instruments, as well as evidence from women who had been patients. These women's trust in their doctors and in hospitals declined; their health care was undermined. Officials focused on regulating the behavior of the unmarried and the working class. The legal system assumed women seeking abortions were victims. Many of those who died in the process were poor, married women like Anna Bilinski. Anna's husband, John, sought out an abortionist, telling him "that his wife was in the family way; was getting old; that they had five children and asked him to do something about it." Instead of prosecuting the women or their husbands, police harassed doctors who performed abortions, publicly exposing them.[11]

But the courts' reluctance to punish was clear; it remained difficult to obtain a conviction or a jail sentence for abortion. In New York City between 1925 and 1950, almost half of 111 convictions resulted in probation. Chicago prosecuted only thirty-eight cases over a ten-year period in the 1940s and 1950s, with only nine guilty verdicts. Nationwide, state supreme courts affirmed only slightly more convictions than they reversed. The public and the courts still accepted the toleration story. Courts usually reversed license revocations or convictions when a woman whose abortion was uncomplicated refused to testify against the abortionist. The courts usually affirmed convictions only when a woman died in the hospital after a botched abortion or when a nonphysician practitioner or a physician who specialized in abortion was charged.[12]

Occasionally, on the basis of a defendant's story of well-meaning attempts to avoid shame and the death of a loved one, an appellate court reversed an abortion conviction even when the woman died. In Florida the supreme court reversed the 1957 conviction of two friends of a high school coach who helped him to obtain an abortion for a high school student he had impregnated. Harold Johnson was found guilty of third-degree murder and his brother Alton Johnson of being an accessory before the fact. William Hamilton, the coach, admitted to having routine sexual intercourse with an eighteen-year-old student. Alton and Harold's story was that they located an abortionist in Pensacola and drove the girl to a tourist motel cottage they rented there. Harold testified that while he was trying to get in touch with the abortionist, the girl asked him to leave. When he returned, she seemed ill and appeared "faint." Harold and Alton took her to the hospital, where she was pronounced dead. An autopsy revealed that she had died of complications from the apparent introduction of a sharp object through the cervix. "A piece of wire, apparently part of a coat hanger, was later found . . . in the cottage Harold and the girl had occupied." Harold and Alton were both charged "with inserting a wire into the womb of decedent with intent to produce a miscarriage," causing her death. The court interpreted legal rules to reverse both convictions. They were just trying to help out the coach.[13]

In the 1960s, the public accepted a changed story about abortion and the empowerment of women. As a result, judicial treatment of those who prevented childbirth or interrupted an unwanted pregnancy became even more positive. Sherry Finkbine, an Arizona housewife and local talk-show host, fled to Sweden in 1962 to obtain an abortion because she had taken thalidomide during her pregnancy. The episode helped change public opinion. Fifty-two percent of respondents in a Gallup poll thought she had done the right thing. The Pill, which appeared in 1960 and offered women an easy method of contraception, also influenced public opinion. By 1965, over 30 percent of Gallup respondents approved of the idea of a health officer giving birth control pills to women in college. In addition, most Americans, 77 percent, wanted abortion legalized "where the health of the mother is in danger."[14]

Catholics and Protestants substantially agreed that saving the life of the mother was a valid reason for abortion. In 1955 seven out of ten U.S. Catholics used the rhythm method alone. By 1970, with the advent of both the Pill and the liberal teachings of Pope John XXIII, 68 percent of Catholics admitted using contraception. Kinsey reported that 2 percent of his sample of married couples had procured an abortion. Among women who had premarital sex, the vast majority who became pregnant sought an abortion. Single African American women with a college education were as likely as white women to abort. However, most abortions were performed on married women who had families.[15]

Law enforcement reflected public attitudes. By the early 1960s, police experts called abortion the third most extensive criminal activity in the country, surpassed only by narcotics and gambling. Prosecution remained sporadic and infrequent. Abortion cases continued to result in convictions of physician and nonphysician abortionists, however, until after *Roe v. Wade,* in which the U.S. Supreme Court agreed that the Texas statutes punishing abortion abridged a constitutional right of privacy when applied in the first trimester of pregnancy.[16]

In comformity with the decision in *Roe v. Wade,* states began to declare their abortion statutes unconstitutional. Courts also reconsidered related issues. In 1976, the California Supreme Court reversed the conviction of Karl Andrew Smith for the criminal abortion that resulted from his brutal beating of his wife. The high court declared that the criminal-abortion statute applied only to the killing of a "quick child." They believed that to hold otherwise would be inconsistent with *Roe v. Wade.* If the destruction of a nonviable fetus was "the taking of human life and therefore murder, then the mother no more than the father would have the right to take human life." (This did not preclude punishment for Smith. His conviction for assault and wife-beating stood.)[17]

Even after *Roe v. Wade,* abortion opponents continued to press the story that abortion was sin and murder. They advanced a constitutional amendment to overturn the decision and enacted various state laws in an attempt to prevent abortion. One new antiabortion story, that parents could control the bodies of their daughters who were not legal adults, became popular. A Michigan case involving that state's parental consent law showed the tension between the new abortion rights stories and attempts to perpetuate the old story of outlawry. A Michigan judge who displayed his adherence to the old story that punished abortion was also mired in the old story of racial differences. In a 1991 telephone interview, Francis K. Bourisseau, a probate judge in Mason County, Michigan, objected to the state's Parental Rights Restoration Act, which required pregnant underage girls who wanted an abortion to have written permission from a parent or guardian. As a probate judge, Bourisseau had the right to waive the consent provision. He declared that he did not want to make the decision, "to be the fall guy and have blood on my hands." However, he went on, "one of the circumstances in which he might permit a minor to have an abortion would be the rape of a white girl by a black man."

These remarks were "widely disseminated in the news media, and were subsequently criticized as insensitive and racist." Bourisseau responded, "I just told it like it was."[18]

Civil liberties and civil rights groups complained to the Michigan Judicial Tenure Commission about Bourisseau's statements.

In an attempt to remain on the bench, he wrote an apology, in which he stated, "Contrary to the way in which my remarks have been construed, I believe that the race of the victim and the race of the perpetrator of a rape have no bearing on the reprehensibleness of the crime." The commission decided on censure instead of removal, and the state supreme court upheld this sanction, although Bourisseau had undermined public perception of the "impartiality of the judiciary, and exposed the judicial system to contempt and ridicule." A chastened Bourisseau remained on the bench to decide other cases involving race, gender, and abortion.[19]

Throughout the 1980s and 1990s, the public battle over abortion rights still raged in state legislatures, the Congress, and the courts, and in violent and nonviolent protests at abortion clinics. The story of abortion as sin and murder contended with the story of women's empowerment and choice. As a result of the tension, the Alan Guttmacher Institute reported that the U.S. abortion rate fell in 1992 to 25.9 abortions per 1,000 women of childbearing age, its lowest level since 1976. In the latest statistics available, the Institute reported that the abortion rate remained about level, at 26.2 in 1996. Researchers cited greater use of condoms because of AIDS, a desire for birth control, the increasing acceptability of unmarried motherhood, and a decline in the percentage of the population consisting of women under the age of twenty-five.[20]

In the 1990s, violence began to constrain abortion rights. Between 1993 and 1998, antiabortionists murdered two doctors who performed abortions, two clinic receptionists, a volunteer clinic escort, and two security guards. Two other doctors and six other clinic employees or volunteers were shot and wounded by abortion opponents. On March 10, 1993, Dr. David Gunn, forty-seven, was shot in the back three times by Michael Griffin as he walked from his car at the Pensacola, Florida, Women's Medical Services clinic. On July 29, Paul Hill killed Dr. John Bayard Britton, sixty-nine, and his protective escort, retired Air Force lieutenant colonel James Barrett, seventy-four, in Pensacola. Griffin was sentenced to life imprisonment and Hill received the death penalty.[21]

In addition, John C. Salvi III, armed with a rifle, fired inside two Brookline, Massachusetts, abortion clinics on December 30, 1994. He killed two clinic receptionists, Shannon Lowney, twenty-five, and Lee Ann Nichols, thirty-eight. He also wounded five other people, including a security guard who tried to stop him. Salvi was arrested in Norfolk, Virginia, after firing repeatedly into the lobby of another abortion clinic, hitting no one.

Despite the 1994 Federal Access to Clinics Act, federal officials were unable to end the terrorism against clinics that provided abortion services. In January 1997, a security guard was killed when an Atlanta clinic was bombed; a guard and a nurse were killed in a Birmingham clinic bombing that same month. Attorney General Janet Reno, in October 1998, charged Eric Rudolph with the bombings, as well as with bombings at a gay bar in Atlanta and at the 1996 Olympics. Lack of access to abortion services; the refusal of many medical schools to train physicians to perform abortions; the resulting shortage of medical personnel, exacerbated by threats and violence, undermined the right to choose. The new story of women's liberty and sexuality was far from fully accepted.[22]

While there is no way to know how often newborns are killed and secretly disposed of, infanticide has historically been accompanied by stories of poor women unable to afford abortion. Because of increased access to low-cost abortion services and birth control, discussion of infanticide largely disappeared in the 1970s. A resurgence of reported cases in the 1990s involved parents ranging from affluent college students, who presumably had access to counseling, to drug addicts, the severely mentally disabled, and incest victims. At the end of the twentieth century, experts saw no typical profile for parents charged with killing their infants at birth.[23]

In the post–Civil War South, reports of a great number of killings of newborns reflected the predicament of the largely poor defendants, whether white or African American. Some perpetrators went undiscovered. For example, a Virginia newspaper reported on April 3, 1873, that a body "unearthed by a dog in a Lynchburg field" was a "supposed infanticide, colored." No investigation or prosecution was announced.[24]

State supreme court justices generally accepted the gendered story of poor unfortunates as the victims of male desire. Therefore, they hesitated to affirm women's sentences for infanticide although the crime was murder. They also sympathized with male defendants who expressed concern for the pregnant woman. By the very nature of their crime, usually the defendants in infanticide cases appeared in desperate straits.

The story of Mrs. Harriet M. Nelson (née Allen) evoked the kind of local interest and sympathy usually accorded white fallen women. Allen, who lived in the village of Whistler, Alabama, was "a handsome young woman," according to local newspaper stories. She was in her early twenties, of medium height, "with soft expressive eyes, and a fair gentle and intelligent face." Her manner of dress was also appealing. She wore a neat calico dress and a green checked gingham bonnet to court. During her infanticide trial, in 1869, "she frequently pressed a white linen handkerchief to her eyes which were now and then suffused with tears." Her predicament displayed perfectly the narrative of the exploited, respectable white woman, which could not help but elicit sympathy from the public and the courts.[25]

Thomas Nelson, the infant's father, whom Harriet married during the trial, did not appear in court: he had "stepped over to Mississippi to await the blowing over of the storm." At trial, a neighbor testified to finding a nude newborn infant in an open field between her house and the Allens' one night after hearing it cry. Women in the vicinity discussed the incident and decided that "somebody should go and talk to the accused and endeavor to find out whose child it was." The local midwife and several other women visited Allen, who admitted the child was hers. She testified that she had left it in the field because "her mother would scold her" for having become pregnant and delivering a baby. She first took it to a neighbor's house, she insisted, but no one was at home. The infant lived four or five days.[26]

Two physicians examined the corpse and attested to the cause of death. One testified that he could not say it would have lived in any case. The other physician found the corpse emaciated, much like a "child that had died from inattention and neglect." From its appearance, "if it had been the child of rich parents and had plenty of attention, it might have been raised," but not otherwise.[27]

Allen's mother told the court she had been "unwilling" for her daughter to marry Nelson, whom she thought "unworthy." She testified further that Harriet was fifteen or sixteen, in poor health, and would "never consent to marriage" before her arrest. On cross-examination, the prosecutor pointed out that the mother's testimony was unreliable; Harriet had been married for two years and her husband was dead. The prosecution also insisted that Harriet deliberately exposed the child to danger: a neighbor testified that hogs could get into the field where the infant lay unprotected. The jury consulted for about half an hour and brought in a verdict of not guilty. The absence of violence in the baby's death protected Allen from a murder conviction. The jury was troubled by the infant's death; however, the story of dishonor for a respectable woman widowed young and then exploited by a neighbor youth demanded Allen's exculpation.[28]

An 1871 case that presented intersecting stories of race, class, and gender drew almost daily newspaper headlines until it was resolved. In this instance, Newton Smith, a Virginia "man of color," admitted to fathering the infant of a white chambermaid at the hotel where both worked. The mother's family did not want to care for a mixed-race infant. Neither they nor the mother wanted public acknowledgment of her interracial relationship with Smith. Besides, she could not support it alone.[29]

Smith took the baby, saying he would leave it with his mother in the country. Soon afterward, the body of a female mulatto infant was found in a city pond, wearing only a shirt and a band around its body. The physician who attended the birth of baby Smith heard of the discovery and told the police that the dead infant might belong to the chambermaid. The police arrested Smith when he could not produce his baby.[30]

At the trial, no eyewitnesses to the alleged infanticide appeared. A hotel boarder, the steward, and two "colored waiters" all attested to Smith's good character. After the mayor testified that Smith had confessed, an all-white jury convicted him of first-degree murder. He was sentenced to hang.

The Virginia Supreme Court reversed his conviction. The child delivered by the physician was described as very light in color, but the dead infant was not so described. Also, the prosecutor offered no proof that the dead child was the defendant's and no one had seen him with it. The confession allegedly made to the mayor consisted of Smith's response that "he did not know why he did it," to questioning as to why he committed the crime. His answer could have referred to his interracial "criminal intercourse with the mother of the child," for which both could have been imprisoned. She, as a chambermaid, fit the story of lower-class immorality, while Smith reflected the narrative of the black man who lusts after a white woman. However, more was at stake here. The parties did not want to publicly defy the racial conventions society and the courts wanted to preserve. For them to acknowledge the child would have meant acknowledging their sexual relationship.

The chambermaid and her family, as accomplices before the fact, essentially left Smith to dispose of the infant—to make the problem disappear. Finally, Smith's witnesses included whites who attested to his character. The court preferred to narrowly interpret the confession and the infant's color, permitting everyone to escape. The judges managed to leave the taboos intact as they used a "legal rules" story to let Smith and the white family avoid punishment.[31]

In the African American community, to commit infanticide for no reason other than one's single status was considered outrageous. An unmarried woman who had a child out of wedlock was not necessarily considered immoral. However, unless particular violence—such as crushing the infant's skull—attended the murder, the high courts would reverse convictions. In an 1881 Alabama case, neighbors reported the birth and mysterious disappearance of an infant. Because of her appearance, they decided that Ann Spicer, an African American woman, had been pregnant and had delivered. They appointed three people to visit her and determine whether their suspicions were correct. The deputation, accompanied by two physicians, told her that "it was the opinion of the citizens generally, that she had been delivered of a child and that she had destroyed it." The physicians insisted on examining her. Spicer refused at first, proposing an examination by "an old colored midwife who was near by." When the group insisted that the physicians examine her, she allegedly confessed, admitting that after the birth of the infant she "administered laudanum to it because it was in misery, and she desired to end its misery." When it died, she buried it in the woods. Considering the manner of death, and empathizing with the defendant—thus reflecting the narratives of female disgrace accepted by whites—the state supreme court reversed her first-degree murder conviction.[32]

Stories of parental shame and disgrace still held sway after the turn of the century. In a 1921 Michigan case, such considerations mitigated the defendant's punishment for the death of a fetus. A physician who had been called to attend Alice Kirby talked to both her parents, who wanted to delay the "operations of nature" until they could take Alice away. He gave Alice an "opiate" to delay labor and went to his office for his instruments. When he returned, Alice was ready to deliver. Throughout the labor, Alice's mother discussed the possibility of a stillbirth. When the doctor handed the child to Mrs. Kirby, she "placed it in a basket on some clothes." On seeing the infant lying "face down in the basket," the doctor told her it could "smother in that position." When she asked, "Do you care?" he answered yes, and "placed the child in the basket in proper position."[33]

The doctor then left—through the back door, at Mrs. Kirby's request. The next day, she told him that her husband had taken the infant away. However, he prepared and filed a birth certificate for Baby Kirby.

Despite Mrs. Kirby's precautions, the cries of the baby that night had alerted everyone in the neighborhood to the birth. In the next few days, when they saw Alice but no signs of the infant, local citizens told the county sheriff that they suspected foul play. Two deputies arrived at the Kirby home to investigate. When asked about the child, Mrs. Kirby replied that "the child was dead, and that her husband had taken it away; that the child had not lived quite an hour." When asked why the baby died, Mrs. Kirby answered that it was because she "couldn't take care of the child and my daughter too, and my daughter came first."[34]

The deputies arrested both parents, but the prosecutor filed charges only against Mrs. Kirby, for first-degree murder. The local jury convicted her of manslaughter. In their view, the murder of the infant only increased the family's disgrace. However, the Michigan Supreme Court had another story in mind. They reversed because "no witness testified that the babe was dead. No one found its remains, though the back yard was dug up, cemeteries were searched, and the furnace was examined."[35]

A concurring justice explained that the story the court had in mind was that of past community crusades that punished the innocent without proof of a corpse. He recalled: "History records many deplorable errors committed when the safe rule has not been observed." For example, "men, women, and children confessed themselves witches and were burned." He also thought that to sustain the conviction would be as perverse as the ancient English rule that any woman whose newborn illegitimate child died "should be deemed to have murdered it, unless she prove it to have been born dead." The community frenzy led the jury to discount the story of perpetual shame that motivated the parents to dispose of the infant. The parents wanted to pretend that Alice had never been pregnant.[36]

By the 1960s, with the advent of the Pill and the legalization of abortion, fewer people were in the Kirbys' predicament. Women could better control unwanted pregnancies. The change in stories of sexuality, however, did not change stories of gender sufficiently to insure that perpetrators were punished. The experiences surrounding pregnancy, labor, and delivery constituted a framework for ambiguous attitudes toward the killing of an infant in the first twenty-four hours of life. When arrests were made, the cases often ended in plea bargains or short sentences, from which defendants did not appeal. From the 1960s on, the narrative in most cases in which women appealed convictions for infanticide presented a married woman who became pregnant at a time when she was sexually unavailable to her husband. These women included those whose husbands were in military service or employed elsewhere for long periods of time. They violated the gender story. Their pleas that they did not know they were pregnant until too late to avoid the delivery of an infant at an inauspicious time fell on deaf ears. They were punished for infanticide. Sexual freedom did not extend to infanticide to avoid the consequences of extramarital sex.[37]

. . .

When a woman brought her out-of-wedlock pregnancy to term instead of using birth control or choosing abortion or resorting to infanticide, child support claims brought race, gender, and class issues into the courts. The story the public understood was that children and mothers were supported by fathers or other relatives. Paternity statutes had the primary purposes of establishing responsibility for child support and protecting men from false accusations. They gave out-of-wedlock children and their mothers a legal way to enforce their rights against the father. Statutes also protected fathers by ensuring an accurate determination of paternity and enabling them to acquire custody or consent to adoption.[38]

A consistent theme of the "out-of-wedlock" narrative has been concern that fathers support their children. Under the 1996 welfare reform law, women who want aid must identify the father of their child. In the nineteenth century, unmarried women who carried a pregnancy to term had to report the father's name to the local court. The principle was the same as that of today's welfare law: to keep the child from becoming a public charge. In keeping with the economic and social position of women, the legal system made fathers responsible for their children's support. Another consistent theme, however, has been the refusal of fathers to pay child support orders.[39]

Until recent years, out-of-wedlock births in the African American community infrequently led to legal proceedings. The issue did not arise during slavery. African American slave children were the property of the master. Deference to white men and racial taboos meant that no white man would be designated the father of a black woman's child against his will. The law took little notice of sexual behavior among African Americans, and illegitimate African American children were supported within the family. Post–Civil War Southern courts, however, using the new "black freedom and responsibility" narrative, applied paternity statutes directed at "free white women" to African Americans, and ordered support.[40]

Paternity and child support disputes almost always involved poor and working-class white men and women. A woman might hope that the father would marry her when confronted with a "bastardy" charge. This was not a criminal proceeding, but the father could suffer incarceration until he agreed to pay court-ordered support. As Arkansas's high court pointed out in 1885, the prosecution was not designed to "punish" the "guilty parties, but to prevent the offspring of the illicit connection from becoming a charge and burden upon the public." The state supreme courts upheld more local-court paternity verdicts than they reversed. Appellate justices were as concerned as locals were about seeing to it that mother and child did not become public charges. When Jesse Broadway, who was accused of bastardy in North Carolina, defended himself by claiming impotence, the prosecutor's only proof was a child born some years before. The state supreme court decided that past potency had nothing to do with the present: "It will not do to infer that the vigor and manhood of youth is always attendant upon more advanced years." Just as in other sexual behavior cases, the support of illegitimates among poor whites became a matter of societal and legal attention.[41]

The story that she had an out-of-wedlock child made courts question the credibility and character of a woman in other legal proceedings. According to an 1868 North Carolina case, defense counsel could ask a woman who claimed rape whether she had had a "bastard child," in order to determine whether her rape allegation was believable. Racial themes also carried weight. The Alabama court reversed an arson conviction in 1871 because the trial judge refused to order an unmarried white woman with an illegitimate African American child to say whether she was not of "such ill fame as to be excluded from society." A woman's promiscuity tarnished her more than that of a man, "but doubtless this has been occasioned rather from the fact that men make the law, and women are compelled to obey it than any just distinction in principle for the difference." The court accepted the tradition that women were expected to remain chaste and men to make the rules in enforcing patriarchy. Because of accepted stories of gender and power, only women suffered punishment for their sexual activity.[42]

Narratives of the immoral poor and the needs of children underlay the treatment of out-of-wedlock pregnancy after the turn of the century. Until the late 1930s, both black and white unwed mothers were expected to keep their children. Some states even enacted laws requiring six months of breast-feeding to ensure this goal. Social workers and legal officials urged the parents of out-of-wedlock children to marry; doing so would cleanse them of their immorality and create a home for the child. Of 163 Chicago cases studied by Hull House resident Louise De Koven Bowen in 1914, one-third ended in marriage. Fourteen of the men she studied agreed to marry to settle child support and paternity cases, and forty married in court. If a jailed man reconsidered, he could marry and gain his freedom.[43]

Female conformity and concern about reinforcing male power and gender relations became prominent themes in the "out-of-wedlock children" discussion in the 1940s. These concerns also reflected cultural uneasiness with single women, who had been more liberated during the war. Single women who became pregnant were redefined. If they were white they became, by definition, unfit mothers, whose children should be taken away. But if they wanted to keep the baby, they were mentally ill. So unmarried white females increasingly put their babies up for adoption. There were many homes for white unwed mothers, as well as adoption services and families eager to adopt white children. The Florence Crittenton Homes for unwed mothers and Salvation Army national offices announced the racial integration of their services in the 1940s, but locals maintained racial exclusion except in large Northern cities. The white public still viewed black women as licentious and immoral; their unwed pregnancy only confirmed the judgment. However, black women's social organizations established maternity homes, such as the Phillis Wheatley home in Columbus, Ohio, and the Talbert Home in Cleveland. They saw these as refuges for pregnant girls, who could not attend school. They kept the homes open despite severe financial problems that repeatedly threatened their closure.[44]

Aid to Dependent Children (ADC), established by the Social Security Act of 1935, at first had little relevance to out-of-wedlock children among African Americans. Like state-allocated mothers' pensions, the ADC program was meant to provide assistance to white widows with children. To foreclose help for African American mothers, states enforced surveillance laws and in many cases simply denied eligibility in a period in which the federal government was unwilling to intervene. Few blacks, even those who met eligibility criteria, received benefits until the 1960s civil rights and welfare rights movement.[45]

From the 1920s until the late 1960s, about 50 percent of never-married people were sexually active. This rate remained constant. However, decreasing the ADC, or welfare, caseload, which now included large numbers of previously excluded African American women and children, attracted public concern. Prosecutors became greatly interested in determining paternity and securing court orders for child support. The white public accepted the story that promiscuous, licentious black women who became pregnant out of wedlock caused the explosion in illegitimacy and raised welfare costs.

Historian Ricki Solinger concludes that the Florence Crittenton Homes and other services for white unmarried mothers continued to provide a great resource for white mothers and for the many persons who wanted to adopt white children. Public and private agencies and government policies viewed both black and white women who had children out of wedlock as "breeders." But racial disparities and marketability conjured different stories. Black babies were defined as unmarketable, and black women as socially unproductive, undeserving persons who required punitive legal sanctions. White women were socially productive: their babies, though conceived out of wedlock, could offer infertile couples their only chance to have families. Solinger notes that blacks were referred to as living in "zoological tenements" that served as "breeding warrens," characterizations that might justify sterilization. White women, being deserving, could be rehabilitated and redeemed through casework, adoption, and return to the marriage marketplace. Public and private social service agencies facilitated adoption services for whites, ADC for African Americans. The different attitudes reflected and reinforced the story of black immorality and dependency.[46]

The new narrative of greater freedom and mobility of women, which led to the repeal of seduction as a cause of action, also led state appellate courts to reject some charges of paternity and suits for child support in the twentieth century. However, by the 1950s medical testimony and blood tests came into use, which made paternal identification relatively easy. Prosecutors no longer relied on showing that a child "looked just like" the father or was his "spitting image." In the 1960s, fathers began to concede paternity without disputation. For example, in 1965, 83 percent of the 2,034 defendants in Philadelphia admitted paternity without the need for a trial. Themes of immorality no longer consumed the energies of the courts; children's financial support by fathers rather than the government was the issue.[47]

Despite scientific advances, in 1980 a Texas man tried to use a racial story to counter blood test results and disclaim the child of the woman he married. The couple began having a "meretricious relationship" shortly after her first divorce, and were having sex in

October 1966 when the disputed child was conceived. In 1971, they married and had another child. When the mother sought a divorce and support for both children, the husband disputed her claim, arguing that she had had sex with other men. The trial judge granted the divorce and support for the younger child, but refused to order support for the older child, deciding that the date of the mother's divorce was in doubt and that the child was fathered by her first husband.[48]

The appeals court found that the presumption that a married woman's child was fathered by her husband was valid, but a certified copy of the divorce decree showed that the divorce preceded the beginning of her relationship with the second husband. Additionally, an expert witness testified that blood tests showed a 98.5 percent probability that the defendant was the father of the child. The father offered no evidence that the test was inaccurate. His major claim was that "the child is lighter in color than he and is pigeon-toed, although he is not. . . . no evidence was introduced concerning the probability of a black child being the same color as his father, or the probability of the child being pigeon-toed when his father is not." Besides, debates over color and likeness belonged to the past; science had ruled out such stories. The court made the defendant pay child support.[49]

Because blood tests made determinations of parentage more certain, a trial court that refused to order tests was almost guaranteed reversal. In a Pennsylvania case, however, the appeals court rejected blood test evidence, holding that the alleged father was the parent of an illegitimate child and that the trial judge had mistakenly ordered the testing. Joseph P. Ascero paid child support for Joseph Michael Wachter after admitting paternity when Donna Wachter named him as the father and asked for a support order. Before blood tests were done he voluntarily and in writing acknowledged paternity and agreed to support the child. He admitted that he "lived together with [Donna Wachter] during the early years that this child was born and he had grown to love the child, the child had grown to love him."[50]

After Ascero moved out, he still visited the child and paid support. However, in 1986 he asked for an order to determine paternity by blood tests because of "the doubts that were raised by the mother on the one hand, [and] by someone else who admitted being the father." His lawyer expressly agreed that Ascero would "continue paying support even if it is determined that he is not or likely not to be the father of the child by virtue of the blood testing. So that he is here really because he would like to settle his mind."[51]

The Landsteimer series of red blood cell grouping tests could conclusively exclude a putative father but could not determine whether a particular individual was the father. Unsurprisingly, when the blood test excluded Ascero as a possible father of the child, he filed to vacate the support order. The appeals court rejected his request. The law could not "permit a party to renounce even an assumed duty of parentage when by doing so the innocent child would be victimized." The trial judge should not have ordered blood tests in this case, "even for humanitarian purposes," given the facts. The appellate judge refused to undertake a problematic effort to identify another father to assume the support burden.

Soon the increased reliability of blood tests and the use of DNA profiling and other genetic tests made arguments over paternity exceedingly rare. However, Ascero was a volunteer parent.[52]

Because the theme of immorality had receded in the out-of-wedlock narrative as a result of sexual liberation, courts in child support cases, beginning in the 1960s, rarely admonished parties for their sexual conduct. Further, unfocused attempts by the defendant to prove that the mother had sex with other men had little impact. In a 1968 Chicago case, attempts to show that Andrea Elkin had sex with other men did not undermine the evidence of paternity against Joseph Rimicci. Elkin admitted she had been picked up by the police at age thirteen for being a "runaway." The defense produced witnesses who claimed to have visited her apartment for sex. However, they could not identify or remember any "physical characteristics" of the apartment. The state appeals court believed the true father had been identified; other evidence was irrelevant. Rimicci had to contribute $10 a week to the support of the child.[53]

However, proof that the mother had sex with other men at or around the period of conception was acceptable. It was a question not of immorality but of practicality. In 1977, the Oregon Court of Appeals reversed a decision that Emmet H. Hogan Jr. was the father of Kim Leonard's child. The trial court mistakenly excluded evidence concerning Leonard's sexual relationship with another man around the time of conception. Hogan wanted to show that she had had not only an opportunity to have sexual intercourse, "but also the inclination to do so." The court saw no reason to deny his request, because of its limited and relevant focus. Neither the public nor the courts were interested in the mother's sexual activity, but only in determining who should pay child support.[54]

In the 1970s, high rates of divorce and illegitimacy, combined with perpetual taxpayer concerns about the support of dependent women and children, drew attention to paternity and child support actions. The story of the welfare mother, identified as a licentious black woman who had illegitimate children and lived off the taxpayers, generated public concern. Government agencies brought most paternity suits, either directly or on behalf of the mother, seeking the father's support of the child. Occasionally, however, the father brought the action to establish his visitation rights or the right to object to adoption. Courts focused on the best interests and support of the child.

As they drew more attention, paternity actions began to reflect a different story, with less gendered and maternalist assumptions, designed to affirm and bolster the father's interest in and responsibility to his offspring. The change in the story reflected, in general, men's greater interest in retaining ties to their children. As in other areas of the law, the U.S. Supreme Court's review of state laws under the federal Constitution ratified the changed story. In the 1972 case of *Stanley v. Illinois,* the Supreme Court acknowledged the custodial rights of fathers to their out-of-wedlock children, striking down a statute that presumed unwed fathers unfit for custody. The Court held that the statute violated the equal protection and due process clauses of the Fourteenth Amendment. After *Stanley,* the father received a hearing before the termination of his parental rights.

In later cases, the Supreme Court refined its views. An unwed father could lose his parental rights if the court deemed it in the child's best interests. However, even an unwed father who did not live with his children might have a relationship with them comparable to that of the mother. The Court extended constitutional protection if the father developed a substantial personal relationship with his child, beyond the biological tie.[55]

In 1979, the Michigan Supreme Court, reflecting the new "caring father" story, gave an unwed father, Kevin Robards, the right to refuse adoption and the right to custody. The justices asserted that it was in the best interest of the child to respect the father's rights, asserting that "[the] time has long since passed" when children born out of wedlock had no rights with respect to their father and the father had no rights with respect to the children. Out-of-wedlock children, like those born in wedlock, belong to their parents. The mother "is the natural guardian of her child and has a primary right to his or her custody." However, "subject always to the child's best interest," after the mother the father has custody rights "paramount to those of any other person."[56]

The higher court reversed the lower court's decision, which had been based on the view that Robards was "young, immature and unmarried," with a nebulous plan to care for the child. The state supreme court found this judgment too superficial, declaring, "Youth and marital status are not evidence of either an incapacity or disinclination to assure that a child will receive adequate care and supervision." Although Robards might have only "minimal knowledge of the fundamental requirements involved in raising a child," the record did not suggest that he was "incapable of learning what most adult human beings quickly learn upon the birth of a first child."[57]

The views expressed in the *Robards* case reflected a shift in the narrative concerning gender roles. It remained to be seen how the narrative would embrace custody and support claims by "unwed" same-sex parents. Dealing with pregnancy put on display narratives of class (the poor had more difficulty than others and were viewed differently) and of gender (the assumptions underlying differential treatment for murder in neonaticide cases, for example). The courts also displayed narratives of race—in their responses to out-of-wedlock pregnancy, for example. The stories were changing, as in the eroding of maternalist assumptions in child custody cases, but the old stories still had resiliency.

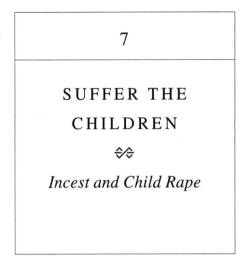

7

SUFFER THE CHILDREN

⇜⇝

Incest and Child Rape

C hild sexual abuse has come increasingly to public notice in recent years. Day care center operators are accused of molesting the children left in their care; one parent accuses another of abuse; adults want to prosecute a parent for abuse they believe began at an early age but that has just been remembered. These complaints are disputed as concocted or as false memories. The rights of teachers, psychiatrists, fathers, families, and children are all contested in what have become huge media stories, told as though the sexual abuse of children and the basis for assigning blame are new phenomena. However, these narratives are not new. They have been told repeatedly before, but from the perspective of adult concerns instead of harm to a child's psyche. In the child rape story the desire to protect the adult's reputation from false charges has been modified to include a concern for not letting persons who injure children go unpunished. The incest story has evolved; where once it expressed a need to protect the patriarch's property rights, it now identifies the patriarch as a monster. The child has evolved from merely a species of property to a person endowed with human rights, who the state must intervene in the family to protect. The story has not completely changed. We test the child's story strictly, to see if it is fantasy. Also, we have not completely replaced the old Freudian story of Dora, the seductive child, with a new feminist psychiatric story of the child who is not to blame.[1]

Child rape and incest cases have always brought dramas of male sexual aggression and power into the courtroom. Incest stories dwelled on the need to protect patriarchy and on the allegedly precocious girls who seduced their fathers. Rape cases did not involve the sex-fiend rapist of media and popular imagination. The rape stories acted out in the courtroom presented men who were acquaintances, or family members not closely enough related for the rape to constitute incest. On the other side were fathers, injured because their property in their children had been invaded by another man. Defendants routinely characterized child victims as "sexual actors." They told elaborate stories to prove consent, especially as the child neared the border to the artificially decreed age of majority. When the child was African American, the theme of racial promiscuousness embellished the defendant's tale of enticement.

The 1879 case of Liney King, a black girl "about three and one-half feet high," brought to court the intersecting narratives that influenced decisions in child rape cases. Liney worked as a house-maid and lodged across the street from her white employer, Conrad Anschicks, with two of his white women friends. Anschicks had a live-in lover who feared he would make sexual advances to Liney. Instead of confronting Anschicks, however, she warned Liney to take care around him, threatening to whip her if he "did anything." A few weeks after this, Anschicks asked Liney to have sexual intercourse. She told him "she was too young and too small," but he carried her into the bedroom and forcibly raped her. She bit him on the arm and "hallooed" to attract help, but none came. Afterward, Anschicks told her that if she kept quiet he would give her a pair of shoes.[2]

When Liney returned to her lodgings, the women residents saw blood on her nightgown and asked her what had happened. With the warning from Anschicks's mistress still on her mind, Liney told them "it just came that way at school." Reassured that they would not punish her, she confessed that she had been raped. The women told Anschicks's mistress, who threatened to whip Liney if she reported the incident. When Liney did not stop bleeding, the two women became frightened. One thought Liney might die and feared they might be charged as accomplices to murder. They then confronted Anschicks, asking why he raped Liney. He calmly replied, "Someone had to be first."[3]

The women reported the rape. Anschicks was indicted in Robertson County, Texas. The incident stimulated considerable excitement in the county, which had a majority of black residents and where blacks continued to hold political office. Anschicks avoided a statutory rape charge because Liney's father, like other former slaves, had no records to prove the birthdates of any of his three daughters. Liney thought she was ten or eleven. Anschicks's lawyer emphasized that the age of consent in Texas was ten years, and that therefore Liney had to prove she did not consent to intercourse. Now that Liney had recovered physically, her two landladies testified for Anschicks that the child seemed "very forward" around him. She "had commenced to dress, fix up her hair and act like a woman." However, the jury convicted Anschicks, sentencing him to twenty years' imprisonment. He appealed to the state supreme court, which reversed the decision and ordered a new trial. The high court thought the trial judge should have changed the venue, because the furor the case aroused might have influenced the jury to convict. A new trial, heard in white-majority

Milam County, resulted in another conviction, but this time the judge sentenced Anschicks to five years' imprisonment. Milam County whites devalued Liney's claim but were willing to punish Anschicks, lightly.[4]

Anschicks's counsel appealed again. He argued that the prosecutor's racially biased closing remarks in the new trial prejudiced the jury against his client. The white prosecutor had said: "The defendant, though his skin is white, his heart is blacker than the midnight of hell. He is more of a brute than any negro in the jungles of Africa." The appellate court did not find these comments prejudicial, but nevertheless reversed the conviction, using a rationale offered by Anschicks's counsel to support the decision: without firm proof that she was underage, Liney had to prove she did not consent. She had failed to complain promptly after the injury, behavior acceptable for a child below the age of consent but not for an adult woman. The court knew she could not prove her age, because slaves lacked records to prove the birth of their children. Liney King's rape went unpunished.[5]

The proceedings in Anschicks's case displayed narratives of race, class, and gender. His mistress and the "ladies" across the street had the advantages of whiteness, but as unmarried women in a ménage centered on Anschicks's control over them, they lived at the margins. "His" women came to his defense because they were dependent on him. The case was prosecuted because Anschicks and his entourage were disreputable and they lived in a community with a politically empowered black majority. Otherwise, Liney would have been completely ignored. The local court, telling the story of black exploitation, would not let Liney suffer simply because slaves had no birth records. The high courts, uninfluenced by blacks as political actors, repeated the story of white male power and indulgence and the subordination of African Americans. Anschicks's reversal reinforced the social order: white men could indulge themselves sexually with black women and girls.

In the nineteenth and early twentieth century, every child rape and incest case brought into the courtroom a drama in which judges, lawyers, and defendants protected male sexual proclivities and power. In rape cases, when force or violence was used, judges sided with the father as property owner and emphasized the abuse of the child in their decisions to uphold convictions. When no physical force was used, the court sided with the accused. Like Liney King, until recent years most complainants of child sexual abuse, whether it involved rape or incest, were lower-class or otherwise marginal. Usually the victim and the accused were of the same race; few cases involved African Americans.[6]

The age of consent determined by law, at issue in Anschicks's case, reflected uncertainty about the punishment of males and how much to protect girls from sexual abuse. Among the Southern states, the age of consent ranged between ten and eighteen but generally was kept very low, a trend that erred on the side of protecting males accused of abuse. Most cases of child sexual abuse by nonrelatives involved actual rape or carnal knowledge unaccompanied by threats or force, not attempts or assaults. The child rapist usually accomplished his purpose and physical evidence rather than problematic charges by the child proved the case.[7]

Some of the cases of white male abuse of white children arose from bloody acts done in drunkenness and with excessive brutality, circumstances that persuaded juries and courts that conviction was necessary. In such cases, the courts emphasized the innocence of childhood and depicted the white offender as the prosecutor described Anschicks—as a man with a soul "blacker than the midnight of hell." The abuser was "more of a brute than any negro in the jungles of Africa."

A man was much more likely to receive punishment for rape than for incest. Men who by force or persuasion had intercourse with children under the age of consent were almost uniformly friends or acquaintances. Typically, males established a trust relationship with the children and then took advantage of them.

Whether the victim was a child in foster care, or a neighbor's child, the convicted men took advantage of the opportunity to have sex with girls under the age of consent. In upholding convictions, courts repelled repeated offers to prove lack of chastity. The state wanted to protect white girls under eighteen from "conscienceless men." It was as much a crime to have sex with an unchaste girl as a chaste one.[8]

While this rule applied to adult men, courts were prepared to ignore sex perpetrated by a teenager as mere play, even when parents called it rape. Hearing a noise, the father of a six-year-old girl went into a barn, where he found the defendant "on top of the child, she being on her back with her clothes up, and discovered other evidence of improper intercourse." There was no evidence of force. The boy, who was fifteen, and the girl were both "chastised by the father." The North Carolina Supreme Court reversed the boy's conviction in 1878, finding that he was engaged in sexual play, not attempted rape. The court noted: "It was certainly an offence which called for the severe discipline of the domestic forum, and to a certain extent, that seems to have been inflicted." In one sense this is the original patriarchal story: from the standpoint of the court, the boy was merely a patriarch in training.[9]

Most child rape victims bore the scars of physical abuse. John Williams, a Mississippi man, seduced a ten-year-old girl by using his friendship with her family. After the intercourse, the girl's mother discovered the child's legs covered with blood. The girl refused to say what happened until her mother whipped her severely. Then she explained that Williams raped her and afterward gave her a nickel and told her to wash her clothes. The rape was observed by the girl's friends, who told her mother that the man had her "down." At trial, the prosecution showed that Williams not only raped the girl but also infected her with a venereal disease. Williams's attorney insisted that she consented to have sex. The Mississippi Supreme Court upheld his conviction in

1873, denouncing him for statutory rape with "some shocking, as well as disgusting features."[10]

The rape story of ten-year-old Amanda Clark and her twelve-year-old sister, Emma, was tragic, but a confusion in the story line delayed help for them: their neighbors thought the rapist, C. D. Sharp, was their father; so they were his property, and patriarchy was at stake. Sharp came to live in the Clarks' house in Dallas County, Texas, after their father left the family. Sharp and Mrs. Clark took Emma, Amanda, and three younger children and moved to a nearby county. Mrs. Clark made the children call Sharp "Pa." Amanda resisted, explaining: "He is not my Pa; my pa is named Jimmy Clark." In the winter of 1882, Mrs. Clark died and Sharp began routinely raping the two girls. When he was finally arrested and placed on trial, the girl's father, Jimmy Clark, whom no one had seen since he had left the family, came to witness the proceedings.[11]

Amanda testified that Sharp warned her and her sister that he would kill them if they told anyone that he and their mother were not married. Sharp whipped Amanda many times with switches and sticks. Sometimes, she reported, "He beat me with his fist and kicked me with his foot; knocked me down several times with a hoe handle." He made her and Emma sleep with him after their mother died, and told her that if she refused to have sex with him "I will burst your head open."[12]

Amanda had not told anyone because "I had no kin in that country, I knew no one to go to." His beatings led to such loud screams and left such bruises that while the sisters were "hoeing cotton last spring, the neighbors told us to come to them if he abused us." Finally, Amanda went to the neighbors on the pretext of "going after some water," told them Sharp was not her and Emma's father, and asked them to have him arrested. The key element here was the discovery that Sharp was not the girls' father and no paternal rights were involved. Otherwise, despite their offers of help, the neighbors would have been reluctant to intervene.[13]

A physician named Riley testified that whenever he had occasion to be at the house he had noticed "the terror with which the children, and especially Amanda," reacted to Sharp. Jeff Sires, who was present when Mrs. Clark died and continued to visit for a few days, said Sharp explained that he was having the girls sleep with him for their own good. Sharp told Sires that "they were subject to fits" and claimed that they were his children. Another witness, who worked in the fields for Sharp, reported that he saw him kick Amanda in the stomach and tell her he would "stamp her haslets [viscera] out."[14]

The jury sentenced Sharp to fifty years' imprisonment for the beating, choking, and rape of Emma and to death for the beating and rape of Amanda. Sharp's lawyer appealed, claiming the girls consented. The disreputable relationship between their mother and Sharp was the linchpin of his argument. The girls had seen their mother "living in perpetual shame and adultery." Furthermore, a mother's example, whether for good or evil, "impresses itself so firmly upon daughters that they can never be freed from its influences." The girls were therefore "bad seed." The mother's behavior had taught them to consent to sexual and physical abuse by a man.

Refusing to accept such a convoluted story line, the appellate court upheld the sentence. It determined that the girls related to Sharp like "slave[s] to a cruel and unmerciful master," and that they lived "in awe and fear." It was especially wrong for Sharp to defy racial strictures by treating white girls as if they were slave girls. The court agreed that their mother was the epitome of poor white immorality, but rejected the crude social Darwinism advanced by the defense; their mother's behavior did not automatically make the girls immoral. The case shows the acceptance of fathers' rights over their children, extending even to excessive force to gain sexual access. Whatever Sharp did to Amanda and Emma was ignored by the neighbors until they were assured he was not their father.[15]

White men convicted of statutory rape—which was almost uniformly acquaintance rape—offered every excuse in their defense. In a Missouri case, thirteen-year-old Freddie Ewings's mother permitted her to visit the Adamses' house one afternoon. They prepared dinner, and while they ate Adams engaged in "a very lascivious conversation." Freddie got up to go home. The Adamses induced her to go outside to plant some peas; later, all three went back into the house. The Adamses began showing Freddie pictures, and Adams exposed himself to her. He pushed her onto the bed, where he and his wife tried to persuade her to submit sexually. When Freddie's mother knocked at the door and Mrs. Adams went to answer, Freddie jumped up. Freddie's mother said her daughter "won't look any worse when she is dead than she looked when she came to the door."

The Adamses denied any lewd conduct toward Freddie. However, when asked why they had the doors to the house closed and the room's windows covered in the middle of May, they answered that they were trying to keep pigs out of the house. In upholding Adams's three-year prison sentence, the court said, "Such an explanation is, to say the least, absurd. It is hard to believe that pigs would force themselves into a room where there were three persons and where they were not tempted to enter by the presence of food of some kind."[16]

In many instances, only evidence of injury or disease disclosed the rape. In a 1927 Virginia case, the repeated rape of a nine-year-old by a boarder in her family's house came to light when her mother noticed pus and blood in her vaginal area. In a 1925 Washington State case, three young girls were sexually assaulted by a man who owned and operated a taxicab headquartered at the hotel where their mother worked. The cabbie, who was charged only with the rape of the eldest child who could better testify to the violation, was a respected local citizen known to be especially fond of children, who liked him. He "would frequently load his vehicle with children and take them to picture shows." He had a venereal disease, the same as that contracted by the girls. They also had "scars and abrasions" from the sex. These girls were all below the age of ten and bore physical signs of their abuse.[17]

In the 1930s and 1940s, the courts continued to reject rape claims made by girls near the age of consent, under ambiguous circumstances, and without signs of physical injury. In Illinois in 1948, Phillip A. Ritchie Jr. gained a reversal of his thirty-year sentence for statutory rape because the girl consented to go for a ride with him. The victim, a resident of Chicago, was employed in a local drugstore. Ritchie, nineteen years old at the time of the incident, drove a cab. She told police that a month before her sixteenth birthday he picked her up in his cab, took her to a secluded spot, beat her, and forcibly raped her. There were no witnesses.[18]

The court believed Ritchie's explanation rather than the complainant's charges. He was a military veteran and his employer, Joseph M. Stern, president of the Individual G.I. Livery Company, supported his story. The victim and a female friend told Stern that they were walking near the naval armory and Ritchie "drew up in a cab and asked, 'You want a ride in my cab?' " They ended up riding with him as he delivered another passenger and then "went riding around, stopping in a quiet place where they engaged in sexual intercourse." Stern testified that four days later, "when [the complainant] came to the office of the cab company[,] she had no marks or bruises on her face; that she stated she desired a medical examination to see whether she was pregnant, and that money would take care of everything." Stern also explained that, immediately after Ritchie's conviction, she filed an unsuccessful civil suit against the cab company for damages of $20,000, "based on an alleged assault."[19]

Even if Ritchie had committed statutory rape, the court thought thirty years' imprisonment was excessive. They downplayed the whole purpose of the statutory rape law, which was to punish men who had sex with females who could not legally consent. The court accepted the story that pitted a decent military veteran against a girl who accepted a ride with a stranger and was close to the age of consent. Even if the two had had sex, there was no violence and she did not appear to the court to have suffered harm.[20]

The death penalty was rarely imposed for child rape, unless the offense was perpetrated by an African American male upon a white victim. Few such cases reached the appellate courts. However, when they did the incidents evoked stories of the black beast rapist, which excited the public and the judges. In analogizing him to a "black brute," the court embraced a reason for reversing Conrad Anschicks's conviction in 1879 for the rape of Liney King. However, a similar description did not help the defendant in 1956, when the Texas Supreme Court, influenced by racial fears, upheld the execution of a black defendant, Junior Williams, for the rape of a fourteen-year-old white girl. The evidence seemed to support Williams's guilt. However, Williams's portrayal as an animal-like rapist led the court to ignore serious due process questions raised by the defense. Williams was tried twice; at first, the appellate court reversed his conviction, applying the rule that the venue should have been changed because too many prospective jurors had heard of the incident and of other crimes Williams had allegedly committed. The second trial took place in the next county where the sheriff had incarcerated Williams the night he was arrested for the rape. During the first trial, the press reported that Williams had been indicted for other offenses, that "many prowlings and peepings had been reported in the area" where the rape occurred, and that "sentiment was running high," so much so that the sheriff had asked the newspapers not to publish Williams's picture. The press described the case as "one of the most vicious in recent Texas history." Williams had a definitely unappealing story.[21]

According to the prosecution, the fourteen-year-old victim was brutally raped by a nighttime intruder, who fled when her cousin entered the room. It was the cousin who gave the police a description of the suspect; the girl "remembered nothing save that she had been choked into insensibility." She spent ten days in the hospital recovering.[22]

The prosecution relied primarily on Williams's confession at the police station. Williams's attorney argued that the confession was invalid. He tried to use the "coerced confession" story, explaining that the sheriff had moved Williams to jail in another county because "a crowd had gathered around the jail, that some man came in the jail armed with a shotgun" and that "at one stage of the questioning the sheriff had told him that he would 'let the people get me' and at another time someone told him that they were going to put him out on the courthouse lawn." When police demanded a confession, Williams said, he hoped that if he gave them what they wanted "they won't bother me." He told the sheriff to get a typewriter and he would tell them "all about it." The police, on the other hand, denied any threat of a lynching. The appeals court upheld Williams's conviction. The description of the rape, in combination with racial stereotypes, overcame any procedural errors.[23]

In contrast to the *Williams* case, in 1967 William Nilsson, a white Texan, avoided the death penalty for raping the eleven-year-old daughter of a friend. Except for the racial difference, his story was at least as disgusting as Williams's. The rape occurred during the night, when he was a guest in his friend's home. Because both were white, racial fears were no part of the story, which instead was the tragedy of the white friend who, because of drunkenness, behaves like a fiend. Even though the child was left bloody and semiconscious, Nilsson escaped with only a twenty-year prison sentence.[24]

In 1972, the U.S. Supreme Court decision in *Furman v. Georgia* declared capital punishment, as practiced in Georgia and Texas, illegal because it was racially discriminatory. Then, in the 1976 decision *Gregg v. Georgia,* the Court ratified the use of the death penalty with certain procedural safeguards. Texas and other states now reenacted a penalty. However, only three states, Florida, Mississippi, and Tennessee, left intact the whole range of capital crimes, as in the earlier laws, including child rape by an adult rapist. In these states, the theme of patriarchy in child-rape cases—that the law must sternly punish the invasion of a man's property in his child by another man—remained strong.[25]

In incest cases, the focus shifted from what was required to protect a man's property to defenses based on the need to avoid interference with a man's responsibility for and control of his wife and children, and on the need to maintain healthy families. Prosecutors countered with alternative stories about power: the fear mothers and other female kin felt because of their dependence on husbands and fathers. When the evidence of sexual abuse was irrefutable, women relatives, because of their dependence, often reinforced the defendant's tale of seduction by a child. The indulgence of men and the latitude allowed them by judges covered domestic sex as well as adultery and prostitution.

Incest prosecutions, like other sexual misconduct cases, involved almost exclusively poor whites and an occasional poor black. The wealthy classes did not expose their intrafamilial sexual abuse to the scrutiny of the legal system. The courts decided cases within the framework of concern about maintaining gender roles and male control in the family. Until recent years, gender prescriptions led the courts to decide most frequently in favor of the father. With the advent of the women's rights and children's rights movements, judicial decisions began to reflect stories of the need to protect children. Many courts, however, continued to privilege male power in the family.[26]

Incest took many forms. It ranged from voluntary adult intercourse between close relatives to sex between young siblings to violence against the helpless and institutionally committed. Most of the cases, however, involved father-daughter or stepfather-daughter relationships. The social requirement that girls be good and pure, as well as obedient—especially to men—made girls susceptible to claims of consent. Traditional patterns of parental authority, combining with equally powerful expectations of male domination of females confused decisions about culpability for incest. Because the injury occurred within the family and because victim and perpetrator were related, punishing the harm done was complicated. Commonly, as in child rape cases, incest victims were too afraid to complain; or they purposely blocked the memory of their abuse, especially if it happened when they were very young. Unless disease or bleeding betrayed him, the offender might avoid detection.[27]

State legislatures forbade sexual relationships with close kin, and local juries willingly convicted. However, in the late nineteenth century, state supreme court justices convicted incest defendants only reluctantly, interpreting the laws narrowly, as they did in other sexual behavior cases, and permitting male sexual indulgence even when the offense was incest. They found the "need to protect the father's control of the family" story most persuasive, unless evidence of resistance and force or a pattern of threats accompanied by force was undeniable. Otherwise they reversed defendants' convictions. Courts obsessed about whether the girl had invited the abuse. Was she complicitous? Had she really consented? Was she a seductress? Appellate justices regarded the incest victim as an unindicted accomplice, and the uncorroborated testimony of an accomplice could not be used to convict an offender. White girls were treated as if they were black girls, attracting suspicion when they charged incest. The needs of patriarchy required this skepticism and suspicion.[28]

Stepdaughters were particularly at risk and usually had no recourse. Courts often indicated deep disgust with incest in principle, even while acquitting defendants on narrow interpretative grounds. In Mississippi, Bobbie Weaver saw S. I. Chancellor, her stepfather and rapist, escape punishment in 1872 because the prosecutor charged incest, even though the statute did not mention step relationships. Evidence of forcible intercourse had persuaded the jury to convict. The state supreme court, however, declared: "As much as we regret that a man should go unpunished, if guilty of so gross a violation of moral law of domestic virtue, of the obligations of a citizen, and of the honor of manhood as charged in this case, we are left no other alternative than to reverse." They thought these cases were "so rare" that legislators had believed they did not require specific mention in the legislation. The justices hoped, however, that the defendant "cannot escape the just judgments of that Higher Court, where the sin and the secrets of all will be exposed, and swiftly adjudged." Here on earth, however, their narrow interpretation permitted Chancellor to go free.[29]

Paternalism—the story of "the good African American whose white employers stand up for him"—permitted an African American father in Alabama to avoid punishment for the brutal abuse of his daughter. Isaac Smith, in episodes like those in Alice Walker's novel *The Color Purple,* forced his daughter Judy to have sexual intercourse with him on at least three occasions. Witnesses testified that he threatened murder if she did not submit. A younger sister said she heard their father threaten to cut Judy's throat. She also observed that he "whipped her with a stick and beat her with a fire shovel before she would consent to go with him."[30]

An older sister who lived elsewhere testified that Judy confided in her and asked for help. She filed a complaint and had Smith arrested.

Smith denied having intercourse with Judy. He had "the pock"—venereal disease—and the prosecution had not offered proof that his daughter had it. The defense also decided to attack the victim's chastity. One witness testified that Judy's "character . . . was not good." However, a local physician, who testified for the state, reported that it was "as good as any girl's character of her condition."[31] Finally, five white witnesses, including the son of Smith's plantation "mistress in slavery times," attested to his integrity and "good character."

The Alabama Supreme Court reversed his life sentence. The justices rationalized that while the indictment charged a single offense, the evidence proved repeated acts of intercourse, and the prosecutor had not identified which testimony related to the indictment. They also explained that the trial record failed to specify that the required jury oath was taken. The court was more concerned to respect paternalism in matters of race—the patriarchy of whites protecting one of their "boys," and a father's right to the bodies of the women in his home—than to protect Smith's daughter from his abuse.[32]

Reluctance to interfere with a father's role often deterred friends and neighbors from intervening in family matters, no matter how unusual the circumstances. In Arkansas, witnesses finally reported a father's intercourse with his daughter, "a damsel ten years of age," because they were disturbed repeatedly by her screams and cries. His "defence was insanity." The state supreme court decided in 1887 that "the proof to sustain [the insanity plea] was meager." The girl was "bruised and lacerated at the time from former attempts by the prisoner to commit the act, and she consented to enter the paternal roof on the evening of the offence only upon the command of her unnatural father." The tumult occasioned by the father's abuse had become undeniable and he did not deny the acts. His behavior had exceeded the boundaries of the "need for father control" narrative. The Arkansas Supreme Court upheld his death sentence.[33]

In a 1907 Kentucky case involving African Americans, Horace

Webb, the stepfather of Hattie Thomas, used color distinctions to attack his fourteen-year prison sentence. Hattie was just sixteen when Webb raped her on frequent occasions, in her mother's absence. He threatened to kill her if she did not submit. Becoming pregnant, she told the doctor who delivered the baby that Webb had impregnated her, and she charged him with rape.

Webb claimed that since the child was a "lighter mulatto" than the mother it could not have been "begotten by a full-blooded negro" like him. Two physicians testified that it was unlikely but not impossible for a child of Webb's to be the color of this baby. One physician said the child was of a "color about that of the mother." (The color defense had served other defendants well in cases when the court wanted to acquit. Newton Smith had used it effectively in his 1871 Virginia infanticide case.) Webb had no white witnesses to attest to his good character and no racial subordination story to exculpate him. The court upheld his conviction.[34]

After the turn of the century, punishment for incest still collided with a tradition that supported the father's right to control his children. The family was still patriarchal, and no feminist critique had yet been developed on the subject of intrafamilial abuse. The few incest cases reported remained the province of the poor, as the well-to-do continued to shield their problems from the glare of publicity. A witness in a Kentucky case concerning a poor white father who was sentenced to prison for two years "could neither read nor write" and "signed with his mark." The woman in the case "admitted to being the mother of five children, although unmarried," but could not identify their fathers "with much certainty." The court did not feel the need to exact severe punishment; the daughter's lack of virtue fit the story of poor white immorality. But for the father's poverty, the case would not have appeared in court.[35]

In a poor West Virginia family, an aunt's report of incest subjected her to spousal abuse. V. L. Wright began having sexual intercourse with his daughter, Iris Wright, when she was about thirteen. He continued to abuse her over the next two years, while they lived in various parts of West Virginia, until the latter part of July 1945, when they moved to a "two-room shack in Francis." Wright's other children "had been taken from him by the public assistance authorities of Mercer County, because of his failure to support them." Susie Wright, V.L.'s brother's wife, wrote to Special Officer Everett Shutt, asking for an incest investigation. Shutt complied and then had V.L. charged with statutory rape.[36]

When Shutt and another officer tried to arrest him, V.L. fled to Mercer County, where his father lived. He was captured a day or two later and returned to Raleigh County. Several women testified to "suspicious circumstances" showing that Wright engaged in illicit relations with his daughter. Susie Wright told the court that in V.L. and Iris's home in Mercer County, the father and girl "slept in the same room which contained only one bed, though places had been prepared for them to sleep in separate quarters."[37]

Susie Wright, who reported the incest and testified against her brother-in-law, faced retribution from her husband, Claude. When he saw that she had been summoned to appear as a witness for the prosecution, he burned the summons "and then began to beat her," asking, "Who are you going to swear for—you are going to swear for us?" She answered, "I am going to swear the truth." Claude and one of his sisters, along with other male relatives, gave the usual testimony that Iris falsely accused her father because he tried to discipline her. For female relatives to stand shoulder to shoulder with their men in hiding sexual abuse was the usual expectation. Susie Wright violated the convention and subjected her family to shame. The court affirmed V.L.'s sentence of five to ten years in prison.[38]

In some states, reforms instigated by civil libertarians to give more protection to defendants changed the treatment of incest in ways that sometimes did more harm than good to complainants.

New York decriminalized incest as part of the domestic law reforms of the 1960s. In 1962 the Family Act began to cover sex offenses. The idea was to heal the family rather than to punish the perpetrator. Incest victims and perpetrators might, it was thought, step forward to seek help if they knew no punishment would result. The legislature believed that otherwise, much incest, hidden from public view, would remain untreated. Under the new guidelines, the Court of Appeals (New York State's highest court) in 1969 reversed a conviction of assault with intent to commit incest, deciding that the case belonged in family court rather than in criminal court. After this decision, a family court judge in New York City accepted jurisdiction over a case of incest between a sixteen-year-old male and his twelve-year-old sister that led to the birth of a child. The judge concluded that only the family court could "restore the various members of this family to useful and less encumbered lives."[39]

In most states, no decriminalization occurred and criminal courts continued to try incest cases. Fathers and stepfathers caught in the act, or faced with overwhelming testimony showing abuse, hoped the courts would free them on technicalities. In 1961, a Kentucky man sought to overturn his twenty-one-year prison sentence for impregnating his sixteen-year-old daughter; he argued that the daughter's confusion about the date showed the whole thing was "untrue." Just in case this theory did not hold, he noted that if they had intercourse, she was an accomplice.[40]

Some daughters were so conflicted psychologically that they refused to testify against their fathers. A Texas father, sentenced to five years' imprisonment, confessed to abusing his seventeen-year-old daughter while his wife was in the hospital. He repudiated his prior confession at trial. The daughter refused to testify, but changed her mind after spending a night in jail. Thereupon, she took the witness stand and testified that while her brothers and sisters were asleep one night in April 1961, her father came into the kitchen and "took me by the arm and we went to his bed-room. . . . there we went to bed." She insisted that she "never con-sented to this act of intercourse and that she feared" her father. Her story was that of the dutiful daughter who was ashamed of what had happened and afraid of how her father would respond if she told.[41]

Even when social workers and police knew that a child was in a vulnerable position within the family, the "father's prerogatives" story brought professional intervention too late. Lacy Brown's rape of his daughter was suspected by authorities, who had identi-fied the family as troubled. Brown lived alone with seven of his children in Westminster, California, after their mother left the home. His nineteen-year-old daughter suffered from cerebral palsy. Social workers had Richard Grodt, a detective on the Westminster police force, assigned to monitor the home "to determine its fitness as a place for the children to live, the only question being the physical fitness of the premises." About nine months later, on March 10, 1969, Royal Allen, a probation officer, told Grodt he had "heard there was sexual activity" between Brown and P., the disabled daughter. Grodt then visited the home occasionally, until one night Brown's son, Donald, called him to report the abuse of his sister. Grodt and a police officer arrived to discover Brown having sex with his daughter as she sobbed uncontrollably.[42]

Brown was easily convicted on the testimony of the police offi-cers and his children. When he appealed, his attorney tried to turn the arrest into an "invasion of civil liberties" story: he claimed that the police entered the house illegally. The court rejected this argu-ment, explaining that even though privacy is important, there is "no impenetrable protective cloak against the prevention of a felo-nious assault upon a helpless victim whose right to physical and mental integrity outweighs the right of the aggressor to remain secure in his domestic sanctuary when used for such a purpose."

The daughter was mentally disabled as well as "crippled," and she "had a bad heart. She was physically weak and had never been to school." The court fit the case within the story of a child's need for protection rather than that of a man's right to control of his family, which had delayed intervention by the authorities.43

Reports of incest, once an anomalous and obscure crime, increased significantly in the 1970s. The changed story of gender roles, sexuality, and the rights of children influenced the shift in the court decisions. Women's liberation empowered some mothers to challenge male control over the family by reporting incest. Also, premarital sex, even if incestuous, was less likely to permanently harm a girl's reputation. In the 1980s, researchers estimated that as many as one out of four girls was molested before reaching the age of eighteen. By the 1980s, the trend toward decriminalizing incest along with other forms of family violence had been reversed. Widely publicized incidents and a well-developed feminist critique attacking male violence in the family accelerated the change in focus. The number of reports increased, but not the likelihood of punishment. The appellate courts became less receptive to defenses based on the need to uphold male control of the family. However, they remained sensitive to the possibility of false charges instigated to punish the father or to gain custody and support in divorce cases.44

Appellate courts carefully assessed the child's story when family members closed ranks to insulate the father from charges. The California court in 1979 reversed a conviction for the abuse of a twelve-year-old girl, "L.," when the grandmother and L.'s brother maintained that L. lied because her father would not let her go out in the evenings. A court-appointed psychiatrist interviewed L. and concluded that she had no psychiatric disorder. However, he agreed that she might be lying because she could not say whether the intercourse was distasteful or pleasurable, only that it was painful. Also he was impressed by the contradictions between her brother's statements and her denials. The entire proceeding showed little understanding of the psychological trauma of incest and the willingness of family members to keep it hidden.[45]

Georgia's high court was also reluctant to accept the new "child protection" incest story, reversing a stepfather's conviction upon charges brought by his fourteen-year-old stepdaughter, "M.," despite strong evidence that M. left home because of the abuse. M.'s mother took her to the county mental health department for counseling. The high court found that testimony about the stepfather's refusal to take a state-administered polygraph test after agreeing to have the results admitted as evidence might have prejudiced the jury.[46]

While courts appeared eager to exonerate fathers, signs of violence encouraged them to side with the complainant. In 1980, the Colorado Supreme Court upheld the conviction of Robert Fierro for sexual assault and incest, the victim being his eleven-year-old daughter. The daughter complained that when she and her two sisters visited her father at home, he sent her sisters to bed and took her with him, ostensibly to a store. When they were outside, he told her that he needed something from a camper trailer parked nearby. After they entered the trailer, he raped her while holding a pistol to her head and threatening to shoot her. The incident was not disclosed until over a year later, when the younger sister told her grandmother. The use of violence, along with separate testimony from the two children, who confirmed each other's stories, led the court to affirm Fierro's conviction.[47]

Gradually, the "child protection" incest story began to gain ascendancy in the courts. In 1989, the North Carolina Supreme Court affirmed Harry Hewett's conviction for molesting his "natural daughters," "A.H.," nine, and "T.H.," eight, when the girls independently told of the abuse. Both girls testified that Hewett abused them in the car, while they waited for his girlfriend and mother, who had gone shopping, and also at his house, when they were alone with him. T.H. testified that "she and her sister took turns getting up on Daddy" and that each child took turns "keeping an eye out to see if anybody would come." Hewett's brother and girlfriend supported his denials; however, the county child medical examiner supported the children's story and testified that he believed they were telling the truth. Hewett complained that the judge erred in permitting the children to use anatomical dolls during their testimony. He also insisted that the judge mistakenly let A.H. testify about a drawing she had made and allowed the drawing to be admitted in evidence. The appeals court, finding these practices routine in such cases, ordered him to serve two consecutive life sentences.[48]

Stories of poverty, immorality, gender, race, and class permeated incest and child-rape proceedings in the courts. Even when social change led to increased reporting of incidents, that did not necessarily translate into increased convictions. While nonreporting was a concern of reformers, courts remained wary of stresses on families that might lead to false reporting. A confused panoply of aims and feelings—desire to maintain the nuclear family as whole; adherence to the mythical good family; awareness of male sexual aggression; and mothers' unwillingness to acknowledge incest—all swirled about the courtroom in these cases. Judges interpreted the legal rules to make sense of the stories, weighing the "child protection" and "father deference" narratives to reach conclusions. Their decisions reflected the flux in gender and power relationships that dominated public discourse on the subject.

8

THE PIG FARMER'S
DAUGHTER

⊰⊱

Rape and Rumors of Rape

R ape cases teach us that race, class, and gender are not simple
or straightforward entities or characteristics—especially
when woven into stories of sexual violence and sexual transgression. We saw earlier that the decisions in the rape trials of William
Kennedy Smith and Mike Tyson were informed, not only by gendered expectations but by class and racial stories. It is this interplay of narratives of race, gender, and class that this chapter will
focus upon—and on the tangled web of convictions and acquittals
that American juries and judges wove over the one hundred years
between the case of the pig farmer's daughter and today. What
does this tangled web tell us about justice and the deployment of
power in the United States? Patriarchy colored judges' visions
when they saw poor white women's charges of rape, especially
when those charges were directed at middle-class white men. On
the other hand, race could easily efface class, so that white judges
and juries seeing African Americans on the stand saw not the class
respectability those African Americans had struggled to acquire

but lustful black animals capable of violent rape or licentious and sexually available black women. The complex ways race, gender, and class informed the courts' understanding of the status of the victim and the accused affected both original and appellate decisions. With so many stereotypes interacting, decisions were neither predictable nor simple. What we can see, overarching all else, is that the law preserves class privilege, which usually means white male class privilege.

The familiar story of rape and race, the "high-tech lynching" image that Clarence Thomas invoked in his confirmation hearings, accurately reflects long-standing popular beliefs. Public discourse promoted the myth that a large number of African American "black beast rapists" were assaulting white women. In movies such as *The Birth of a Nation* and *Gone With the Wind*, African Americans are not citizens with legal rights but animalistic, sexual objects. As objects they can be exchanged among white men in the making of political alliances. The lynching story justified the rise of the Ku Klux Klan, the overthrow of Reconstruction in the South, and the segregation and subordination of African Americans in the years thereafter.

There was a lynching industry despite the reality that most of the interracial rape charges against black men turned out to be false. Lynching and mob violence were usually unrelated to any sexual assault on a white woman. The antilynching crusader Ida C. Wells-Barnett editorialized in 1892 that although hundreds of black men had been lynched, their alleged crime was rarely rape. Rather, the typical lynch victim had been too "uppity," meaning he strayed from the black man's subordinate place and challenged white male privilege. As historian Jacquelyn Dowd Hall explains, rape and lynching remained conceptually tied together whether rape actually occurred or was falsely charged. Historian Glenda Gilmore argues that white men used the construct of the black male rapist to reinforce white women's fear and dependency on them. Pointing to one example of the falsity of popular notions, historian Samuel Pincus noted that of sixty-four persons lynched in Virginia between 1880 and 1897, fifty-one were black, but only twenty-six were accused of rape. Historian Diane Somerville suggests that the lynching of black men for alleged rape occurred more frequently and was more discussed than before the Civil War because whites no longer completely controlled the legal system. However, the high judiciary in every former Confederate state was Southern-controlled throughout Reconstruction; few carpetbaggers ever served on the courts. Furthermore, in the period of the greatest number of lynchings, African Americans were disenfranchised and excluded from participation on juries and as local judges. The difference between illusion and reality was underscored when, during 1893, twelve black men were lynched in Virginia. Governor P. W. McKinney attributed the lynchings largely to white fears of blacks following emancipation. However, whites had completely controlled the courts and law enforcement in the state at least since 1873. In reality, lynching symbolized white men's control of African Americans—and of white women. Rape was a sexual story that legitimized violence.[1]

The myth of the black beast rapist dominated not only popular culture but medical discussion of African Americans. It was generally accepted among physicians as scientifically based. For example, Hunter McGuire of Richmond, president of the American Medical Association, published in 1893 an exchange of correspondence on the subject with G. Frank Lydston, a professor of genitourinary surgery and syphilology at the Chicago College of Physicians and Surgeons. McGuire, after reading Lydston's 1889 article "Clinical Lecture: Sexual Perversion, Satyriasis and Nymphomania," asked Lydston if he agreed that perverted African Americans raped white women because the control and discipline they had experienced during slavery had disappeared, so that they were "deteriorating morally and physically." Lydston responded that the "savage civilization" of Africa and the "bad example set by whites" accounted for rape by African American males. He explained that a white man who fornicated would not "injure his social status," even if his "indiscretions" were known, "provided he confined his indulgences to prostitutes and negroes." Lydston thought that lynching and death sentences were ineffective in controlling the African American; "a few emasculated negroes scattered around through the thickly settled negro communities in the south would be more effective."[2]

Yet torture, castration, and lynching of African Americans do not constitute the whole story of the American justice system in the late nineteenth century. Despite popular culture, some African Americans accused of interracial rape had trials and avoided the rope and faggot. White male class and race privilege protected them. The case of Annie Knuppel, a fifteen-year-old German immigrant who lived in Washington County, Texas, in 1886, shows how other stories complicate the lynching narrative. Washington County, in southeastern Texas, northwest of Houston, sat on a rolling prairie of sandy loam and alluvial soils, irrigated by the Brazos River and its tributaries. Farmers in the area raised cattle, hogs, and poultry and grew cotton and corn. Annie lived with her parents, Frederick and Sophia Knuppel, her older brother, Frederick, and her sister, Lizzie, in an area four miles from the town of Brenham. The Knuppels grew a little corn and cotton, and raised cows and pigs. There was a sizable German immigrant community in the area, including Annie's uncle, her father's brother, and his family.[3]

On the morning of January 26, 1886, Annie started into Brenham to see the doctor and to get some medicine. Along the road, two family friends, Henry Kramer and Gottlieb Roemer, came by in a wagon and gave her a ride into town. The group arrived in Brenham before lunch. Annie saw the doctor and started home again after lunch. As she was walking home along the tracks of the

Gulf, Colorado and Santa Fe railway about two miles south of Brenham, near where a public road crossed the track, she reported being "overtaken by a colored man." According to her story, he struck her, threw her down, and forcibly raped her. After he left, she continued home and told her family of the incident. Her father asked a Dr. G. Becker to examine her. Becker verified that she had been sexually assaulted.

Annie described her assailant to the sheriff as a "knabe"—a young man, or boy—and neither "right white nor right black." She said he had neither whiskers nor a mustache. The police arrested two African-American men on suspicion of the crime, but Annie could not identify either one as the rapist. Seven weeks later, the sheriff arrested Albert Johnson, whom she identified with certainty as the offender. Johnson was an African American "mulatto."[4]

Johnson, who was well-known in the African American and white communities, was not lynched. His trial took place at a time when suppression of the black vote by violence and other means had been effective in Washington County and elsewhere in the Texas black belt. Between 1886 and 1892 the Republican vote declined by 40 percent in the county and black officeholders became practically nonexistent. At Johnson's trial, however, some influential witnesses testified in his defense. Six witnesses, "some white and some black—including the sheriff, the county attorney and the judge and ex-judge of the county court," insisted upon his innocence. They were well acquainted with Johnson and agreed that he had never been clean shaven but "had always worn a mustache for several years continuously up to the time of this trial."[5]

These same witnesses also testified that they had "never seen the defendant dressed in clothing similar to that which, according to the testimony of Miss Knuppel, was worn by her assailant." None of this impressed the local jury. They convicted Johnson, and the trial judge sentenced him to ninety-nine years imprisonment. The appeals court, far from the political transition in Washington County, reversed and ordered a new trial. They found that the verdict was contrary to the evidence.[6]

After the second trial, in which Johnson was sentenced to death, the appeals court saw ample reasons to reverse again. In addition to a reprise of the same evidence, the trial judge let the prosecutor ask repeated questions about whether the defendant had written a letter confessing to the rape, though he never produced the letter or evidence that it ever existed.

This time, the appeals court decision relied heavily on a legal due process story. The judges decried the introduction of the new testimony. They acknowledged that a rape case "arouses public indignation and fires the minds and passions of a community with a desire for vengeance"; therefore, "counsel engaged in the trial should be scrupulously cautious to accord to the defendants a fair and impartial trial, as free as possible from excitement and prejudice." Revealing the most important reason for its decision, the court emphasized that among the white and black witnesses who denied that Johnson was the assailant were "men of prominence" whose testimony carried great weight. When the case was sent back a second time, the local prosecutor, reflecting the local racial-subordination story, proceeded to retry it. However, in October 1889 the trial judge accepted a change of venue by agreement of the parties to Milam County, where the political suppression episodes that erupted in the black belt had not been prominent. The Milam County prosecutor, in view of two reversals, refused to retry the case. The appeals court's paternalistic concerns prevailed.[7]

The Texas appellate judges who reversed Johnson's convictions were neither Republicans nor carpetbaggers. They were ex-Confederates who had fought for the South in the Civil War. They had been appointed to the court by Democratic governors after the state was Redeemed from the Yankees. In their deliberations, they sided with Johnson's well-to-do white patrons; that he was their "boy" weighed heavily on the appeals court's scales of justice. Annie Knuppel was a pig farmer's daughter. The year before, the same judges had reversed the conviction of a black man accused of the attempted rape of a poor Polish farmer's daughter, because his employer said he was "always an humble, respectful negro, never disposed to fudge on the rights of the white people." Local juries and prosecutors, polarized by race, valued even a poor immigrant white woman's words against a black man—but not so elite appellate judges, who had competing concerns. For them, class was the telling issue. Among conflicting stories, they chose to affirm white male privilege and paternalism in race relations.[8]

Not only the Texas courts but judges in other states decided cases in which African Americans were adjudged not guilty of rape. For example, in the Mississippi black belt, in 1889, a white woman went horseback riding alone about two miles from town. As she approached a railroad crossing she reported seeing a "negro man" standing there. As a train approached, she turned her horse toward him, thinking that "he could assist her if the train frightened her horse." She rode on two hundred or three hundred yards after the train passed and noticed he was following her on foot. He came up behind her and caught her riding skirt. She "immediately uttered an outcry" and sped the horse on. The man, who ran in the other direction, was captured and identified by the woman as her assailant. On this evidence, the circuit court jury convicted him of attempted rape.

In deciding to reverse the conviction, the state supreme court embraced a due process story. The judges reasoned that there was not enough evidence that the defendant intended to rape the woman who filed the complaint: "We can conjecture the purpose of the defendant to have been to commit a rape but on the facts disclosed it is conjecture only." They decided that "mere probability of guilt of a particular crime and that, too, springing more from instinct than from proved facts, cannot support a verdict of guilty." This court responded differently from North Carolina Chief Justice Richmond Pearson, who, in an 1875 attempted rape case, linked a black man's sexuality with a barnyard animal's: "I see a chicken cock drop his wings and take after a chicken and my experience and observation assure me that his purpose is sexual intercourse, no other evidence is needed." The Mississippi justices, instead, agreed essentially with the defendant's counsel that "unless violent presumptions be drawn from the race instinct of the African, the verdict is wholly unsupported by the evidence."[9] They noted that there was a "great danger of improper convictions in cases of this character, and, while the court should not for that reason invade the province of the jury, the danger admonishes us of the necessity of standing firmly upon the right and duty of proper supervision and control of them."[10]

The records of the trial are unavailable, which makes it difficult to determine whether powerful white friends intervened on behalf of the accused, or whether the lower-class status or foreign birth of the woman told the whole story. However, to judge by what we know, the court told the most elite story of all: that of impartial common-law justice, which complicates the lynching story. Wilford Smith, a well-known late-nineteenth-century African American lawyer, explained how some judges consciously projected the paternalism touted in the Southern gentlemanly tradition. Adopting a posture of detachment in contrast to the racist attitudes prevalent at every level of the courts, they were identified as "noble exceptions" and "high-toned honorable gentlemen," who, whatever the consequences, "stood for fairness and justice to the Negro in their courts." Smith cited in particular Justice Josiah A. Patterson of the Mississippi Supreme Court, who was in the majority in this case. An emphasis on the need for fairness characterized his opinions. The approach taken by appellate judges in the Texas and Mississippi cases produced a result similar to that produced by the justices who upheld inheritances to African American mistresses and their mulatto children. They reinforced the subordinate status of the "Negro" rather than enhancing it. Their decisions did not make the African American a full citizen in the court; instead, they emphasized how the paternalist must take particular care of his "good Negro."[11]

Every rape case, whether interracial or not, required the courts to manipulate long-standing rules constituting the "legal evidence of rape" story. Their rulings, whether broadly or narrowly interpretive concerning the evidence, defined rape in ways that upheld white male privilege and traditional gender roles. A rape conviction required proof of penetration achieved by force and violence—that is, lack of consent. In the absence of penetration the charge could be only assault with intent to rape. How the complainant's appearance accorded with the judge's story of how a vulnerable woman should appear became the major determinant of the outcome on appeal. The pig farmer's daughter looked like a rape victim to the local judge and jury, but the defendant's prominent friends were more appealing to the appellate judges. A woman who reported her assailant saw herself as a victim of violence and wanted the legal system to vindicate the harm. Courts distinguished between pure and impure women and allowed accused men much latitude. When both the accused and complainant were white, the victim's sexual and class history determined whether the convicted rapist would win or lose on appeal. As one late-nineteenth-century court explained, the absence of intimate acquaintance between the two and "the [good] character, repute and position of the woman" signified that a man who had sex with her could not have done so by invitation. Bourgeois women confined to the domestic sphere knew men intimately—or not at all.[12]

If a defendant presented a convincing narrative that a complainant was a "loose" woman, he would invariably win, because the rape story included the presumption that a loose woman, having no morals, loses the right to refuse sex. A public woman, she circulated in a sexual market as a negotiable item. She could not have sex against her will. She must have solicited—that is, provoked—the attack. Racist stereotypes reinforced this theory: loose white women—and all African American women—were tarnished, in the view of the white legal system; they were defined by patriarchal imagination as sexual objects, available and thus without rights. This was a classic patriarchal story that dated at least as far back as the rape of the Sabine women or of the Levite's concubine. Appellate courts imposed the patriarchal narrative. Late-nineteenth-century judges were very sensitive to the possibility of false accusations of rape by a woman deemed too "forward." They used biblical and common-law stories and repeated English Lord Chief Justice Matthew Hale's seventeenth-century admonition that rape is "an accusation easily to be made, and hard to be proved, and harder to be defended by the party accused, tho never so innocent." Other Hale formulations tested the veracity of the complainant: "If she be of evil fame and unsupported by others, if she concealed the injury for any considerable time after she had the opportunity to complain, if the place where the act was alleged to be committed was where it was possible she might have been heard and she made no outcry, these and the like circumstances carry a strong but not conclusive presumption that her testimony is false or feigned."[13]

The story the judges demanded of complainants to support their accusations was based on the idea that male relatives of a respectable woman would seek vengeance for her rape. (Similar expectations arose when a woman was seduced.) The legal process sought to preclude personal combat or other extralegal punishment. Often, however, sexual assaults were resolved without appearing in the appellate courts or even in the lower reaches of the legal system. The nature of the crime and social expectations affected the reporting of rape offenses to the police. In these cases, emotions ran high, more because rape compromised the honor of a husband or father than because the woman had suffered; she was merely the occasion of the injury. Rape meant the physical violation of the woman, but it meant violation of family honor as well. Given the concern with male honor it should not surprise us that patriarchal stories laid great emphasis on men's sexual prerogatives. As they did with respect to other sex offenses, well-to-do women avoided the publicity of a trial. Rape defendants and complainants were usually poor. Affluent women either were not raped or did not report it, or their assailants escaped, suffered lynching, or did not exercise the right to appeal.

To charge a man with attempted rape, or with assault with intent to commit rape, did not bring shame upon the accuser, because she had not had intercourse with the assailant. Therefore, a respectable woman would not report rape unless she had no alternative. Instead, even when she *had* actually been raped, she would report that she had been assaulted with intent to rape. Only if pregnancy or venereal disease exposed her secret, would she charge rape. Also, women who were discovered in the embrace of a class or race inferior might claim they were raped.

Even in the infrequent cases when a black man was convicted of the rape of an African American woman, the deference to white male privilege, seen through the lens of race, was apparent. African Americans took the rape of a black woman by a man of any race seriously, and were as prone to take drastic action as any white mob. In Virginia in 1870, after a "colored boy" was convicted of "choking and thrusting dirt" into the mouth and throat of a "colored girl," a large number of African Americans, "some of whom were armed," watched his arrest and "threatened to hang the accused." The state supreme court reversed the defendant's death sentence. Where enfranchised blacks were a majority of the population, trial courts willingly convicted accused rapists, but the higher courts usually reversed these decisions. However, very few men were ever arrested, much less tried, for the rape of an African American woman. African American men were objects instead of persons, and so were "their" African American women, unprotected by a powerful white person. Appeals courts usually reversed the convictions of both white and black men who were convicted of raping black women.[14]

In 1885, when Eliza McGee charged Joe Favors, a black laborer on the Texas property where they both lived, with rape, she suffered from the old skeptical stories that plagued black women, and from the deference paid to her white employer's views. Favors, McGee claimed, had forced her to the ground and raped her, despite her protests, as she passed through a field on the way to a friend's house. Charley Johnson came upon McGee in the field after Favors let her go, and they went together to report the assault to Mr. Dick Ward, the owner of the place at Honest Ridge where they lived and worked. Favors's brother, Sam, reinforced McGee's devaluation by the court. He testified that he saw his brother and McGee in the field having intercourse and passed on, "laughing," after commenting to his brother that he had caught him. He also claimed that McGee had had intercourse with him earlier. Charley Johnson, however, corroborated Eliza McGee's testimony. He heard her cry out and say she would take Favors to jail if he did not stop.[15]

McGee was victimized at every turn by the official acceptance of stories of African American licentiousness and by patriarchy—the power of white males to bind and loose and to place their protection over men both black and white. The official court reporter wrote jokingly that McGee insisted she had "no appointment to meet the defendant at any place on that night for copulative or other purposes. She had not passed her promise to accommodate the defendant with horizontal refreshment on that or any other night." He also reported that he thought Favors might have winked at McGee, and that she "dropped her head and laughed." He implied strongly that McGee should be ignored; she was sexually interested in Favors, in his view.[16]

Mr. Ward preferred his laborer Favors and showed no interest in protecting McGee. He testified that she had worked at his house for about eight years in exchange for food and clothing, and he characterized her as a "simple, silly-minded, childish negro." The appellate court noted without objection that the district attorney had asked Ward whether McGee's reputation resembled that of other "unmarried darkies." He answered that McGee's reputation for chastity was "about on an average with that of other unmarried negro women."

The appellate court reversed Favors's conviction. White men did not care what "promiscuous" African Americans did among themselves. African American men could freely satisfy their lust for a black woman without worrying about complaints that the sex was involuntary. The court believed Mr. Ward, who was in the best position to know his "darkies." He did not take the matter seriously, despite the verdict of the local jury in Limestone County which had only a 20 percent black population.[17]

The narrative of white male dominance and black promiscuity also led the courts to refuse punishment for a white man convicted of raping an African American woman. In an 1886 Texas case, Mrs. Jennie Webb charged rape by William Bryson. She was by all accounts a respectable married woman, despite her blackness. Mr. Webb was sitting on the porch when his wife left on an errand to her brother-in-law's house. About 400 yards from the Webbs' house, Bryson stopped her, dragged her into the weeds, and forced her to have intercourse with him by threat of murder. Her husband heard her shout, "grabbed his gun and ran toward the sound, forcing Bryson to release her." The Webbs immediately reported the assault.

Mrs. Webb testified that she had never seen Bryson before in her life. Bryson's lawyer followed the usual pattern of undermining Mrs. Webb's reputation by presenting witnesses who claimed to know that her chastity was suspect. This testimony amounted only to a rumor that her father had engaged in incest with her and that she might have engaged in illicit intercourse at some time in the past. Nevertheless, the appellate court reversed Bryson's conviction. The justices, disinclined to punish a white man for assaulting a black woman, advanced a procedural story to rationalize their decision. They ruled that the prosecutor used "clap-trap or sharp practice" in his closing argument, when he mentioned other rapes that had occurred in the area recently. These comments might have inflamed the jury to convict the defendant.[18]

The importance of white male privilege and gendered stories of race was also reflected in the court's treatment of a marital rape case. In 1890, the North Carolina Supreme Court affirmed the conviction of T. N. Dowell, "the white husband of a white wife," who held a loaded gun on his wife and one Lowery, a black man, forcing them to have intercourse. But "fright and excitement rendered him [Lowery] incapable of consummating the outrage." Also, at "perhaps the critical moment," the gun discharged in the hands of the "unnatural husband," permitting Lowery to escape. The court rejected Dowell's claim that because a husband could not rape his wife he was not guilty. The story of racial inferiority evoked disgust at Dowell's insistence that an African American violate white womanhood. He had violated the narrative that required the upholding of white male power in the family and the protection of his wife's purity; some punishment was necessary. However, Dowell's behavior was designed to gratify his own desires, so the charge was only assault with intent to rape—a misdemeanor.[19]

The justices' psychological pain over the conflicting visions and stories they had to weigh led them to declare the episode so "disgusting" that they would not "stain the pages" of the state supreme court reports with the details. They wanted it clearly known that a husband might have forcible intercourse with his wife, but this was a nontransferable privilege. As Hale explained,

"For though in marriage she hath given up her body to her husband, she is not to be by him prostituted to another." The court found the idea that a white woman could suffer violation in this way as offensive as permitting someone to kill an innocent person in order to save his own life. Therefore, Lowery would have been punished if he had consummated the act.[20]

The court's conclusion appalled Chief Justice Augustus Merrimon, who dissented, but not because of any sympathy for the wife or the African American man. He believed that to rule that a husband could not rape his wife would impair the narrative requiring male power over the family. The husband also could be an accessory in aid of a rapist, but Lowery did not actually intend anything. At best, the law could punish Dowell for assault with a deadly weapon. This case shows the confluence of three conflicting white male stories: One, white men needed to protect white women from black men. Two, a husband had the right to rape his own wife. Three, the sexual purity of a white female meant that a Victorian husband should not rape her. Merrimon thought that strict adherence to the legal story of the husband's authority over his wife would better serve patriarchy and the protection of female virtue in the long run.[21]

The same white male privilege that confounded poor white women who accused black men of rape, and African American women in every situation, operated when a white man was convicted of raping a white woman. Assertions of white female virtue were of no avail; late-nineteenth-century judges eagerly accepted stories of consent in these cases. Only when a prominent person witnessed the crime in progress or substantial evidence of force or violence existed were justices willing to affirm convictions. Social status clearly counted. Patriarchy required protecting the purity of respectable women, but also required leeway for men.

In an 1871 Georgia case, the power of a respected professional and the court's characterization of the woman's own story worked against her claims. The Georgia Supreme Court reversed the conviction of a physician for the rape of Mary Meyer, a patient. Meyer said she went to the doctor's office with her husband. While Mr. Meyer was seated in an adjoining room, Dr. S. B. Innis asked whether Mrs. Meyer had ever had sexual relations with anyone except her husband. She answered positively and admitted she had a child by another man. Innis took her into a room with a bed and raped her. The court emphasized Lord Hale's admonition about men "put in the power of abandoned and vindictive women." The defense established a very appealing story of a respected physician and a fallen woman with an illegitimate child. They embellished the story by offering to introduce—but not actually tendering—evidence that Mrs. Meyer had gonorrhea a short time before the alleged rape.[22]

A white woman already regarded as disreputable in the community would receive little sympathy when she reported an unwitnessed rape. Unchaste women, those who had an illegitimate child, prostitutes, and many poor women fell into this category. Poor white women had even less chance with charges against a white man than with charges against a black man who was protected by paternalism. A Georgia court discounted a poor white woman's insistence that she was totally chaste until being raped in her first encounter and rejected her claims of abuse. She was too frightened to tell anyone of the incident until four days later, when she told a sister-in-law. Her father testified that he was advised by the sheriff to wait until court term to file charges. By that time, the woman "was known to be pregnant." Cortney Crockett, the accused rapist, had a different story. He explained that he had invited the eighteen-year-old complainant into his house while his wife was not at home. They had "a little dram" and then had voluntary intercourse, agreeing not to tell anyone. He subsequently went to Atlanta and "bought ten cents worth of snuff and give it to her," to show his appreciation. The court reversed Crockett's conviction, noting that although the alleged rape took place in daylight along a mill road busy with traffic, no witnesses were brought forward by the prosecution. In any event, the court expected that dissolute poor whites would have extramarital sex, which might lead to claims of rape when pregnancy resulted.[23]

The "poor farmer's daughter" cases were exceptional among the rape decisions because black defendants escaped punishment, but they are important because they underscore the power of white male privilege. They show how paternalism could lead to protection of an African American defendant accused of raping a white woman even at a time when public discourse gives the impression that lynching was the usual remedy. They show how devalued poor white women were, and how valued was the influence of powerful white males.

Victorian presumptions and stories about race, gender, and class in rape cases persisted into the twentieth century. Courts usually had little difficulty accepting a white woman's complaint of rape when the attacker was a stranger, which presumptively included all black males. However, judges remained reluctant to exact severe punishment when white women claimed rape by acquaintances, such as dates, ex-husbands, and ex-lovers. Punishment of these men violated white male privilege and male patriarchal bonding. Judges accepted a story that the woman probably wanted sex and that the man naturally became aroused and had to be satiated. They wondered whether the woman provoked the attacker or whether she really consented.[24]

An Idaho court in 1907 showed the impact of these gendered stories. Frank Neil, a traveling salesman, admitted attempting to rape Annie Fuchs, whom he met at a German community picnic. His excuse was that, although she said no to his hugging and attempts to pet her, "she liked it." He was "trying to inflame her passions." The court found the ten-year sentence imposed by the trial judge too severe. Neil was twenty-six at the time, while Fuchs was twenty-eight and had been a professional nurse for several years. She was mature enough to know she should not walk home alone with him at night, and had more worldly experience than usual for a woman. Therefore, she knew enough not to expose herself to an unwanted attack. Fuchs was by all accounts "a virtuous woman and not the character her actions and conduct indicated to him." Although her conduct was "undoubtedly free from any evil purpose or intent," it was "indiscreet and ill-advised."

The court had specific views concerning rehabilitation. Ten years in prison "would practically ruin [Neil] for life," while two would not only be enough protection for society but should also reshape and reconstruct his views and give him some "higher and better notions" than gratifying his lust. Annie Fuchs's unorthodox status as a mature professional woman did not fit the story of the vulnerable, dependent female entitled to the court's protection. The angle of the court's vision shifted to make her assailant the victim.[25]

When an African American was accused of the rape of a white woman, racial stories and "pure white womanhood" themes remained at center stage. Well into the twentieth century, lynching could still occur, and not just in the South. One example displayed the confluence of stories in a poisonous eruption of violence and legal unfairness in the nearly all-white Iron Range community of Duluth, Minnesota, in 1920. The Duluth story inverts the ethnic, working-class, "pig farmer's daughter" stories. There we saw middle-class males bonding to protect one of their "boys," an object rather than a person, against women who were not really white because they were foreigners and members of the working class. In Duluth we see immigrant working-class men using lynching to whiten their own identity. *They* become really white by lynching blacks, while their women become really white and possessed of legal and political rights because black men are lynched in defense of their honor. In the process, the women are transformed into respectable white women.[26]

On June 14, 1920, the Duluth newspaper announced, "Hey,

Skinny! [The] Circus Is Here," heralding the arrival of "John Robinson's Famous Circus, the oldest in the world." The glow of the circus dissipated early on June 15, when complaints that six or seven blacks had raped a seventeen-year-old white girl on the circus grounds spread throughout the city. In the next twenty-four hours three African Americans were lynched—the first reported lynchings in Duluth—and soon three others were convicted of rape.

Late on June 14, eighteen-year-old James Sullivan told his father, with whom he worked on the night shift at the "ore docks," that six or seven African Americans had "held a gun to his head" and raped his girlfriend, Irene Tuksen, earlier that evening at the circus. James's father called the police, who in turn called Irene's home and discovered her parents knew nothing about the alleged incident. Irene was in bed, asleep.[27]

James Sullivan and Irene Tuksen, accompanied by the police, "picked out" some twelve of the men working as unskilled laborers for the circus as possible perpetrators, after looking over the 100 to 120 African Americans who were gathered at the circus train waiting to move on to the next town. Six were arrested. Word of the alleged rape spread rapidly throughout Duluth, and a mob gathered, whipped up by the angry cry "To hell with the law!" Rioters threatened "to get those negroes and hang them." They claimed that six "niggers" raped the girl and she was critically ill at the hospital. "What if it were your sister?" someone in the crowd asked, asserting that "south of the Mason Dixon line they would have worked faster than we are here tonight." Real white men would have protected the honor of real white women sooner. The men of Duluth must confirm their whiteness.[28]

A riot ensued as the crowd used crowbars, sledgehammers, railroad rails, and steel bars to force its way into the jail. The lynchers held a "kangaroo court" and allowed a news reporter to enter the cell to take notes of the "stories of the doomed men." The "court" declared three of the men, Isaac McGhie, Elmer Jackson, and Nate Green guilty and sentenced them to lynching. The other three detainees—Lonnie Williams, John Thomas, and Henry Richardson—they determined should not suffer immediate execution; the three were turned over to the police, who took them to Superior, Minnesota, for safekeeping. After the three condemned men were taken out of the jail and hanged before the crowd, the governor sent in the militia to restore calm. Two black prisoners arrested elsewhere by police searching for the rapists were joined in jail the next day by a seventh, an African American man who was arrested while walking along the railway on his way to Canada to look for work, oblivious to the events in Duluth. Meanwhile, the circus went on to Fort Francis, Ontario, where no disorders marred the circus day as the "large numbers of negroes employed continued at work."[29]

Once the mob's immediate thirst for revenge was satisfied, the good people of Duluth blasted the lynching. They worried about the image of their town; they preferred to believe the story that lynching was restricted to other, less civilized places. The local paper editorialized that Duluth had sustained a "Horrible Blot" it could never erase. Local businessmen in the Commercial Club, Rotary, and Kiwanis passed resolutions of condemnation. Calling the lynching a "shocking outrage," the Commercial Club asked for an investigation of "the adequacy and efficiency" of the police. County Attorney Warren E. Greene convened a grand jury immediately on June 17. Judge W. A. Cant Jr. told the grand jurors that the lynching was the most "atrocious" example in Duluth history of open defiance of law. Essentially, the city's elite sought to distance itself by arguing that the immigrant laborers involved in the riot and lynching were still not fully white, not possessed of white male privilege.[30]

Duluth's small African American population did not know which story line would prevail. They were justifiably wary of speaking out until whites had denounced the events. On June 22, the black women's Interstate Literary Club of Duluth and Superior announced that "the colored People of Our City do regret the outrage committed upon the men." Mrs. Odessa A. McCullough, Mrs. Laura Colby, Mrs. Jessie Williams, and Mrs. Minnie Adams expressed their "sadness mingled with painful surprise and regret" at the lynchings. They wanted it known, however, that they felt no "animosity" and were "thankful" for the resolutions of Kiwanis and other groups.[31]

The lynching was followed by farcical judicial proceedings. The local courts held eight trials of the accused lynchers, but in the end no one was imprisoned. Population numbers, and therefore public sympathy, lay not with the elites' effort to withhold the cloak of whiteness but with the perpetrators.

Greene, the county attorney, then decided to prosecute the alleged rapists before concluding the remaining lynching trials. He put Max Mason on trial first. Mason was charged with holding a gun to Sullivan's head while the others raped Tuksen before he also assaulted her. The recently founded NAACP sent the Chicago lawyer Ferdinand L. Barnett, the husband of antilynching crusader Ida Wells-Barnett, to town to aid local attorneys in representing Mason. News of the Duluth lynching excited great interest in the black community nationwide.[32]

Gender and race determined who heard the proceedings. The public was excluded from the courtroom only for the testimony of the girl and her mother, but was otherwise permitted open access. The press reported that half the audience consisted of African American men and women. Because of the delicacy of the subject, no white women were in the crowd that "filled every inch of sitting and standing room in the rear of the court." In summing up for the defense, Ferdinand Barnett told a racial story in an attempt to undermine Sullivan's credibility. He insisted that Sullivan's failure to make an immediate report was peculiar, because "Anglo-Saxon blood never permitted attacks on its women without a protest." He suggested: "Something did happen at the circus grounds. . . . The girl's ring may have been stolen and the boy's watch taken; the offense charged in the indictment against this defendant did not happen." Barnett did not "ask any favor for a black man—only justice." Objecting to the identifications at the circus train, he asked the all-male, all-white jury, "Is it fair to send a man to the penitentiary for thirty years on that identification?" Prosecutor Greene warned the jury that they must convict the defendants. He used a different racial story, about demonstrating that the legal system would exact retribution so that whites did not need to lynch alleged perpetrators: "Why do we have mobs, it's because people think the negroes won't be convicted. That's why they take the law in their own hands." After five hours of deliberation, the jury brought in a verdict of guilty.[33]

In upholding the conviction, the state supreme court announced that the defendant's story and the complainant's story were equally plausible. However, finding refuge in a narrow interpretation of the rule that they should not lightly overturn a jury verdict, the justices upheld the conviction. The court referred casually to the lynching as "the lamentable occurrence of a frenzied crowd taking the law into their own hands." In dissent, Judge Dibell, appalled at the decision, argued that "the story upon which the conviction rests is a strange one." He found inexplicable "the fact that they [Tuksen and Sullivan] spent time sitting, talking, went home she making no report of the incident and going to bed and to sleep making no complaint." In rape trials, evidence was routinely required that the victim report the crime within a reasonable time. Dibell announced his gender story, stating: "While the rule was not inflexible it was so natural as to be almost inevitable that a female upon whom the crime has been committed will make immediate complaint, if she have a mother or other confidential friend to whom she can make it. The rule is founded upon the laws of human nature."[34]

Dibell noted that neither Sullivan nor the girl identified Mason, stating: "There is testimony that the girl shook her head when Mason was presented." Dibell was not dismayed by the inability of Sullivan and Tuksen to clearly identify an assailant. He thought the police officers, who had experience making identifications, should have done a better job. Showing the influence of a racial story, he declared it common knowledge that "colored men are not easily distinguished in daytime and less readily in the dark or in the twilight. Young southern negroes, such as these, look much alike to the northerner." The identification by Sullivan and Tuksen long after the event, when the grand jury had been in session for a protracted period, was unsurprising. For the police and everyone involved by that time any African American would do: "The identification of a guilty negro was rightly enough to their liking," because—referring to the riot and lynching—"some distracting things had happened since."35

Dibell's adoption of a due process story left him in a decided minority at the time. As the Duluth episode showed, stories of black male bestiality and the need to protect white female vulnerability remained influential, not just in the South but in the North, and even in areas where the black population was quite small. Size did not inoculate against the racial-lynching disease. Of the 98,917 persons living in Duluth in 1920, only 495 were African Americans.36

In the decades after the Duluth lynching, social reform movements gradually displaced some of the old stories with new ones. As a result, legal and extralegal responses to rape charges underwent change. Due process stories and racial equality stories, and women's autonomy and equality stories, partially broke down the gender and racial subordination stories on which patriarchy depended. Reformers did not entirely succeed—old stories die hard—but they made significant progress in advancing the goal of justice in the courts.

To begin with, antilynching campaigns successfully focused on due process and judicial fairness stories to displace the "black beast rapist" story. Reform groups consisting of white and black women worked to undermine the practice. In addition, continued campaigns by the NAACP for a federal antilynching bill accelerated the decline. With the media spotlight on lynching, white men increasingly began to use the legal system to punish black men accused of raping white women. According to Tuskegee Institute records, there were only twenty-one reported lynchings in 1930—with twenty black victims and one white—and three in 1955, all African Americans. Between 1956 and 1968 there were only seven reported lynchings, four of them black men. After 1968, in view of the shift to legal action, organizations stopped tracking lynching.[37]

Media reports on lynchings that did occur underscored the vibrancy of the deeply imprinted racial stories, but also helped to hasten the practice's decline. In 1935, Claude Neal, a black man arrested in Marianna, Florida, for the murder of his white mistress, was kidnapped from jail in Alabama, where he had been placed for safekeeping. While the kidnappers traveled toward Florida, Southern newspapers announced the date of the coming lynching and the movements of the mob. The lynchers tortured Neal for twelve hours, hanged him until he was almost dead, castrated him Lydston style, forced him to eat his own penis, burned him with red-hot irons, and cut off his fingers and toes before they hanged his body in the Marianna courthouse square.

Cleo Wright of Sikeston, Missouri, accused of raping a white woman in her home in 1942, was captured by a mob that dragged him through the black community and burned his body. Townspeople remarked they had taught him "not to fool with white women."[38]

The new racial equality and due process stories brought African Americans accused of interracial rape into court and affirmed that the men were persons with agency, not objects. In some cases, recently founded civil rights organizations mounted national campaigns in the men's defense. In response, the U.S. Supreme Court in the 1930s began to enunciate a due process story that aided defendants. These factors were at work in the most celebrated episode of the 1930s, when nine African American youths were prosecuted at Scottsboro, Alabama, after two white women, reportedly prostitutes, claimed that the "boys" had raped them. After long court battles and an accompanying national campaign by civil rights organizations, however, charges against five were dropped; four men were convicted, and three of these were later paroled. Along the way, U.S. Supreme Court decisions increased the likelihood that defendants in such cases would have effective counsel.[39]

However, the Scottsboro cases were unusual. The reformers had achieved a diminution in lynching, but lynching was displaced by discriminatory and certain judicial punishment. Most white women who claimed rape were not prostitutes, and in the conflict between racial and due process stories, the accused often lost. In a widely known case described by historian Charles Martin, Willie McGee avoided the rope and faggot, but the state of Mississippi nevertheless executed him under the influence of old racially charged stories. A married white woman, Willamette Hawkins, charged him with rape; he claimed she brought the charge when he tried to abandon a voluntary relationship with her. Three separate juries convicted McGee, a black World War II veteran in his thirties, of the 1945 rape before his execution in 1951. His lawyers tried to imprint a "legal rules" story. They submitted affidavits offering to prove that he and Hawkins had had a liaison, initiated by her, for some nine years before the alleged rape. But the defense lawyers succeeded only in further infuriating Chief Justice Harvey McGehee. He told McGee's defenders, "You not only do not know what you are talking about, but you are insulting us the whole south." The journalist Carl Rowan, who reported on the case, elicited evidence supporting McGee's claim that the complainant was angry at his efforts to terminate their relationship. He concluded that "local blacks were too intimidated to give this evidence in court."

In May 1951, McGee was executed in a portable electric chair in the Laurel courtroom, while Mr. Hawkins and several relatives looked on. About five hundred whites gathered on the courthouse lawn cheered when undertakers removed the body.[40]

The fear and loathing contained in the interracial rape story led a court to convict a black sharecropper in Yanceyville, North Carolina, in the same year as McGee's execution, for "rape by leer." Although he was seventy-five feet away, Matt Ingram was convicted of assault because of the way he allegedly looked at a white girl. He obtained his freedom only after two and a half years of court maneuvers.

Leering by a black man at a white woman was apparently more significant than a white man's assault of a black woman: Ingram's imprisonment was longer than that of W. H. Gerrard, a white Mississippian charged with assaulting a black woman with intent to rape. He admitted the offense, which remained incomplete only because neighbors gathered in response to the woman's loud screams and prevented him from penetration. He received a one-year sentence.[41]

In most cases, the new due process stories were more problematic than the old paternalism for an accused African American. Conviction was practically certain, and in every state African American men convicted of raping white women received prison terms three to five times longer than those handed down in any other kind of rape case. An investigation of rape cases in Philadelphia in the 1950s discovered that only 3 percent involved black men who allegedly raped a white woman. However, execution was reserved almost exclusively for black men accused of raping white women. Of 455 men executed for rape between 1930 and 1968 in the United States, 405, or 89 percent, were black. Data from 1950 showed that no white man had ever been executed for rape in Virginia. Fifty-three black men had been sentenced to death in the state since 1908, and forty-four were executed. Between 1900 and 1949, the state appeals court upheld death sentences for seven men accused of rape, denied appeals in five other cases, and reversed only one. In this one case, class trumped race. The white couple who accused a black man of rape lived in a two-room house across from a "negro" restaurant in the "negro" section of Leesburg. The husband worked as a manual laborer on the town dump truck. The accused, unarmed, supposedly entered the house and raped the wife while the husband offered only "a shameful surrender and capitulation descending almost to complacence." The couple were essentially "poor white trash."[42]

The slow but steady progress of civil rights reform in changing stories and outcomes in interracial rape cases was apparent in two Maryland cases. In 1961, the state supreme court relied on old stories of race and gender in approving the conviction and twenty-year prison sentence of Charles L. Humphreys for raping Jane Linton Kennedy, a married white woman. She charged that the automobile in which Humphreys was riding crowded her car off the road. Then, she said, he forcibly entered her car, drove it into a wooded area, and raped her after threats and physical violence. Offering a story that had been presented unsuccessfully in the McGee case, Humphreys contended that Kennedy voluntarily submitted to his advances.[43]

Humphreys's lawyer, Robert Powell Cannon, thought the new due process and racial equality stories gave him license to explore Kennedy's behavior, "for the light it would shed on whether she consented to the intercourse." Cannon also attempted to ask prospective jurors whether they would give equal punishment to a white man and a black man who were charged with interracial rape. Eschewing the latitude allowed the defense when a white male was a defendant, the appellate court agreed with the trial judge's refusal to ask whether Kennedy had a "reputation for associating with colored men." The court rightly noted that even if she did associate with "colored men" it would not suggest that she was unchaste. Furthermore, asking jurors about equal punishment went too far afield. New stories were not part of the court's agenda.[44]

Cannon told a newspaper that his client had not confessed and said "that the woman submitted to his advances willingly."[45] So potent was the racial story that a white woman who had sex with a black man was doubly damaged goods, Kennedy successfully sued Cannon for damages. Kennedy claimed that Cannon's statement caused her "humiliation and harassment by annoying phone calls from unknown persons" and that she and her family were "forced" to move out of the state. Cannon argued that "the physical safety of his client" and the possibility of a "lynching if only the state's attorney's charges were published" justified his response. The state supreme court overturned the trial verdict in Cannon's favor, noting that the proper response would have been to ask for Humphreys's transfer to another jurisdiction for safe-keeping until trial.[46]

Whether or not Humphreys raped Kennedy, he and Cannon had exceedingly bad luck in the assignment of Judge C. Ferdinand Sybert to write the appellate opinion. Sybert's prior experience with another interracial rape case led to the incarceration of an apparently innocent man. The episode is incomprehensible unless one understands the importance of race and gender stories in the courts; its eventual outcome shows the power of reform movements in changing stories.

In July 1957, a thirty-one-year-old white housewife from Glen Burnie, Maryland, filed rape charges against twenty-one-year-old Gus Merchant, "a negro laborer." She claimed he entered her home and, wielding a knife, overpowered and raped her. The police arrested Merchant later the same day at his sister's house. In those pre–*Miranda* warning days, they questioned him for several hours with no defense counsel present. Merchant made a statement admitting only to voluntary sexual intercourse with the complainant. He pointed out that he knew her and her neighbors and had worked for them.[47]

The case went to trial before a judge alone, without a jury. Merchant's court-appointed counsel, Noah A. Hillman, "an experienced and respected member of the bar," was assisted by a younger associate, John A. Blondell. On the housewife's testimony, the judge convicted Merchant. Before sentencing him to the maximum penalty then available for rape, death by lethal gas, the judge expounded on the fairness of the legal process. He also commended the willingness of the good people of Glen Burnie to let this case be tried in court with no talk of lynching. The Maryland Court of Appeals, with Attorney General C. Ferdinand Sybert briefing and arguing for the state, let stand Merchant's conviction and sentence.[48]

Gus Merchant's conviction occurred at a time when the reform movements that eroded old racial inequality stories were just beginning their work. The "black beast rapist" and "pure white woman" stories still prevailed. Merchant wrote to Governor Theodore McKeldin, insisting on his innocence: "I know I had a defense that would stand up in any court of law when a man is supposed to get a fair trial." The governor, who had commuted thirteen out of the eighteen capital cases he had reviewed, commuted Merchant's sentence to life imprisonment. He languished in jail for thirteen years; meanwhile, different stories emerged.

In 1968, Eldridge Cleaver published *Soul on Ice*, in which he described his "rape psychosis." This did not help to erase the image of the African American man lusting after white women. However, there were also countervailing influences. The civil rights movement imprinted more egalitarian race stories, and the due process revolution afforded defendants more civil liberties protection. Increasingly, scholars discussed racial stereotyping, disparate sentencing, and discrimination in the selection of jurors. Changes in rape law and criminal justice were designed to alleviate race, gender, and class bias in the punishment of the offense.[49]

Gus Merchant soon benefited from these trends. In 1970, the state Court of Special Appeals reviewed his case and vacated his sentence. The context and the story of race had changed by this time. The earlier court and Sybert's brief obscured salient points in the transcript that undermined the validity of his conviction. The judges concluded that the transcript showed that neither the police nor Merchant's court-appointed attorney ever questioned the housewife's claim that she did not consent. During the special appeals court review, the counsel who defended him in the first case explained: "It didn't make sense [to question her on this point]. Here was a married woman, of a different race, in her own home, in bed, in the early morning, and he wanted us to believe, and have a court or a jury believe, that he came into that home and had intercourse with her voluntarily. We didn't believe it, or I didn't." Everyone involved agreed, however, that Merchant had never deviated from his insistence that the housewife consented to intercourse.[50]

The Court of Special Appeals called attention to facts that earlier courts would have ignored or discounted: The woman's rape story did not match the facts. The trial transcript showed that she made no outcry and did not report the assault until hours later. She cooked, removed the bedsheets "and put them in the clothes hamper; took off her nightgown and put it in her bureau drawer, changed her clothes, and washed herself before going over to her sister's to report the rape." She also testified that after the rape, Merchant asked her for "five dollars for bus fare. She gave him eleven dollars and continued to converse with him while fixing herself a cup of coffee." Merchant "did not behave as if he felt in any danger of being apprehended for the commission of a crime." He stopped at the home of Mr. and Mrs. Jesse Quarles to pay Quarles $1.90 for a previous loan, using the money given him by the alleged victim. The Quarleses noticed "nothing unusual about his behavior." Merchant did not attempt to "flee or secret [*sic*] himself until the police surrounded his house." Furthermore, there were "no signs of a struggle or of torn clothes." Also, "the doctor reported his examination [of the woman] was absolutely negative as to evidences of violence or of rape." In addition, "the woman's protestations, which she characterized as 'kind of loud,' failed to awake her children asleep in the next room."[51]

The court also accepted the defense lawyer's positive story about Merchant. They could not fathom why the accused, "a married man with two children, with no prior criminal record or record of mental instability, and with an honorable discharge from the army," would rape the complainant. After all, she "could easily identify him since they had spoken to one another over the backyard fence on at least two occasions as he passed by her house on his way to work."[52]

Significantly, the complainant testified that she locked the door before going back to bed after her husband left that morning. "Yet no testimony was offered as to any breaking and entering on the part of the accused. His access to the house was completely unaccounted for." It seemed to the court that "presented with the above-listed facts and circumstances, a court might properly have entertained the probability that the accused may have been telling the truth." At least, the justices insisted, an investigation should have been undertaken. The court's conclusions were reached because social change symbolized by the civil rights movement had made new, positive racial stories acceptable. Under the old stories, the actions of the earlier law enforcement officials and the court were routine and not unexpected.

The state's attorney, C. Ferdinand Sybert, who wrote the brief used to uphold Merchant's conviction and death sentence in 1957, prospered. He went on to become a state supreme court justice. He wrote the opinions upholding Humphreys's conviction and the slander verdict against his lawyer, who had suggested that a white woman might have consented to sex with a black man.[53]

Before the modern women's rights movement, social change left mostly untouched the old stories of patriarchal privilege when a white man was accused of the rape of a white woman. Legal approaches reflected the popular culture, the story everyone accepted. It was expressed, as legal scholar William Nelson points out, in the lyrics of a 1950s Mitch Miller song: "Your lips tell me No! No! But there's Yes! Yes! in your eyes." Not all courts responded in this fashion. However, many judges continued to devalue a woman's right to reject forcible sex.[54]

In 1941, these themes dominated the discussion when the Illinois Supreme Court affirmed a one-year sentence for Charles Bakutis and John Petkus. The story told by the twenty-year-old woman who filed the complaint was that when she left the theater in Chicago late one evening strangers forced her into their car. As she "struggled and screamed and endeavored to get out of the car," they drove out into the country to a secluded place, where they raped her. An examining physician testified to "bruises about the face, mouth and neck, and that the private parts were inflamed and swollen." Also, part of the clothing the woman was wearing "bore spots of blood."[55]

The defendants' story was that she agreed to go drinking with them and consented to the sex. None of their witnesses, however, provided corroborative testimony. There were too many conflicts as to where and when they had been drinking. The trial court acknowledged these discrepancies but seemed to believe that the complainant was at fault because she was out late at night carousing in the streets. The court also discounted the testimony of two police officers that they had known Bakutis for some considerable time and knew his reputation for veracity, which was "bad." The judge sentenced the defendants to just one year in jail, and the appellate court upheld the sentence. Clearly the trial court rejected the complainant's story and did not take her charges seriously.[56]

In 1953, the Illinois high court went further in relying on stories of appropriate gender behavior when it reversed the rape convictions of three young men by a judge sitting without a jury. The high court made clear its contempt for the victim's complaint. Her story was that she met the defendants at a tavern; after dancing and drinking with one of them, she started home by streetcar. They forced her into the backseat of a Buick and drove into an alley, where they beat her severely and in turn raped her. When the last assailant was in the backseat with her, preparing for his turn, the police approached and arrested them. Their story was that none of them did "anything that remotely resembled rape." She had consented.[57]

The appellate court accepted their story and concluded that the woman was crying when the police approached the car only because of the "shame, surprise and shock of being arrested, rather than the pain produced by the assault." More important, the complainant described herself as a married woman, forty-five years of age, who had a son eleven years old and worked as a food service employee in a Chicago hospital. The narrative the court told was quite different. The complainant's husband, from whom she "did not regard herself as legally separated," lived apart from the family, working in St. Louis. She had gone out alone after work, seeking "recreation and amusement." She was a woman who "left her husband and son behind her, traveled from tavern to tavern drinking intoxicating liquors and dancing with strangers and teenagers." The court thought the trial judge was "exceedingly charitable" when, in announcing the "harsh sentences on the boys," he referred to the victim "as a lady and as a girl." The appellate justices believed she had been out looking for a good time and was not "averse to meeting someone interested in the field of sex."[58]

Stories of appropriate gender behavior remained largely resistant to change even when the modern women's rights movement began to demand gender equality. Patriarchal privilege made it extremely difficult to convict white men of rape. Only when white women's stories included overwhelming evidence of force and violence did they have a chance to overcome stories of consent. In 1968 and 1969, Iowa's supreme court twice upheld Ronald Pilcher's conviction for a "shocking" rape, only because witnesses saw him rob a woman at gunpoint, then force her to accompany him to a secluded spot, where he forcibly had sexual intercourse with her. A Maryland court convicted George Rice of raping a twenty-two-year-old Baltimore art student in 1968. Rice forced his way into her apartment, took her to his own apartment a few blocks away, raped her several times, and made her the subject of a variety of obscene photographs. The court rejected Rice's consent argument because the woman's screams were heard when he first entered her apartment and a witness saw him on the street, hurrying her along and pushing her. Furthermore, she fit the narrative of the unsuspecting easily intimidated female: "a rather curious mixture of sophistication and naivety. Sophisticated in many ways, naive in many ways." Her confusion over whether to report the rape resulted from "natural hesitation," if the matter was publicized. The court could understand why "a young girl would not want her parents to know about something like this having happened."[59]

Courts also understood naive women like Mary Beth Fatheree, who in the early afternoon of Thursday, April 28, 1966, let a white man named Vessels enter her house in Pampa, Texas, to check for a gas leak. He told her he was a gas company employee. In raping and robbing her, he assaulted her with a knife, cutting her so severely that she required hospitalization. The court accepted the narrative that a white woman, accustomed to deferring to white men, would let a white man enter her house for repair work without requiring him to establish his credibility.[60]

In the 1970s the confluence of reform movements made a major change in the use of race, gender, and class stories in the court. Believing that too many rapes went unpunished, in the 1970s conservative and feminist activists agreed that punishment for rape and family violence needed to become more certain. They succeeded in imprinting new stories about the vulnerability of women and children and what counted as consent to sex. They influenced legal changes that made it easier to prosecute male perpetrators of rape and violence, even in states where substantial decriminalization had occurred in the 1960s. In the 1970s most state legislatures significantly revised their rape laws.[61] The reforms in rape law seemed to punish even acquaintance rape seriously, although the reforms took some time to affect the cases that reached the state supreme courts.

In 1975 Susan Brownmiller published *Against Our Will,* in which she persuasively described rape as an exercise of power in which a man forced a woman to submit. She explained that the aim of rape was control and that sexual satisfaction was generated by the assertion of power. The book helped to erase or soften the edges of some of the traditional stories. It raised consciousness about the necessity for dealing seriously with rape charges. The new statutes treated rape as a crime of violence, not as sex. Police and prosecutors who wanted to gain more convictions and arrests joined women's groups in urging the passage of new legislation. The statutes undermined a requirement that the woman resist physically to show nonconsent, and dispensed with the need for corroboration of the complainant's testimony. They also eliminated mandatory jury instructions to scrutinize the woman's testimony with caution.[62]

In 1974, Iowa, Florida, Michigan, and California enacted the first rape shield statutes to protect women from defense questioning about their past sexual behavior. By 1993, forty-eight states and the federal government had enacted rape shield laws, and one additional high state court had approved a similar procedure. The new evidentiary standards were rationalized as necessary because the humiliation suffered by those who reported rape made it the most often unreported crime.[63]

In addition, a joint effort by women's rights advocates and civil rights reformers worked to imprint different stories to abolish the death penalty for rape, a particular object of their efforts. Some reformers were motivated by concern about racial bias in sentencing, and others by the difficulty of gaining convictions for intraracial rape. There was the possibility that the availability of the death sentence might lead a jury to acquit in such cases. Efforts to abolish the death penalty gained impetus after the 1972 Supreme Court case of *Furman v. Georgia,* which declared capital punishment, as exacted under the statutes of Georgia and Texas, illegal as racially discriminatory.[64]

In the 1977 case of *Coker v. Georgia,* the U.S. Supreme Court adjudged the death penalty illegal in adult rape cases, unless severe bodily harm occurred. Director Counsel Jack Greenberg of the NAACP Legal Defense Fund saw the decision as a milestone in the group's long effort to end the death penalty, or at least, minimize its disparate impact on African Americans, even though Coker, the defendant, was white. The concern of civil rights groups about racism in sentencing coincided with the belief of women's groups that the death penalty for rape discouraged jurors from convicting. In *Coker,* U.S. Supreme Court Justice Byron White denounced rape as, short of homicide, the "ultimate violation of self." He also acknowledged that rape is violent and is "very often accompanied by physical injury to the female and can also inflict mental and psychological damage. Because it undermines the community's sense of security, there is public injury as well." However, "in terms of moral depravity and of the injury to the person and to the public, it does not compare with murder, which does involve the unjustified taking of human life." Rape "by definition does not include the death of or even the serious injury to another person." The murder victim's life is over, but "for the rape victim, life may not be nearly so happy as it was, but it is not over and normally is not beyond repair." Therefore, the death penalty was excessive punishment. However, the abolition of the death penalty did not end disparate sentencing. It modified the rape story but not the race story. Instead of being executed, black defendants convicted of interracial rape began to receive longer prison sentences than whites.[65]

Social reform movements and the due process revolution were limited in their effectiveness at gaining fairness in the justice system. Although stories are subject to change under political pressure, they are stubbornly resistant. Reforms designed to protect victims of sex crimes not only left the racial story alive, but made it no easier for white women to gain convictions of white men charged with rape. Courts continued to find ways to let in evidence of past sexual behavior, and white men continued to receive light sentences for raping white women. This was true even though many of the rapes included extreme brutality. In most cases, men assumed that they could force a woman to have intercourse and then simply leave without punishment. Often the victims trusted the rapist's motives and consequently fell into harm's way. One woman met a man in a bar who invited her to go with him to a "pig pulling" in North Carolina, where he and his friends gang-raped her. Another woman left her date at a party and accepted an invitation to go motorcycle riding with a stranger, who threatened her with a knife, raped her twice, and left her stranded while he returned to the party, oblivious to the possibility of punishment.[66]

Reforms designed to alleviate discrimination in jury selection were no more effective than the rape shield laws. Racial stories limited their impact. Discrimination simply took another form. In *Batson v. Kentucky* (1986), the U.S. Supreme Court decided that the Fourteenth Amendment's equal protection clause forbids striking African Americans from the jury pool on the assumption that they would be biased in a particular case simply because the defendant is black. Even after *Batson,* trial courts excluded jurors for some reasons that clearly reduced disproportionately the opportunity for African Americans to serve. Sometimes the cases involved black-on-black crime but often they were interracial. In 1993, the New York Court of Appeals ordered a new trial for Willie Dabbs, a black man convicted of rape, grand larceny, and kidnapping by an all-white jury. However, the basis of the decision offered little promise generally to African American defendants. First, the court, in accord with usual practice, approved the prosecution's challenge to a potential black female juror "who had relatives who had been convicted of crimes and who would [therefore] likely be sympathetic toward defendant." This outcome meant that, given the high incarceration rates of African Americans for drug offenses, large numbers of blacks would be excluded from jury service. Second, the court reversed the conviction because of the challenge to the other black female potential juror. According to the prosecutor, she was struck "because she worked for the affirmative action unit of a State agency and, as such, has a frame of reference that carries over into everyday life that the system doesn't work; at least as far as giving minorities fair shakes." The prosecutor did not ask her if she shared this view. If she had, she could legitimately have been excluded. But this view is shared by a majority of African Americans.[67]

The continued resistance of race stories to discrimination in jury selection stories was shown in a 1990 interracial rape case. Jane Smith and her fiancé, John Jones, joined thirty-two friends at a crawfish festival in Breaux Bridge, Louisiana. During the festivities, Smith left her group to watch a helicopter landing near the festival grounds, and there met Eric Porter and Todd Aubrey. After chatting for several minutes, they told Smith they were leaving to buy beer and she accepted their invitation to ride along. They drove around for a time, passing several stores, until it became dark. Smith began to worry that she would miss her ride home and asked Porter and Aubrey to take her back. Instead, she claimed, they drove into a field and raped her while she "pleaded with them to stop." They then left her on the highway. She walked to a nearby house to call the police, who traced the car and arrested Porter and Aubrey.[68]

The two men insisted that Smith had consented. However, in separate trials both were convicted of kidnapping and rape. The court sentenced Porter to twenty-one years at hard labor, seven without benefit of parole; Aubrey received concurrent terms of twenty-five years and five years, the first fifteen to be served without probation, parole, or suspension of sentence. These sentences were harsh for a rape case in Louisiana—unless the defendant was black and the victim white.[69]

In his 1993 appeal of the conviction, Porter complained of bias in jury selection. The jury included eleven women—four black and seven white—and one white man. Porter complained that the prosecutor used peremptory challenges to exclude his peers, black males, from the jury. The court denied his appeal, pointing out that sex discrimination in jury selection was not illegal. In addition, the prosecutor gave acceptable racially neutral explanations for his challenges of other prospective jurors. Among these neutral reasons: Two jurors were single parents, which "indicated sexual casualness." Another candidate, "a single twenty-four-year-old, is too young and seemed infatuated with the defendants." The fact that another "entered the court wearing curlers in her hair" was used to dismiss her. One woman's husband had been imprisoned for drug distribution, and another was "single, young, and was making excessive eye contact with one of the defendants." Among one prospective juror's other problems, she "wore dark sunglasses." The exclusion of jurors who might have known the defendant or of one who was a client of the defense attorney seems reasonable. However, other reasons seem trivial and designed to exclude on the basis of class or race. The appeals court accepted these reasons because they reflected the stories believed by the judge and prosecutors and the stories they believed the jurors might believe, even though these beliefs were based on inference, not fact. The purpose was to exclude poor women and African Americans whom the prosecutor and judge believed might decide in favor of Porter.[70]

Porter also argued that the court should have dismissed two prospective jurors who had stated their opposition to interracial sex. Instead, his attorney had to exhaust his peremptory challenges to avoid their selection. But the appeals court found their statements not disabling, ruling that the jurors had been "successfully rehabilitated" when the trial judge persuaded them to say they "could be fair."

This case was emblematic of a long history of bias in jury selection. The stories the public and judges believed were changing, but not fast enough for Porter. In 1994 the Louisiana court, in compliance with the U.S. Supreme Court decision in *J.E.B. v. Alabama* that same year, overruled the holding in Porter's case in an unrelated proceeding. They decided that in the future gender and race-neutral reasons must be given for striking jurors, and these reasons must be more than vague statements and impressions. They did not, however, specifically forbid the exclusion of jurors whose relatives had been convicted of crimes, or who were clients of defense attorneys as was done in Porter's case. Porter's conviction remained in force. However, in the absence of the *Coker* decision he would most likely have been executed.[71]

Rape cases disclose unambiguously that the prevailing narrative used in the courts is of white male privilege. They also disclose how difficult it is for men and women to avoid punishment or blame for the choices they make about expressing their sexuality. Rape also enhances our understanding that patriarchy is the subtext underlying race, class, and gender. We may think the story is race, but when we look at race dead-on we are looking at a socially constructed distinction used to maintain hierarchical relationships in the society. When an African American man is lynched or executed or imprisoned it is because powerful—most usually white—males defined him as an object—the other—whose punishment, whether he is guilty or not, signs racial subordination through the perpetuation of a negative image of black males. When an African American woman's rape story is discounted, it is because she is a socially constructed inferior. We can see the power relationships most clearly when the race involved is not black but socially constructed whiteness, when a white man is accused of the rape of a white woman. Then she is constructed as the other, who says no when she means yes, and is by definition available for white male desire. Her very being includes vulnerability to rape. Everyone involved is constructed through the angle of vision of the white man's privileged sight.

When the African American man accused of interracial rape escapes lynching or jail, it is because the white man views protecting him as more important than protecting the white woman. The white man's paternalism confines both the victim and defendant. By virtue of her lower-class status, the woman is not really white; and the black man's status as an object, without agency of his own, is affirmed. Black men and women and white women are all dependent on the white man. Rape, in this sense, is just the highest form of white male oppression.

When we apply this angle of vision it is easy to see that the Anita Hill–Clarence Thomas saga was not about two African Americans, it was really about the white male privilege to devalue her, and to elevate him because he was seen by powerful white politicians as the white man's boy, as surely as the rapist of the pig farmer's daughter or my uncle Lincoln was seen that way. The difference was that the stakes were higher—the power to sit on the Supreme Court, to apply legal stories that justify decisions on the most important matters in American life.

Therefore, when we say that changing the law requires changing the stories, we really mean changing the white man's stories about himself and everyone else. The stories are not really about skin color or gender but traditional white male privilege. White men who have become nonracist and nonsexist share in the difficult work of changing the traditional white man's stories. Social movements can affect the stories; it is difficult work, and backsliding is much too easy. But only to the extent that we mount and sustain reform movements can we change the law. The stories must be changed, if we want the law to presume that every adult has the traditional heterosexual white male freedom to make sexual choices.

Notes

Methodological Note

Since most African Americans lived in the South until the twentieth century, the cases used in this study before 1900 were collected by reading the Southern state reporters and the *West Century Digest*. More recent data were collected by taking a random sample of sexual behavior cases reported from throughout the nation in *Decennial Digests* and Westlaw. Using a random-number generator, a sample of 10 percent of the reported cases was drawn. Race and gender were almost always identifiable from the court opinions. Names were checked against the agricultural and manuscript Census of the United States, located in the National Archives, and local police and court records were consulted for additional information when possible. Newspapers were also used to augment the research. Only the cases discussed in the book are listed in the notes. The complete list of cases is filed in the Biddle Law Library at the University of Pennsylvania and on the Internet at the Biddle Law Library Web site (www.law.upenn.edu/~bll/mfberry.htm).

INTRODUCTION

1. On the use of narrative to analyze the law, see Thomas Ross, *Just Stories: How the Law Embodies Racism and Bias* (Boston: Beacon Press, 1996). For the legal debate over the value of narrative, see, for example: Alex M. Johnson Jr. "Defending the Use of Narrative and Giving Content to the Voice of Color: Rejecting the Imposition of Process Theory in Legal Scholarship," 79 *Iowa Law Review* 803 (May 1994).
2. Mary Frances Berry and John W. Blassingame, *Long Memory: The Black Experience in America* (New York: Oxford University Press, 1982), p. 249.
3. Ibid, p. 239.
4. David Benjamin Oppenheimer, "Understanding Affirmative Action," 23 *Hastings Constitutional Law Quarterly* 921 (1996); Tom W. Smith, "Ethnic

Images, General Social Survey Topical Report No. 19" (National Opinion Research Center, 1990).

5. Seth Mydans, "In Simpson Case, an Issue for Everyone: Class and Race Concerns Beginning to Emerge as Dividing Factors," *New York Times,* July 22, 1994, citing poll in which 62 percent of whites but only 38 percent of blacks said that they believed Simpson was "very likely or somewhat likely guilty."

6. Christopher A. Darden with Jess Walter, *In Contempt* (HarperCollins, 1996), pp. 168–69.

7. Ibid.; Sheri Lynn Johnson, "The Color of Truth: Race and the Assessment of Credibility," 1 *Michigan Journal of Race and Law* 261 (summer 1996), on the use of race by judges and jurors with different perspectives; Janet Elder, "Trial Leaves Public Split on Racial Lines," *New York Times,* Oct. 2, 1995, citing poll reporting that just 37 percent of African Americans have a high level of confidence in their local police, while 28 percent of African Americans expected to be treated more harshly than other persons in a hypothetical encounter with a police officer.

8. Elizabeth Shogren, "Clinton 'Troubled' by Racial Gulf over Simpson Verdicts," *Los Angeles Times,* Feb. 12, 1997; William Claiborne and William Booth, "In Los Angeles, Relief It's Over; Clinton 'Troubled' by Racial Division That Grew Out of Simpson Trials," *Los Angeles Times,* Feb. 12, 1997.

9. Sheridan Lyons, "Public Hearing Planned on Charges Against Judge," *Baltimore Sun,* September 8, 1995; Elaine Tassey, "Judge Cleared over Remarks in Sentencing," *Baltimore Sun,* May 4, 1996.

10. Jack M. Morgan Jr., "*Michigan v. Lucas:* Rape Shields, Criminal Discovery Rules, and the Price We Pay in Pursuit of the Truth," 1993 *Utah Law Review* 545; Ronet Bachman and Raymond Paternoster, "A Contemporary Look at the Effects of Rape Law Reform: How Far Have We Really Come?" 84 *J. Crim. L. & Criminology* 554 (1993).

11. Tim Golden, "Palm Beach Police Say They Will Seek a Rape Charge," *New York Times,* May 8, 1991; David Margolick, "Smith Acquitted of Rape Charge After Brief Deliberation by Jury," *New York Times,* Dec. 12, 1991; Mary Jordan, "Jury Finds Smith Not Guilty of Rape," *Washington Post,* Dec. 12, 1991; Janet Cawley, "Smith Cleared in Quick Verdict," *Chicago Tribune,* Dec. 12, 1991.

12. Thomas Stinson, "Tyson Guilty of Rape Boxer Could Get 60 Years in Prison," *Atlanta Journal and Constitution,* Feb. 11, 1992; Sharon Cohen, "Tyson Prays in First Act of Freedom, Then Heads Home to Ohio," Associated Press, March 25, 1995.

13. Ibid.

14. W. Lance Bennett and Martha S. Feldman, *Reconstructing Reality in the Courtroom: Justice and Judgment in American Culture* (New Brunswick,

N.J.: Rutgers University Press, 1981), pp. 179–80, report that 63 percent of a sample taken from a Southern county believed that black women had lower morals than white women; *Meritor Sav. Bank v. Vinson,* 477 U.S. 57, 69 (1986); Christina A. Bull, "The Implications of Admitting Evidence of a Sexual Harassment Plaintiff's Speech and Dress in the Aftermath of *Meritor Savings Bank v. Vinson,*" 41 *UCLA L. Rev.* 117 (1993). The discussion that follows is largely based on Bull's analysis.

15. In *Baehr v. Lewin,* 74 Haw. 530, 852 P.2d 44 (1993), the court found that the Hawaii Revised Statutes at 572-1 denies same-sex couples access to marital status and its concomitant rights and benefits, thus implicating the equal protection clause of article I, section 5 of the Hawaii Constitution.

16. Ibid.; *Baehr v. Miike,* 80 Haw. 341, 910 P.2d 112 (1996).

17. Ibid.; AP wire, *New Times,* Jan. 25, 1997, "Hawaii Marriage Bill Advances." "Judge Says Benefits Must Cover Gay State Workers' Partners," *New York Times,* Aug. 18, 1996; Angela Miller, "Businesses Seek Veto of Benefits Bill," *Honolulu Advertiser,* June 4, 1997; Elaine Herscher, "Same-Sex Marriage Suffers Setback/Alaska, Hawaii Say No," *San Francisco Chronicle,* Nov. 5, 1998.

18. *Evans v. Romer* 116 S. Ct. 1620 (1996); Andrew Sullivan, "Three's a Crowd: The Polygamy Diversion," *New Republic,* vol. 214, no. 25 (June 17, 1996), pp. 10–12; Joan Biskupic, "Once Unthinkable, Now Under Debate; Same-Sex Marriage Issue to Take Center Stage in Senate," *Washington Post,* Sept. 3, 1996; Steve Kloehn, "Definition of Family Elusive/Religious Groups, Academia in Disagreement," *Houston Chronicle,* Sept. 12, 1996.

19. Mary Frances Berry, *Why ERA Failed: Politics, Women's Rights and the Amending Process of the Constitution* (Bloomington: Indiana University Pres, 1986), p. 43, on women's suffrage; Melinda Chateauvert, *Marching Together: Women of the Brotherhood of Sleeping Car Porters* (Urbana, Ill.: University of Illinois Press, 1997), pp. xi–xix; and Evelyn Brooks Higginbotham, *Righteous Discontent: The Women's Movement in the Black Baptist Church, 1880–1920* (Cambridge, Mass.: Harvard University Press, 1993), p. 186, on the politics of respectability.

20. Michael Tackett and Linda P. Campbell, "Thomas Eludes Easy Labels Key to Understanding High Court Nominee Lies in His Roots," *Chicago Tribune,* July 14, 1991.

21. Ibid.

22. Henry Louis Gates, "Comment," "Marketing Justice: What, Really, Are Jury Trials for?" *New Yorker,* Feb. 24–March 3, 1997, pp. 11–12.

23. Jeffrey Rosen, "One Angry Woman: Why Are Hung Juries on the Rise?" *New Yorker,* Feb. 24–March 3, 1997, pp. 54–64.

24. G. Edward White, "The Appellate Opinion as Source Material," *Journal of*

Interdisciplinary History (1971), pp. 491–509, explains the rewards and dangers of using appellate opinions. Most cases are not appealed. Sexual behavior cases were only a small percentage of the types of cases the state supreme courts decided. The cases mostly involved debt, property, and other economic disputes. Robert A. Kagan, Bliss Cartwright, Lawrence Friedman, and Stanton Wheeler, "The Business of State Supreme Courts," 3 *Stan. Law. Rev.* 121–55 (1977–78); see also Stephen Daniels, "A Tangled Tale: Studying State Supreme Courts," 22 *Law and Society Review* 833–63 (1988). Jonathan Wright was the only African American who served on a state supreme court until 1961—South Carolina during Reconstruction. As late as 1995 there were still only twenty-five black judges, six of whom were female, among the total of 335 judges serving on the highest state courts nationwide. In 1995 sixty-three female justices, including the six black females, served in the states' highest courts. 1990 Census Data from the American Bar Association Commission on Women in the Profession, Statistics on Women and Minority Lawyers 1/28/94; see also U.S. Department of Commerce, Economics and Statistics Administration, *Statistical Abstract of the United States,* 1994, p. 407. As late as the 1990 census, when the United States had about 747,077 persons who were trained as lawyers, about 25,067 were African American, 11,006 of whom were female. About 182,745 of all lawyers were women. Black men have served on juries since emancipation, although few were chosen until the late twentieth century, after the civil rights movement. Women rarely served on state court juries until the late twentieth century. Not until 1975, when the Supreme Court decided in *Taylor v. Louisiana* (419 US. 522) that juries should include a fair cross section of the community, did juries routinely include women. A. Leon Higginbotham, *Shades of Freedom: Racial Politics and Presumptions of the American Legal Process* (New York: Oxford University Press, 1996), pp. 127–51.

I   THE PROTECTION OF HOME AND HEARTH

1. *Turner v. Turner,* 44 Ala. 437 (1870).
2. Ibid; Glenda Riley, *Divorce: An American Tradition* (New York: Oxford University Press, 1991), pp. 62–69; Nelson Manfred Blake, *The Road to Reno: A History of Divorce in the United States* (New York: Macmillan, 1962), pp. 119–21. After 1824, Indiana's courts could grant divorce decrees on specific grounds or for "any other cause" they might deem "proper." Also, the state had virtually no residence requirement. In 1873, the law was tightened; the state courts began requiring a two-year residence, strong proof of citizenship, real notice to the spouse, and no remarriage for two years.
3. Thomas Jefferson, *Notes on the State of Virginia* (New York: Harper & Row,

1964), originally published in 1861 as part of vol. viii of *The Writings of Thomas Jefferson*, H. A. Washington ed. (New York: H. W. Derby), pp. 132–34, 138; Annette Gordon-Reed, *Thomas Jefferson and Sally Hemings: An American Controversy* (Charlottesville: University Press of Virginia, 1997). For the colonial period, see William Wiecek, "The Origins of the Law of Slavery in British North America," 17 *Cardozo Law Review* 1711 (1996).

4. Winthrop Jordan, *White Over Black: American Attitudes Toward the Negro, 1550–1812* (Chapel Hill: University of North Carolina Press, 1968), pp. 152–54, 158–9; Deborah Gray White, *"Aren't I a Woman": Female Slaves in the Plantation South* (New York: Norton, 1985), p. 164.

5. Adele Alexander, "She's No Lady, She's a Nigger: The Demeaning Legacies and Images of African-American Women," unpublished paper in the author's possession; Jordan, *White Over Black,* pp. 161–62. Diane Miller Somerville, "The Rape Myth in the Old South Reconsidered," *Journal of Southern History,* vol. 62 (Aug. 1995), pp. 481–518. See also Victoria Bynum, *Unruly Women: The Politics of Social and Sexual Control in the Old South* (Chapel Hill: University of North Carolina Press, 1992), on the importance of class for poor white women.

6. Mary Frances Berry and John W. Blassingame, *Long Memory: The Black Experience in America* (New York: Oxford University Press, 1982), p. 120; Martha Hodes, *White Women, Black Men: Illicit Sex in the Nineteenth-Century South* (New Haven: Yale University Press, 1997), discusses a number of relationships between white women and black men.

7. Peter Bardaglio, *Reconstructing the Household: Families, Sex, and the Law in the Nineteenth-Century South* (Chapel Hill: University of North Carolina Press, 1995), pp. 63–64; *Scroggins v. Scroggins,* 14 N.C. 535 (1832); *Barden v. Barden,* 14 N.C. 548 (1832). The South Carolina legislature established two grounds for divorce: separation and living in adultery, or impotency at time of marriage and still continuing. In 1827, the legislature gave the courts the power to grant divorces. Before 1827, only divorces enacted by the legislature were permitted.

8. Ibid.

9. Ibid.

10. Joel Williamson, *New People: Miscegenation and Mulattoes in the United States* (New York: Free Press, 1980), p. 94 and chapter 10.

11. Leon Litwack, *Been in the Storm So Long* (New York: Knopf, 1979), p. 264.

12. Berry and Blassingame, *Long Memory,* p. 114; Howard Rabinowitz, *Race Relations in the Urban South, 1865–1890* (New York: Oxford University Press, 1978).

13. Berry and Blassingame, *Long Memory,* p. 115; *Hines v. Arkansas and Louisiana Gas Company,* 613 So.2d 646 (1993); James Baldwin, *Going to Meet the Man* (New York: Dial Press, 1965), p. 229.

14. *George, a Slave v. State,* 37 Miss. 306 (1859); Bardaglio, *Reconstructing the Household,* pp. 67–68.

15. Litwack, *Been in the Storm,* pp. 114, 125–43: Jacqueline Jones, *Labor of Love, Labor of Sorrow: Black Women's Work and the Family from Slavery to the Present* (New York: Basic Books, 1985); Samuel Pincus, "The Virginia Supreme Court, Blacks and the Law, 1870–1902," Ph.D. diss., University of Virginia, 1978, pp. 133–36. On the impact of the Civil War on the consciousness of elite white women, see Drew Gilpin Faust, *Mothers of Invention: Women of the Slaveholding South in the Civil War* (Chapel Hill: University of North Carolina Press, 1996), pp. 3–8, 48–53, 246–47.

16. John W. Blassingame, "A Social and Economic Study of Negroes in New Orleans," Ph.D. diss., Yale University, 1971.

17. David Fowler, *Northern Attitudes Towards Interracial Marriage: Legislation and Public Opinion in the Middle Atlantic and the States of the Old Northwest, 1780–1930* (New York: Garland Publishing Co., 1987), p. 221; William E. Foster, "Note: A Study of the Wyoming Miscegenation Statutes," 10 *Wyoming Law Journal* 131–38 (1956); Bardaglio, *Reconstructing the Household,* p. 180; John Blassingame, *Black New Orleans, 1860–1880* (Chicago: University of Chicago Press, 1973), pp. 203, 207, 210; Williamson, *New People,* pp. 91–92; Pincus, "The Virginia Supreme Court," chapter 4; Rabinowitz, *Race Relations in the Urban South,* pp. 34–35; George Tindall, *South Carolina Negroes 1877–1900* (Baton Rouge: Louisiana State University Press 1966; orig. published 1952), pp. 296–300.

18. Fowler, *Northern Attitudes Towards Interracial Marriage,* appendix, pp. 339–439, summarizes state legislation; Tindall, *South Carolina Negroes,* pp. 296–300.

19. Fowler, *Northern Attitudes Towards Interracial Marriage,* appendix, pp. 339–439. Interracial marriage first became illegal in this country; it was not illegal under the common law or statutes in England when the colonies were established. Pioneers from the Eastern Seaboard venturing west enacted such statutes where they settled. According to Blassingame, "A Social and Economic Study of the Negro in New Orleans," pp. 303–321, 25 of the 29 white women were Anglo-Saxons and 14 were natives of New Orleans; 110 of the white men were Anglo-Saxons. So neither Catholicism nor Latin background, often used to rationalize interracial sex in the literature, accounts for the numbers.

20. Litwack, *Been in the Storm,* p. 243.

21. "War on Back Creek," *Staunton* (Virginia) *Vindicator,* Nov. 26, 1870.

22. Pincus, "The Virginia Supreme Court," chapter 4; Rabinowitz, *Race Relations in the Urban South,* p. 45.

23. *Scott v. State,* 39 Ga. 321 (1869); *Pace and Cox v. State,* 69 Ala. 231 (1881).

In *Pace v. Alabama,* 106 U.S. 583 (1883), the Supreme Court upheld Alabama's statute despite its disparities in punishment.

24. Michael Grossberg, "Guarding the Altar: Physiological Restrictions and the Rise of State Intervention in Matrimony," 26 *American Journal of Legal History* 206–26 (1982), points out that states promoted more stringent tests of marital fitness to protect the health and well-being of the public. See also Bardaglio, *Reconstructing the Household,* pp. 176–85.

25. Bardaglio, *Reconstructing the Household,* pp. 183–88; Derrick Bell, *Race, Racism and American Law* (Boston: Little, Brown & Co., 1972), pp. 258–84. Between 1868 and 1900 there were thirty-two criminal cases reported, and convictions were upheld or indictments approved in twenty. There were twelve reversals, mainly on technical grounds. Ruben Sinins, "Justices of the Ex-Confederate State Supreme Courts," unpublished documentary collection, University of Pennsylvania, 1990, copy in the author's possession. Arkansas had a number of carpetbagger appeals court judges during military Reconstruction, while Florida, Tennessee, Louisiana, Mississippi, and South Carolina had one each. But in general the justices both before and after Reconstruction were Southerners, mostly ex-Confederates.

26. *Ellis v. State,* 42 Ala. 525 (1868); see also *Ford v. State,* 53 Ala. 150 (1875–76); Peter Wallenstein, "Race, Marriage and the Law of Freedom: Alabama and Virginia, 1860s–1960s," 70 *Chicago-Kent Law Review* 371 (1994).

27. *Burns v. State,* 48 Ala. 195 (1872).

28. "Intermarriage of the Races," *Mobile Register and Advertiser,* Sep. 8, 1874; Alabama Code of 1876, section 4189.

29. *Green v. State,* 58 Ala. 190 (1877); the couple challenged the jurisdiction of the court in an attempt to avoid trial, but their appeal was rejected, *Green v. State,* 59 Ala. 68 (1877).

30. Ibid.; the United States Supreme Court upheld the constitutionality of the Alabama antimiscegenation statute in *Pace and Cox v. State,* 106 U.S. 583 (1883).

31. "They are inferior in physical development and strength to the full blood of either race": *Scott v. State,* 39 Ga. 321 (1869). Insisting on the narrowness of his role, a concurring judge said: "I do not go into the policy of the law. I think the courts have nothing to do with that."

32. *Stewart and Another v. State,* 64 Miss. 626 (1887).

33. *Richardson v. State,* 34 Tex. 143 (1870); *Sullivan v. State,* 32 Ark. 187 (1877–78).

34. *Sullivan v. State,* 32 Ark. 187 (1877–78).

35. *Oliver v. State,* 34 Ark. 632 (1879).

36. *Hambey v. State,* 11 Tex. Crim. App. 1 (1881); *Mays v. State,* 88 Ga. 399 (1891).

37. *State v. Carroll,* 30 S.C. 85 (1888); between 1877 and 1900, of forty-three

fornication cases in this category, the high state courts affirmed twenty convictions and reversed twenty-three; see also Mary Frances Berry, "Judging Morality: Sexual Behavior and Legal Consequences in the Late Nineteenth-Century South," 78 *Journal of American History* (1991), pp. 835–56.

38. *State v. Brown,* 100 N.C. 519 (1888); see also *Haley v. State,* 63 Ala. 83 (1879); *Finch v. Finch,* 21 S.C. (1883–84) Shand 342.

39. *Etchison v. Pergerson,* 88 Ga. 620 (1891).

40. *State v. C. D. Butner,* 76 N.C. 117 (1877).

41. Berry and Blassingame, *Long Memory,* pp. 350–52.

42. Bram Dijkstra, *Evil Sisters: The Threat of Female Sexuality and the Cult of Manhood* (New York: Knopf, 1996), pp. 217, 228–9.

43. Ibid, pp. 434–44.

44. These states repealed interracial marriage bans: Arizona, California, Colorado, Idaho, Indiana, Maryland, Montana, Nebraska, Nevada, North Dakota, Oregon, South Dakota, Utah, and Wyoming. The bans are discussed in *Loving v. Virginia,* 388 U.S. 1 (1967).

45. *Loving v. Virginia,* 388 U.S. 1 (1967); Barbara K. Kopytoff and A. Leon Higginbotham Jr., "Racial Purity and Interracial Sex in the Law of Colonial and Antebellum Virginia," 77 *Geo. L. J.* 1967 (1989). The state modified its laws on the subject (which dated from 1785) in the Preservation of Racial Integrity Law of 1924. The 1924 law defined a white person as one with no trace of any other than Caucasian blood or no more than one-sixteenth American Indian blood. A 1931 law made an African American anyone with any ascertainable "negro" blood.

46. *Loving v. Virginia,* 388 U.S. 1 (1967).

47. Ibid.

48. Berry and Blassingame, *Long Memory,* pp. 351–52.

49. Ronald Reagan, *Ronald Reagan's Call to Action* (New York: Warner, 1976), p. 137; Janet K. Boles, "Women's Rights and the Gender Gap," in Tinsley Yarbrough, ed., *The Reagan Administration and Human Rights* (New York: Praeger, 1985), pp. 55–81.

50. Note, "Constitutional Barriers to Civil and Criminal Restrictions on Pre- and Extramarital Sex," 104 *Harvard Law Review* 1660, and notes there cited.

51. See, e.g., *Doe v. Duling,* 603 F.Supp. 960, 962–63 (E.D.Va. 1985), reversed on standing grounds, 782 F.2d 1202 (4th Cir. 1986). Note, "Constitutional Barriers to Civil and Criminal Restrictions on Pre- and Extramarital Sex," 104 *Harvard Law Review* 1660, and notes there cited. See Joan Beck, "Sexual Behavior: A Survey Confirms Moral Majority," *Chicago Tribune,* Feb. 22, 1990. In *Commonwealth v. Stowell,* 389 Mass. 171, 449 N.E.2d 357 (1983), the Massachusetts court fined two persons married to others $50 each for having sex in a van in an isolated wooded area, in violation of the state

fornication law. Even though the statute was rarely used, the public could address its "disfavor" with the statute to the legislature, "which has the power to change or repeal the statute." In other words, if the public no longer supported this story, the legislature could change its mind.

52. *Doe v. Duling,* 603 F.Supp. 960, 962–63 (E.D.Va. 1985), reversed on standing grounds, 782 F.2d 1202 (4th Cir. 1986). There were eight fornication arrests in Virginia between 1982 and 1985. Police in Virginia and elsewhere did not often seek out heterosexual fornication, but when they discovered such activity many officers aggressively enforced fornication laws. See, for example, "Sex Among Singles Is a No-no in Utah" (Aug. 29, 1986) (NEXIS, UPI file) (reporting prosecutions and noting that prosecutor argued that "it was his duty to file charges because the laws were on the books"). Note, "Constitutional Barriers to Civil and Criminal Restrictions on Pre- and Extramarital Sex," 104 *Harvard Law Review* 1660 (1991).

53. James Brooke, "Idaho County Finds Ways to Chastise Pregnant Teen-agers: They Go to Court," *New York Times,* October 28, 1996.

2   THE CRIME THAT HAD NO NAME

1. *Darling v. State* 47 S.W. 1005 (1898), affirmed. Another Texas court referring to a defendant's conviction, described oral sex as "vile and detestable," but not the crime of sodomy at which the law was directed: *Prindle v. State,* 31 Tex.Crim.App. 551 (1893), reversed. In *Medis v. State,* 27 Tex.App. 194 (1889), the court found a defendant who complained of being sodomized "evidently consenting" to the "bestial act."

2. *State v. Vicknair,* 52 La.Ann. 1921 (1900): sodomy is a "carnal copulation by human beings with each other, against nature, or with a beast."

3. Carroll Smith-Rosenberg, *Disorderly Conduct: Visions of Gender in Victorian America* (New York: Knopf, 1985), p. 220. Lesbian sex was tied to social structures of male dominance and female subordination throughout the Mediterranean world of the Roman and early Byzantine periods. Lesbian identity in the ancient world was condemned as gender transgression. See Bernadette J. Brooten, *Love Between Women: Early Christian Responses to Female Homoeroticism* (Chicago: University of Chicago Press, 1996).

4. Michel Foucault, *The History of Sexuality,* Robert Hurley, trans. (New York: Pantheon, 1978), pp. 43, 101. *Bowers v. Hardwick,* 478 U.S. 186 (1986), at 192–93; but see Rhonda Copelon, "A Crime Not Fit to Be Named: Sex, Lies and the Constitution," in David Kairys, et al., eds. *The Politics of Law: A Progressive Critique* (New York: Pantheon, 1990), pp. 177–94; Vern Bullough and Bonnie Bullough, *Sin, Sickness and Sanity: A History of Sexual Attitudes* (New York: New American Library, 1977), pp. 55–73, 201–209. For the

antebellum period, see Martin Bauml Duberman, " 'Writhing Bedfellows' in Antebellum South Carolina: Historical Interpretation and the Politics of Evidence," in Duberman, Martha Vicinus, and George Chauncey Jr. eds., *Hidden from History: Reclaiming the Gay and Lesbian Past* (New York: New American Library, 1989), pp. 153–68. Duberman discovered letters that show a homosexual relationship between James H. Hammond and Thomas J. Withers, two of the "great men" of the antebellum South. Hammond, the better known of the two, was a major proponent of the proslavery argument and served South Carolina as governor, congressman, and senator. Harriet Jacobs writes of a master who sexually abused a male slave, in Linda Brent, *Incidents in the Life of a Slave Girl*, L. Maria Child, ed., with an introduction by Jean Fagan Yellin (Cambridge, Mass.: Harvard University Press, 1987), pp. 288–9. Jonathan Katz, "U.S. Census Department of the Interior Report on the Defective Dependent and Delinquent Classes of the Population of the United States, Including Statistics Collected at the Tenth Census, June 1, 1880," in Jonathan Katz, ed., *Gay American History: Lesbians and Gay Men in the U.S.A.* (New York: Thomas Crowell, 1976), pp. 36–37. Thirty-three of the 63 prisoners jailed for sodomy were in the South: one each in Alabama and South Carolina, three each in Georgia and Louisiana, seven each in Mississippi and Tennessee, four in Texas, two in Virginia, and five in Florida. One white prisoner was female.

5. Jonathan Katz, "U.S. Census Department of the Interior 1890 Report on Crime Pauperism and Benevolence in the U.S. at the Eleventh Census," in Katz, ed., *Gay American History*, p. 39. Two of the cases Katz cites were not actually sodomy cases; one was a robbery and the other larceny by trick. Some cases used in this study were catalogued under sodomy, or cross-referenced with divorce, libel, and slander.

6. Foucault, *The History of Sexuality*, pp. 43, 101; Smith-Rosenberg, *Disorderly Conduct*, pp. 245–97. Stephen O. Murray, *American Gay* (Chicago: University of Chicago Press, 1996), pp. 18–19, argues that Foucault was mistaken in regarding homosexuality as a conceptual entity invented by nineteenth-century medical science for control purposes. Murray believes he was mistaken because homosexuality existed and was already labeled before that time.

7. Smith-Rosenberg, *Disorderly Conduct*, pp. 245–97; Brooten, *Love Between Women*, pp. 143–45, points out that ancient writers without as much power as trained medical practitioners labeled homosexuality a sin and proposed treatments including clitoridectomy.

8. John D'Emilio and Estelle Freedman, *Intimate Matters: A History of Sexuality in America* (New York: Harper & Row, 1988), p. 172; Smith-Rosenberg, *Disorderly Conduct*, pp. 167–73.

9. D'Emilio and Freedman, *Intimate Matters*, pp. 223–29.

10. *Jones v. State,* 17 Ga.App. 825 (1916).

11. George Chauncey, *Gay New York: Gender, Urban Culture, and the Making of the Gay Male World, 1890–1940* (New York: Basic Books, 1994); Eric Garber, "A Spectacle in Color: The Lesbian and Gay Subculture of Jazz Age Harlem," in Duberman, et al., *Hidden from History,* pp. 318–31.

12. Lawrence R. Murphy, "Defining the Crime Against Nature: Sodomy in the U.S. Appeals Courts," *Journal of Homosexuality,* vol. 19, p. 49 (1990); Lawrence Friedman, *Crime and Punishment in American History* (New York: Basic Books, 1993), pp. 343–44; *Jones v. State,* 17 Ga.App. 825 (1916).

13. *People v. Singh,* 93 Cal.App. 32, 268 P. 958 (1928); *State v. Hubbard* (Missouri), 295 S.W. 788 (1924); *People v. Peck,* 314 Ill. 237, 145 N.E. 353 (1924); *State v. Pitman,* 98 N.J.L. 626; 121 A. 597 (1923). Prosecution occurred so infrequently that these cases were not in the sample drawn for this study. But the descriptive language shows the effect of the emerging due process stories.

14. *People v. Robbins,* 171 Cal. 466, 154 P. 317 (1915).

15. Allan Bérubé, "Marching to a Different Drummer: Lesbian and Gay GIs in World War II," in Duberman, et al., *Hidden from History,* pp. 383–94; "Homosexuals in Uniform," *Newsweek,* June 9, 1947, p. 54.

16. *Barton v. State,* 79 Ga.App. 380, 53 S.E.2d 707, 708 (1949).

17. George Gallup, *The Gallup Poll: Public Opinion 1935–1971,* 3 vols. (New York: Random House, 1972), II, pp. 1162–63.

18. Estelle Freedman, " 'Uncontrolled Desires': The Response to the Sexual Psychopath, 1920–1960," *Journal of American History,* vol. 74, pp. 83–106 (1987), dates the interest from 1931, when, in the film *M,* Peter Lorre played a former mental patient who stalks innocent school girls, luring them with candy and balloons and then murdering them off-screen to satisfy his desires. After the film opened in New York, the media began clamoring for stories of violent sexual murder by the mentally unbalanced. In 1937 the *New York Times* published 143 articles on the new subject of sex crimes.

19. Ibid.; *The Gallup Poll,* II, p. 1129.

20. *People v. Ross,* 407 Ill. 199, 95 N.E.2d 61 (1950); 344 Ill.App. 407, 101 N.E.2d 112 (1951).

21. *People v. Sellers,* 103 Cal.App.2d 830, 230 P.2d 398 (1951); *People v. Triggs,* 106 Cal.Rptr. 408, 506 P.2d 232 (1973).

22. *State v. Cooper,* 114 Utah 531, 201 P.2d 764 (1949).

23. "Pennsylvania's New Sex Crime Law," 100 *University of Pennsylvania Law Review.* 727 (1952). In 46 out of 48 states, sodomy was a felony; 8 of the 46 had maximum penalties of less than 10 years. Thirteen states, including Illinois, as well as the District of Columbia, had recently passed sexual psychopath laws.

24. D'Emilio and Freedman, *Intimate Matters,* pp. 290–94.

25. D'Emilio, *Sexual Politics, Sexual Communities: The Making of a Homosexual Minority in the United States 1940–1970* (Chicago: University of Chicago Press, 1983), pp. 115–18; Eric Garber, "A Spectacle in Color," p. 319.

26. William E. Nelson, "Criminality and Sexual Morality in New York, 1920–1980," 5 *Yale Journal of Law & Humanities* 265 (1993); *People v. Doyle*, 304 N.Y. 120, 106 N.E.2d 42 (1952).

27. *Stoumen v. Reilly*, 234 P.2d 969 (1951).

28. Ibid.; *Arenella v. People*, 139 N.Y.S. 186 (1954); Patricia A. Cain, "Litigating for Lesbian and Gay Rights: A Legal History," 79 *Virginia Law Review* 1551 (1993); *Woody v. State*, 95 Okla.Crim. 21, 238 P.2d 367 (1951); *People v. Ross*, 344 Ill.App. 407, 101 N.E.2d 112 (1951); 95 N.E.2d 61, 407 Ill. 199 (1950).

29. Marc Stein, "City of Sisterly and Brotherly Loves: The Making of Lesbian and Gay Movements in Greater Philadelphia, 1948–72," Ph.D. diss., University of Pennsylvania (1994), chapter 5; *Haifetz v. Rizzo*, 178 F.Supp. 828 (1959).

30. D'Emilio and Freedman, *Intimate Matters*, pp. 316–25.

31. Ibid. The National Committee for Sexual Civil Liberties later became the American Association for Personal Privacy. American Psychiatric Association, *Diagnostic and Statistical Manual of Mental Disorders* (DSM-II), section 302.0, p. 44 (6th printing, 1974); resolution of the American Psychiatric Association, Dec. 15, 1973, reprinted in *Am. J. Psychiatry*, vol. 131, p. 497 (1974).

32. *Beckham v. State*, 103 Ga.App. 719, 120 S.E.2d 341 (1961); *Farrar v. Commonwealth*, 201 Va. 5, 109 S.E.2d 112 (1959). In keeping with the small number of homosexual cases reported, there were no African American cases in the sample in the 1950s and the 1960s.

33. *Franklin v. State* and *Joyce v. State*, 257 So.2d 21 Fla. (1971).

34. Ibid.

35. Ibid.; Patricia A. Cain, "Litigating for Lesbian and Gay Rights"; *Wainwright v. Stone*, 414 U.S. 21, 21–22 (1973).

36. *State v. Sheldon*, 91 Ariz. 73, 369 P.2d 917 (1962); *Eremita v. State*, 420 S.W.2d 609 (1967). The discussion of New York is based on Nelson, "Criminality and Sexual Morality in New York."

37. *Griswold v. Connecticut*, 381 U.S. 479 (1965); *Roe v. Wade*, 410 U.S. 113 (1975). The court could have emphasized that this was Hardwick's home (as an earlier Supreme Court had done in *Stanley v. Georgia*, 394 U.S. 557 [1969]. *Bowers v. Hardwick*, 487 U.S. 186 (1986). Consensual lesbian sex was not an offense under the Georgia law until 1968. See *Hardwick*, 478 U.S. at 200–201, n. 1 (Blackmun, J., dissenting) (describing the earlier Georgia sodomy statute). In *Thompson v. Aldredge*, 200 S.E. 799, 800 (Ga. 1939), the

Georgia Supreme Court held that the earlier statute did not prohibit lesbian activity.

38. *Bowers v. Hardwick,* 487 U.S. 186 (1986).
39. Comment, "AIDS: A Legal Epidemic?" 17 *Akron Law Review* (1984), pp. 717–22; Teresa Eileen Kibelstis, "Preventing Violence Against Gay Men and Lesbians: Should Enhanced Penalties at Sentencing Extend to Bias Crimes Based on Victim's Sexual Orientation?" 9 *Notre Dame Journal of Law, Ethics and Public Policy* (1995), pp. 309–343.
40. *Loving v. Virginia,* 388 U.S. 1 (1967).
41. *Commonwealth ex rel. Bachman v. Bradley,* 171 Pa.Super. 587, 91 A.2d 379 (1952).
42. Ibid.
43. Ibid.
44. *S. v. S.,* 608 S.W.2d 64 (Ky. 1980).
45. *Bezio v. Patenaude,* 381 Mass. 563, 410 N.E.2d 1207 (1980); see also *In re Marriage of Wicklund,* 84 Wash.App. 763, 932 p. 2d 652 (1996), the Washington appellate court overturned restrictions on displays of affection and overnight guests for a gay father who shared custody of his children with his ex-wife. The U.S. Supreme Court reversed a state court decision based on fears of race stigma, in which a white father had obtained custody after his ex-wife married a black man. *Palmore v. Sidoti,* 466 U.S. 426 (1984).
46. *Bottoms v. Bottoms,* 18 Va.App. 481, 444 S.E.2d 276 (1994); *Bottoms v. Bottoms,* 249 Va. 410, 457 S.E.2 102 (1995); Peter Baker, "Lesbian Mother Loses in Va. High Court," *Washington Post,* April 22, 1995. D'Vera Cohn, "Courts Send Mixed Messages in Custody Cases," *Washington Post,* May 9, 1995, the judges cited Bottoms's sporadic employment history as another factor in the decision; *In re Marriage of Wicklund,* 84 Wash.App. 763, 932 p2d 652 (1996).
47. *Bramlett v. Selman,* 268 Ark. 457, 597 S.W.2d 80 (1980).
48. Shirley Eder, "No More Love Match: Navratilova Tells Her Side of Palimony Suit," *Detroit Free Press,* June 18, 1991; "Martina Settles 'Palimony' Suit," *San Francisco Chronicle,* March 14, 1992.
49. In *Thompson v. Aldredge,* 200 S.E. 799, 800 (Ga. 1939), the Georgia Supreme Court held that the existing sodomy statute did not prohibit lesbian activity. Not until 1968 was the "odious and unnatural copulation per lengua in vagina between two women" covered. See also George Chauncey, "From Sexual Inversion to Homosexuality: The Changing Medical Conceptualization of Female 'Deviance,' " in Kathy Peiss and Christina Simmons, eds. *Passion and Power: Sexuality in History* (Philadelphia: Temple University Press, 1989), pp. 87–119; Lillian Faderman, *Odd Girls and Twilight Lovers* (New York: Columbia University Press, 1991), pp. 164–67.

3 OF CONCUBINE AND MISTRESS

1. *East v. Garrett and Wife,* 84 Va. 522 (1888); Samuel Pincus, "The Virginia Supreme Court, Blacks and the Law, 1870–1902," Ph.D. diss., University of Virginia, 1978, pp. 174–75.

2. *East v. Garrett and Wife,* 84 Va. 522 (1888).

3. Ibid.

4. Ibid.

5. Ibid. Benjamin East, a son of Edward's mother by another father, contested Scott Jr.'s claim. As a half-brother and legitimate heir, he prevailed as far as the farm implements and household goods were concerned but not with respect to the property left by Southey Satchell.

6. Ibid.; Nell Irvin Painter, "Three Southern Women and Freud: A Non-Exceptionalist Approach to Race, Class and Gender in the Slave South," in Ann-Louise Shapiro, ed., *Feminists Revision History* (New Brunswick, N.J.: Rutgers University Press, 1994), pp. 195–213.

7. *Riddell v. Johnson,* 67 Va. 152 (1875); *Thomas, Administrator v. Lewis,* 89 Va. 1 (1892); Pincus, "The Virginia Supreme Court," pp. 180–85, *Augusta County* (Virginia) *Argus,* January 13, 1891; *Davis v. Strange,* 86 Va. 793 (1890).

8. See categorical listing in Mary Frances Berry, "Judging Morality: Sexual Behavior and Legal Consequences in the Late Nineteenth-Century South," 78 *Journal of American History,* 835–56 (1991). Southern state supreme courts decided at least twenty-eight interracial inheritance disputes between 1868 and 1900, including the Virginia cases. African-Americans won twenty cases, attesting to the validity of their relationship with the white testator and affirming their inheritances. Peter Bardaglio, *Reconstructing the Household: Families, Sex, and the Law in the Nineteenth-Century South* (Chapel Hill: University of North Carolina Press, 1996) p. 187, and fn 47, p. 293 adds *Hopkins v. Bowers,* 111 N.C. 175 (1892) to the cases. In *Hopkins,* however, the white father died intestate. There was no offer to prove he intended to include his African American children.

9. *Cornelia Hart v. Hoss and Elder,* 26 La. 90 (1874). In Texas, concubines and their children inherited before the overthrow of Reconstruction but not after. They lost in Alabama after Redemption and won in Tennessee, Mississippi, and South Carolina only during Reconstruction. Long after Reconstruction ended, African American women and children in these relationships inherited in Arkansas, Georgia, and Virginia.

10. As in *Hopkins v. Bowers,* III N.C. 175 (1892). Bardaglio, *Reconstructing the Household,* p. 187 and fn 47, p. 293.

11. *Neel v. Hibard,* 30 La. 808 (1878).

12. William Cheek and Aimee Lee Cheek, *John Mercer Langston and the Fight for Black Freedom, 1829–65* (Urbana, Ill.: University of Illinois Press, 1989), pp. 18–20; Adele Logan Alexander, *Ambiguous Lives: Free Women of Color in Rural Georgia 1787–1879* (Fayetteville, Ark.: University of Arkansas Press, 1991). For antebellum examples, see Judith K. Schaefer, "Open and Notorious Concubinage: The Emancipation of Slave Mistresses by Will in the Supreme Court of Antebellum Louisiana," *Louisiana History,* vol. 28 (1987), pp. 165–82; James Hugo Johnston, *Race Relations in Virginia and Miscegenation in the South 1776–1860* (Amherst, Mass.: University of Massachusetts Press, 1970). A. Leon Higginbotham, "Race, Sex, and Education in Missouri Jurisprudence: *Shelley v. Kramer* in Historical Perspective," 67 *Washington University Law Quarterly* 680 (1989). Celia, who killed her master because he had raped her and made her a concubine in Missouri, was tried and convicted of his murder and hanged in December 1855; see Mellon A. McLaurin, *Celia: A Slave* (Athens: University of Georgia Press, 1991). Mary Frances Berry and John W. Blassingame, *Long Memory: The Black Experience in America* (New York: Oxford University Press, 1982), p. 117; *Kingsley, et al. v. Broward, et al.,* 19 Fla. 722 (1883); Phillip May, "Zephaniah Kingsley, Non-Conformist (1765–1843)," *Florida Historical Quarterly* 23 (1944), pp. 145–59.

13. Jonathan Bryant, "Race, Class, and Law in Bourbon Georgia: The Case of David Dickson's Will," *Georgia Historical Quarterly* 71 (summer 1987), pp. 226–42; *Smith, et al. v. DuBose Executors,* 78 Ga. 414 (1886); see also Virginia Kent Anderson Leslie, *Woman of Color, Daughter of Privilege: Amanda America Dickson, 1849–1893* (Athens: University of Georgia Press, 1995); "Amanda America Dickson," in *Black Women in America: An Historical Encyclopedia,* Darlene Clark Hine, ed. (Brooklyn: Carlson Publishers, 1993), pp. 336–37.

14. *Smith, et al. v. DuBose Executors,* 78 Ga. 414 (1886).

15. *Cornelia Hart v. Hoss and Elder,* 26 La. 90 (1874).

16. *Webster v. Heard,* 32 Tex. 686 (1869–70).

17. Ibid.

18. Ibid.

19. *Webster v. Corbett,* 34 Tex. 263 (1870).

20. Ibid.

21. *Betsy Webster and Baker Williams v. George E. Mann,* 52 Tex. 416 (1880).

22. *Jones et al. v. Kyle,* 168 La. 778; 123 So. 306 (1929).

23. Ibid.

24. Ibid.

25. *Dees v. Metts,* 17 So.2d 137 (1944).

26. Ibid.

27. *Bivens v. Jarnigan,* 62 Tenn 282 (1873–74). Although Clara Carter was an unmarried woman, the court referred to her as Mrs. Carter.

28. *Morris v. Swaney,* 54 Tenn. 591 (1871).
29. *Floyd v. Calvert,* 53 Miss. 37 (1876).
30. Ibid.
31. *In re Levengston's Will,* 142 N.Y.S. 829, 11 Mills 411 (1913).
32. *In re Erlanger's Estate,* 259 N.Y.S. 610 (1932); Douglas Gilbert, *American Vaudeville: Its Life and Times* (New York: Dover Publications, 1963), pp. 238–39.
33. *In re Erlanger's Estate,* 259 N.Y.S. 610 (1932).
34. Ibid.
35. Ibid.
36. Ibid.
37. *Lamborn v. Kirkpatrick,* 97 Colo. 421, 50 P.2d 542 (1935).
38. *Parrisella v. Fotopulos,* 111 Ariz. 4; 522 P.2d 1081 (1974).
39. *Marvin v. Marvin,* 18 Cal.3d 660, 557 P.2d 106, 134 Cal.Rptr. 815 (1976).
40. Ibid.
41. Ibid.
42. Ibid.
43. Ibid.

4 THE BUSINESS OF SEX

1. *State v. Shillcutt,* 350 N.W.2d 686 (1984).
2. Ibid. One-third of 1 percent (approximately 380 out of 132,000) of the population was black; Wisconsin Blue Book 1983–84, p. 759 (1983), quoted in dissenting opinion of Judge Shirley Abrahamson.
3. Ibid.
4. Ibid.
5. *State v. Grady,* 93 Wis.2d 1, 10, 286 N.W.2d 607, 609 (Ct.App.1979), was a Milwaukee county case in which the defendant was black and the state struck all three prospective black jurors. The court of appeals affirmed the conviction, concluding: "[There is a] presumption that the prosecutor was using his peremptory challenges to obtain a fair and impartial jury . . . We do not find error merely because the prosecution struck all three blacks on the jury in this case. . . . Nor do we find error because the state's action resulted in defendant being tried by a jury which did not contain any members of his own race."
6. *After Hour Welding Inc. v. Laneil Management Co.,* 108 Wis.2d 739, 740, 744; 324 N.W.2d 686.
7. *McCoy v. State,* 17 Fla. 193 (1879).
8. Ibid.
9. James R. McGovern, " 'Sporting Life on the Line': Prostitution in Progressive Era Pensacola," *Florida Historical Quarterly* 54 (1975), pp. 137–38.

Between 1865 and 1900, the high courts upheld only seven women's convictions from among twenty-eight appeals in cases concerning the selling of sexual favors or running a bawdy house. The courts usually reversed convictions, as in Mollie McCoy's case, on the basis of technicalities. State supreme court justices during and after Reconstruction generally tolerated "common prostitution" in their decisions. The courts were more likely to uphold convictions of male procurers.

10. *Malta Scarborough v. State,* 46 Ga. 26 (1872).

11. Judith Walkowitz, "The Politics of Prostitution," *Signs: Journal of Women in Culture and Society* 6 (1980), pp. 123–35; John D'Emilio and Estelle Freedman, *Intimate Matters: A History of Sexuality in America* (New York: Harper & Row, 1988), pp. 144–56; Thomas Mackey, *Red Lights Out: A Legal History of Prostitution, Disorderly Houses and Vice Districts, 1870–1917* (New York: Garland Publishing Co., 1987), pp. 392–93; McGovern, "Sporting Life on the Line," pp. 131–44.

12. Steven Schlossman and Stephanie Wallach, "The Crime of Precocious Sexuality: Female Juvenile Delinquency in the Progressive Era," *Harvard Educational Review* 48 (1978), pp. 87–88. Ruth Rosen, *The Lost Sisterhood: Prostitution in America 1900–1918* (Baltimore: Johns Hopkins University Press, 1982), p. 4.

13. *Roanoke* (Virginia) *Times,* May 15, 1873.

14. New Orleans even had a 1900 Supreme Court case affirming the legality of districts under state police powers: *L'Hote v. New Orleans* 177 U.S. 587 (1900); see also *Ex Parte Garza,* 28 Tex.App. 381, 13 S.W. 779 (1890), striking down San Antonio's effort to collect license fees from bawdy houses because to do so involved licensing an illegal business.

15. *Peabody v. State,* 72 Miss. 105 (1898).

16. Ibid.

17. 1900 Manuscript Census of the U.S. National Archives and Records Service, Washington, D.C., vol. 10, ED 15, Sheet 7, Line 98; Vol. 51, ED 118, Sheet 4, Line 64. The adults could all read but Peabody did not know how to write.

18. *Fullilove v. Banks,* 62 Miss. 11 (1884), Book 31 annotated. The court noted that Banks's son had lived with her for fifteen months, but the child may not have been his.

19. Rosen, *The Lost Sisterhood,* pp. 16–19, 40–41, 69–71, 156.

20. D'Emilio and Freedman, *Intimate Matters,* pp. 209–210; David J. Langum, *Crossing Over the Line: Legislating Morality and the Mann Act* (Chicago: University of Chicago Press, 1994), p. 245. The act was gendered until amended in the 1970s to apply to transporting persons.

21. Allan Brandt, *No Magic Bullet: A Social History of Venereal Disease in the*

United States Since 1880, with a New Chapter on AIDS (New York: Oxford University Press, 1987), p. 67; D'Emilio and Freedman, *Intimate Matters,* pp. 208–215.

22. D'Emilio and Freedman, *Intimate Matters,* pp. 208–215; Ruth Rosen, *Lost Sisterhood: Prostitution in America 1900–1918* (Baltimore: Johns Hopkins University Press, 1982), pp. 76–81.

23. *City of Shreveport v. Price,* 142 La. 936, 77 So. 883 (1918).

24. *People v. Edwards,* 180 N.Y.S. 631, 635 (Ct.Gen.Sess. 1920).

25. William E. Nelson, "Criminality and Sexual Morality in New York, 1920–1980," 5 *Yale Journal of Law & Humanities* 265 (1993). *People v. Anonymous,* 161 Misc. 379, 292 N.Y.S. 282 (1936). See also *People v. Nelson,* 427 N.Y.S.2d 194, 197 (City Ct. of Syracuse 1980) (finding no evidence of intent to discriminate, therefore no discrimination shown). One court upheld a gender-neutral prostitution law facing equal protection attack by pointing out that "what would be prostitution for a female would be equally prohibited and punished as lewdness for a male." *State v. Price,* 237 N.W.2d 813, 815 (Iowa 1976), appeal dismissed, 426 U.S. 916 (1976).

26. *State v. Ilomaki,* 40 Wash. 629, 82 P. 873 (1905). In *Southwick v. State,* 126 Ark. 188 (1916), the court noted that there was also no "evidence tending to show that the life of prostitution which the woman was leading was any other than voluntary on her part."

27. *Commonwealth v. Shultz,* 111 Pa.Super. 407, 170 A. 462 (1934).

28. *State v. McGinty,* 14 Wash.2d 71, 126 P.2d 1086 (1942). In addition, the court let the jury hear an argument that he "had married her to prevent her from giving testimony which would have been harmful to his defense. That may well have been the fact; but, even so," the privilege was still valid.

29. *Head v. State,* 146 Cal.App.2d 744, 304 P.2d 761 (1957).

30. Ibid.

31. Ibid.

32. *Lewis v. State,* 87 Fla. 37, 98 So. 917 (1924). Florida's white slave law inflicted imprisonment for not more than five years, or a fine not exceeding $1,000, or both.

33. *State v. Carroll,* 33 S.W.2d 900 (1930); see also *Younger v. State,* 160 Ark. 557 (1923) and *State v. Thom,* 92 Kan. 436, 140 P. 866 (1914).

34. Brandt, *No Magic Bullet,* pp. 122, 157–58; George Gallup, *The Gallup Poll: Public Opinion, 1935–1971,* 3 vols. (New York: Random House, 1972), I, pp. 61, 66.

35. Brandt, *No Magic Bullet,* pp. 122, 157–58; *The Gallup Poll,* I, pp. 353–54, 379. By January 1943, 61 percent thought weekly exams should be required, but only 29 percent thought police action should be used. Ten percent were undecided.

36. *People v. Coronado, et al.,* 203 P.2d 862, 90 Cal.App.2d 762 (1949). Coronado did not appeal.
37. Hopkins, a black Kentucky man, for over thirty years ran a "Negro" hotel and restaurant in Hopkinsville, Kentucky. Besides legal customers, the hotel also served those interested in illicit sex. Such activities in segregated black hotels rarely came to the attention of the police, unless some complication arose. *Hopkins v. Commonwealth,* 298 S.W.2d 695 (1957).
38. *State v. Davis,* 244 N.C. 621, 94 S.E.2d 593 (1956).
39. Ibid.
40. Ibid.
41. In the 1960s, Nelson Noel ran a particularly scandalous Indiana operation. The forty-three-year-old Noel "owned a 1951 Chevrolet school bus with a cot or bed therein," from which he sold the services of girls, recruited from parolees of the Indiana Girls School. *Noel v. Indiana,* 247 Ind. 426, 215 N.E.2d 539 (1966); Langum, *Crossing Over the Line,* p. 219.
42. Nelson, "Criminality and Sexual Morality in New York," p. 265.
43. Ibid.
44. Julie Pearl, "The Highest Paying Customers: America's Cities and the Costs of Prostitution Control," 38 *Hastings L.J.* 769 (1987).
45. Ibid.
46. *Shealy v. State,* 142 Ga.App. 850; 237 S.E.2d 207 (1977); *People v. Seabrooks,* 105 Misc.2d 542; 432 N.Y.S.2d 446 (1980).
47. *State v. Peacock,* 725 S.W.2d 87 (1987).
48. Ibid.
49. Mirta Ojito, "38 Men Accused of Soliciting Sex Are Paraded in Front of Camera," *New York Times,* Jan. 12, 1997.
50. A Massachusetts case involved a man convicted of pandering a child prostitute. A Louisiana case involved a man and two boys. Three of the cases in the random sample involved male prostitutes. Appeals courts affirmed each conviction. *State v. Tomlin,* 478 So.2d 622 (1985); *Ephraim v. State,* 629 P.2d 1277 (1981); *Sowell v. State,* 590 N.E.2d 1123 (1992); *Moreno v. State,* 860 S.W.2d 612 (1993).
51. Catharine A. MacKinnon, "Prostitution and Civil Rights," 1 *Michigan Journal of Gender and Law* 13 (1993); Nadine Strossen, "Hate Speech and Pornography: Do We Have to Choose Between Freedom of Speech and Equality?" 46 *Case Western Reserve Law Review* 449 (winter 1996); Drucilla Cornell, *Beyond Accommodation: Ethical Feminism, Deconstruction and the Law* (New York: Routledge, 1991), explains that prostitution should be understood as supporting a woman's insistence on being sexual in whatever way she chooses.

5 PROMISE HER ANYTHING

1. *Wood v. State,* 48 Ga. 192 (1873).
2. Ibid.
3. Ibid.
4. Ibid.
5. Ibid.
6. Ibid.
7. Ibid.
8. Ibid.
9. Ibid. Seduction cases forced some states to refine their laws in response to Wood's defense that he was already married and therefore legally incapable of giving a promise to marry. In Virginia, for example, the code made seduction criminal in 1873 and added a provision in 1878 that made seduction by a married man punishable by no less than two nor more than five years' imprisonment. Virginia, *Acts* 1872–73, p. 178; *Acts* 1877–78, p. 178; Charles Curry, "Seduction by a Married Man," 5 *Virginia Law Register,* 205–214 (1899).
10. Ibid.
11. Ibid. Chief Justice Hiram Warner dissented, because he preferred to keep intact the "all white women are virtuous" story instead of drawing class distinctions. Otherwise, in other cases white females who claimed rape or other assault might have to prove they were virtuous. "If the unmarried females in this State are not, in the eyes of the law, presumed to be virtuous until the contrary is shown, the condition of our unmarried females is quite different from what I have always supposed it to be."
12. *Wooten v. Wilkins,* 39 Ga. 223 (1869). Because it was not a criminal case, her dying declaration that he was the father of her baby could not be accepted as evidence.
13. *Parks v. State,* 35 Tex.Crim. 378 (1894–96). In one case the accused admitted the seduction: *Blount v. State,* 102 Fla. 1100, 138 So. 2 (1931) Florida's court let stand the conviction of R. A. Blount of Jacksonville, "a negro preacher about thirty-seven years of age," for the 1930 seduction of a thirteen-year-old parishioner. He continued the illicit relation until she became pregnant. After Blount's arrest on seduction charges, brought by the mother, he married the girl. Blount's counsel argued that marriage to her cured the offense since the purpose of the statute was to make sure women who became pregnant through seduction were supported. The court, however, believed that the legislature wanted to punish the actual seduction. Unlike Reverend Wood and Ben Parks, Blount conceded the offense when he married the girl.
14. John W. Blassingame, *Black New Orleans 1860–1880* (Chicago: University of Chicago Press, 1973), pp. 17–18, 202; *Carson v. Slattery,* 49 So. 586 (1909).

15. *Carson v. Slattery,* 49 So. 586 (1909).
16. Ibid.
17. Barbara K. Kopytoff and A. Leon Higginbotham Jr., "Racial Purity and Interracial Sex in the Law of Colonial and Antebellum Virginia," 77 *Georgetown Law Journal* 1967 (1989).
18. *Wood v. Commonwealth,* 159 Va. 963, 166 S.E. 477 (1932).
19. Ibid. Earl Lewis and Heidi Ardizzonne, in "A Modern Cinderella: Race, Sexuality, and Social Class in the Rhinelander Case" (*International Labor and Working Class History* no. 51 [spring 1997], pp. 129–47), discuss a widely publicized New York case, in which a wealthy white man unsuccessfully sought an annulment from an African American woman on the basis of her black ancestry. New York did not prohibit interracial marriages, and the dispute ended in a divorce settlement in 1930.
20. Mary Frances Berry, "Judging Morality: Sexual Behavior and Legal Consequences in the Late Nineteenth-Century South," *Journal of American History* 78 (Dec. 1991), pp. 835–56, presents a more extended discussion of the history of seduction; see also Harter F. Wright, "The Action for Breach of the Marriage Promise," 10 *Virginia Law Review* 361 (1924); Lea Vander-Velde, "The Legal Way of Seduction," 48 *Stanford Law Review* 817 (1996); Robert C. Brown, "Breach of Promise Suits," 77 *University of Pennsylvania Law Review* 474 (1929); "Seduction as a Crime," *Criminal Law Magazine* 3 (1882), p. 331; H. W. Humble, "Seduction as a Crime," 21 *Columbia Law Review* 144 (1921); Nathan Feinsinger, "Legislative Attack on Heart-balm," 33 *Michigan Law Review* 979 (1935).
21. Max Radin, *Handbook of Anglo-American Legal History* (St. Paul, Minn.: West Publishing Co., 1936), p. 246; Edward Livingston, *The Complete Works of Edward Livingston on Criminal Jurisprudence,* 2 vols. (Montclair, N.J.: Patterson Smith, 1968), vol. 1, p. 285; Livingston's code was completed in 1824 but not until 1833 was a complete edition published, in Philadelphia. Pennsylvania acted a criminal seduction statute in 1843; discussed in Walter Wadlington, "Shotgun Marriage by Operation of Law," *Georgia Law Review* 183 (1967), pp. 183–204. The criminal seduction statutes expressed ambivalence as to whether the crimes constituted betrayal of public morality or of private interests.
22. Carroll Smith-Rosenberg, *Disorderly Conduct: Visions of Gender in Victorian America* (New York: Oxford University Press, 1986),pp. 109–28; Barbara Meil Hobson, *Uneasy Virtue: The Politics of Prostitution and the American Reform Tradition* (New York: Basic Books, 1987), pp. 66–70; John D'Emilio and Estelle Freedman, *Intimate Matters: A History of Sexuality in America* (New York: Harper & Row, 1988), pp. 144–45. The New York law passed in 1848 is discussed in *Kenyon v. People,* 26 N.Y. 203 (1863) and *Boyce v. People,* 55 N.Y. 644 (*1873*); "Seduction as a Crime," *Criminal Law Magazine* 3 (1882), p. 331.

23. "Seduction as a Crime," *Criminal Law Magazine* 3 (1882), p. 331.
24. Smith-Rosenberg, *Disorderly Conduct*, pp. 217–44; *Ellington v. Ellington,* 47 Miss. 329 (1872).
25. Smith-Rosenberg, *Disorderly Conduct*, pp. 217–44; *Franklin v. McCorkle,* 84 Tenn. 609 (1886).
26. *Smith v. State,* 107 Ala. 139–43 (1894).
27. *Fry v. Leslie,* 87 Va. 269 (1891).
28. *Bottoms v. Commonwealth,* 168 Va. 714, 191 S.E. 682 (1937).
29. Ibid.
30. Ibid.
31. Ibid. Only eight Southern states criminalized seduction; Florida, Tennessee, and Louisiana did not.
32. *Judd v. Commonwealth,* 146 Va. 267, 135 S.E. 710 (1926), Rockingham County. "Susan Jones" is a pseudonym; the courts did not disclose her identity.
33. Ibid.
34. *Kesselring v. Hummer,* 130 Iowa 145 (1906); the Michigan case was *People v. Clark,* 33 Mich. 112 (1876), discussed in Lawrence Friedman, *Crime and Punishment in American History* (New York: Basic Books, 1993) p. 219.
35. *Honnett v. Honnett,* 33 Ark. 156 (1878).
36. *Jack Thornton v. State,* 20 Tex. 519 (1886).
37. Wadlington, "Shotgun Marriage by Operation of Law," 1 *Georgia Law Review* 183 (1967); Nathan Feinsinger, "Legislative Attacks on Heart-balm," p. 970; Jane E. Larson, "Women Understand So Little, They Call My Good Nature Deceit: a Feminist Rethinking of Seduction," 93 *Columbia Law Review* 374 (1993). Nicholson, called Mrs. Meredith Nicholson Jr. in the press, was married to the son of a well-known Hoosier author. The proposal passed the House by a vote of 87 to 7 and the Senate 31 to 15. Nicholson had introduced the bill in two previous sessions, but it failed to pass.
38. "Illinois Bans 'Heart Balm' Suits," *New York Times,* April 18, 1935; "Plans Bay State Anti-Balm Act," *New York Times,* April 3, 1935; "Alimony and Heart Balm for Men," *New York Times,* April 24, 1935; Feinsinger, "Legislative Attacks on Heart-Balm"; Larson, "Women Understand So Little," pp. 453–57. In the South, Mississippi and Alabama retained the right to sue in civil actions, North Carolina kept an arrest and bail provision, and South Carolina, a provision for damages recovery.
39. Feinsinger, "Legislative Attacks on Heart-balm," pp. 979–1008; David Montgomery and Jeff Leen, "The Sinatra Files: Forty Years of the FBI's Frank Talk; Papers Depict Ties to Mob, Hoover and Other U.S. Institutions," *Washington Post,* Dec. 9, 1998.
40. *Carter v. Murphy,* 10 Cal.2d 547, 75 P.2d 1072 (1938).

41. Ibid.
42. Ibid.; Smith-Rosenberg, *Disorderly Conduct,* pp. 227–28.
43. *Carter v. Murphy,* 10 *Cal.2d* 547, 75 P.2d 1072 (1938).
44. Ibid.
45. *Burger v. Neumann,* 69 N.Y.S.2d 661 (1947).
46. Ibid.
47. *Blackman v. Iles,* 4 N.J.82; 71 A.2d 633 (1950)
48. Larson, "Women Understand So Little," pp. 379–81, 453–71; proposes a sexual fraud damage remedy analogized to economic fraud.
49. Ibid.; *Parker v. Bruner,* 686 S.W.2d 483 (Mo.Ct.App. 1984), affirmed 683 S.W.2d 265 (Mo. 1985) (en banc), certiorari denied, 474 U.S. 827 (1985).
50. "Jilted Woman Keeps Ring, Not Jury Award," *New York Times,* January 23, 1995. *Sharon Wildey v. Richard A. Springs,* 47F.3d 1475 (1995). Cir.(Ill.)(1995).

6   THE WAGES OF SEX

1. *Dotye v. Commonwealth,* 289 S.W.2d 206 (Ky. 1956).
2. Ibid.
3. *Richmond v. Commonwealth,* 370 S.W.2d 399 (1963).
4. Carroll Smith-Rosenberg, *Disorderly Conduct: Visions of Gender in Victorian America* (New York: Oxford University Press, 1985) pp. 217–44; James Mohr, *Abortion in America: The Origins and Evolution of National Policy* (New York: Oxford University Press, 1978), pp. 46–84.
5. Smith-Rosenberg, *Disorderly Conduct,* pp. 217–44.
6. John D'Emilio and Estelle Freedman, *Intimate Matters: A History of Sexuality in America* (New York: Harper & Row, 1988), pp. 158–59.
7. Margaret Sanger, *Motherhood in Bondage* (New York: Brentano's, 1928); Jessie M. Rodrique, "The Black Community and the Birth Control Movement," in Kathy Peiss and Christina Simmons, eds. *Passion and Power: Sexuality in History* (Philadelphia: Temple University Press, 1989), pp. 138–55; Leslie J. Reagan, " 'About to Meet her Maker': Women, Doctors, Dying Declarations, and the State's Investigation of Abortion, Chicago, 1867–1940," *Journal of American History* 77, pp. 1240–64 (1991); Leslie Reagan, *When Abortion Was a Crime: Women, Medicine and the Law in the United States, 1867–1973* (Berkeley: University of California Press, 1997); see *People v. Schultz-Knighten* 277 Ill. 238 11b N.E. 140 (1917), involving a black woman prosecuted for abortion.
8. Reagan, "About to Meet Her Maker," pp. 1254–60.
9. *State v. Russell,* 90 Wash. 474, 156 P. 565, conviction for abortion; *Russell v.*

Dibble, 132 Wash. 51, 231 P. 18 (1924), license revocation reversed; D'Emilio and Freedman, *Intimate Matters,* pp. 222–23, 231–33.

10. *People v. Morani,* 196 Cal. 154, 236 P. 135 (1925).

11. D'Emilio and Freedman, *Intimate Matters,* pp. 252–54; Reagan, "About to Meet Her Maker," pp. 1262–64; *People v. Martin,* 376 Ill. 569, 34 N.E.2d 845 (1941).

12. D'Emilio and Freedman, *Intimate Matters,* pp. 253–54.

13. Most cases were still concerned with the prosecution of a physician whose working-class patient sought an abortion with the agreement of a husband and then died from complications. *Johnson v. State,* 91 So.2d 185 (Fla. 1956).

14. Gallup polling data confirmed changing attitudes. In 1947, 64 percent of Americans thought birth control information should be freely available; by 1965, 81 percent thought so. George Gallup, *The Gallup Poll: Public Opinion, 1935–1971,* 3 vols. (New York: Random House, 1972), I, p. 63; Ill, p. 1915; II, p. 1784; III, p. 1967; David Garrow, *Liberty and Sexuality: The Right to Privacy and the Making of Roe v. Wade* (New York: Macmillan, 1994), pp. 300–303.

15. Gallup, *The Gallup Poll,* II, pp. 1654, 1784; II, pp. 1915, 1957, 1967, 1985, 2000, 2044, 2157, 2225. More Protestants (56 percent) than Catholics (46 percent) agreed on abortion when the child was deformed, and both Catholics and Protestants thought that to have an abortion because one could not afford additional children was unacceptable. In keeping with the attitude toward poor unwed mothers on welfare, in 1966 64 percent thought that women who had more children than they could provide for properly should be sterilized. In the same year, 62 percent, including 56 percent of Catholics, thought birth control pills should be made available free to all women of childbearing age on relief. The same poll revealed that only 43 percent of those asked thought the pills could be used safely—"that is, without danger to a person's health." By 1969, 40 percent of those polled favored making abortion legal during the first trimester, 50 percent opposed it, and 10 percent had no opinion. D'Emilio and Freedman, *Intimate Matters,* pp. 252–53.

16. D'Emilio and Freedman, *Intimate Matters,* p. 255. *Roe v. Wade* 410 U.S. 113 (1973); *Mullins v. State,* 240 Ark. 608, 401 S.W.2d 9 (1966).

17. *People v. Palmer,* 181 Colo. 47, 507 P.2d 862 (1973); *People v. Smith,* 59 Cal.App.3d 751, 129 Cal.Rptr. 498 (1976). In 1994 the California Supreme Court prospectively overruled this case, citing a number of other state supreme courts' decisions that feticide by someone other than the mother was not what *Roe v. Wade* intended to protect; *People v. Davis,* 7 Cal.4th 797, 30 Cal.Rptr.2d 50 (1994).

18. Mimi Hall, "Judge Adds Racial Twist to Abortion Law," *USA Today,* April 26, 1991.

19. *In the Matter of Hon. Francis K. Bourisseau, Probate Judge, Mason County,* 480 N.W.2d 270 (1992); *New York Times,* March 4, 1992.

20. Amy Goldstein, "U.S. Abortion Services Drop," *Washington Post,* Jan. 22, 1995; "Abortion: Where Are the Doctors?" (editorial), *New York Times,* Oct. 13, 1994. Twenty-two years after *Roe v. Wade,* more than 500 hospitals and clinics had stopped offering the procedures, and fewer younger doctors were willing to perform it. The numbers of clinics, hospitals, and doctors outstripped the rate of decline in abortions. Hospitals, because of insurance pressure to do procedures on an outpatient basis, did not perform abortions as frequently. Medical schools and training facilities had mostly stopped offering or requiring training in the procedure. Alissa J. Rubin, "Abortion Providers at Lowest Mark Since 1973," *Los Angeles Times,* Dec. 11, 1998; Dan Sewell, "As Abortion Battle Becomes a Shooting War, Fear Intensifies; Doctors Don Bulletproof Vests; Clinic Workers Buy Guns or Personal Alarms as Those on Front Lines Fight for Survival," *Los Angeles Times,* Jan. 15, 1995.

21. Sewell, "As Abortion Battle Becomes a Shooting War, Fear Intensifies."

22. Salvi was arrested in Norfolk, Virginia, after firing repeatedly into the lobby of another abortion clinic, hitting no one. David Weber, "DA: Salvi Fired as Victim Pleaded," *Boston Herald,* Feb. 16, 1995; Kevin Culled and Brian McGrory, "Abortion Violence Hits Home," *Boston Globe,* Dec. 31, 1994. John Salvi committed suicide in prison while serving a life sentence in November, 1996; Ron Martz and Kathy Scruggs, "Feds Mum on Rudolph's Atlanta Ties," *Atlanta Constitution,* Oct. 16, 1998.

23. Leslie Brody, "Experts Wonder Why Teens Didn't Pursue Other Options," *The Record, Northern New Jersey,* Nov. 19, 1996, discusses the case of Amy S. Grossberg and Brian C. Peterson, two eighteen-year-old college students accused of murdering their baby boy. Michelle Oberman, "Mothers Who Kill: Coming to Terms with Modern American Infanticide," 34 *American Criminal Law Review* 1 (1996).

24. *Salem Roanoke* (Va.) *Times,* April 3, 1873.

25. "Trial of Mrs. Harriet M. Nelson (née Allen) for Infanticide," *Mobile* (Ala.) *Register and Advertiser,* March 6, 1867. W. C. Easton, Esq., was her counsel. Solicitor James Reed and M. B. Jonas for the state. The Mobile city court decided the case in March 1867.

26. Ibid.

27. Ibid.

28. Ibid.

29. *Smith v. Commonwealth,* 62 Va. 809 (1871–72); *Alexandria Gazette and Virginia Advertiser,* March 13, March 14, March 15, March 17, 1870.

30. *Smith v. Commonwealth,* 62 Va. 21 Grattan 809 (1871–72).

31. Ibid. According to the physician who delivered the baby, it was healthy. It was dressed immediately thereafter in a flannel petticoat, a slip, and a shirt or gown, and wrapped in a shawl. The court also believed that the color of the child seemed inconsistent with its supposed parentage: "The child delivered to the prisoner is described as a *bright* mulatto; it must have been at three days old almost white. So young a child of such parents would hardly be described as a mulatto." Yet the body was not described as that of a "bright" mulatto.

32. *Spicer v. State,* 69 Ala. 159 (1881).

33. *People v. Kirby,* 223 Mich. 440, 194 N.W. 142 (1923).

34. Ibid.

35. Ibid.

36. Ibid.

37. See *Shephard v. Iowa,* 255 Iowa 1218, 124 N.W.2d 712 (1961), and *Holt v. Wisconsin,* 117 N.W.2d 626 (1962). Both convictions were affirmed.

38. E. Donald Shapiro, Stewart Reifler, and Claudia L. Psome, "The DNA Paternity Test: Legislating the Future Paternity Action," 7 *Journal of Law* 1 (1992–93).

39. Ann Jones, *Women Who Kill* (New York: Holt, Rinehart and Winston, 1980), pp. 42–62. In the colonies bastardy proceedings were used to prevent an economic drain on the community, and coercion was used to obtain the name of the father. The laws encouraged abortion or infanticide. The 1996 welfare reform law is the Personal Responsibility and Work Opportunity Reconciliation Act of 1996, Public Law No. 104–193, 110 Stat. 2105.

40. In *Allen v. Harris,* 40 Ga. 220 (1869), the father failed to give bond for maintenance and was committed to jail. In *Nicholson v. State ex rel. Collins,* 72 Ala. 176 (1882), the defendant admitted sexual intercourse with the mother but offered testimony that "her character for chastity was bad," implying that someone else could have been responsible. The state supreme court upheld the trial court's support order, finding that everyone knew the woman was pregnant and that "it was the result of illicit intercourse." The defendant had "antecedent opportunities for such intercourse"; besides, he had been asking around about "means of making a woman miscarry."

41. *Chambers v. State,* 45 Ark. 56 (1885); Daniel Scott Smith and Michael Hindus, "Premarital Pregnancy in America 1690–1971: An Overview and Interpretation," *Journal of Interdisciplinary History* 4 (spring 1975), p. 570; includes no data for rural areas post–Reconstruction. *State and Hargett, Mary v. Broadway,* 69 N.C. 411 (1873).

42. *State v. Murray,* 63 N.C. 31 (1868); *Boles v. State,* 10 Ala. App. 184 (1871). In *Christian v. Commonwealth,* 64 Va. 954 (1873), a rape conviction was reversed because the woman had two illegitimate children, which meant she lacked "virtuous sensibilities."

43. Reagan, "About to Meet Her Maker," p. 1261; Rickie Solinger, *Wake Up Little Susie: Single Pregnancy and Race Before Roe v. Wade* (New York: Routledge, 1992), p. 21.

44. Solinger, *Wake Up Little Susie,* pp. 20–26; Linda Gordon, *Pitied but Not Entitled: Single Mothers and the History of Welfare* (New York: Free Press, 1994), pp. 85, 273.

45. Ibid.

46. Lawrence Friedman, *Crime and Punishment in American History* (New York: Basic Books, 1993), pp. 331–34, 343; David Langum, *Crossing Over the Line: Legislating Morality and the Mann Act* (Chicago: University of Chicago Press, 1994) pp. 164–65, 221–22; Solinger, *Wake Up Little Susie,* pp. 20–26.

47. Solinger, *Wake Up Little Susie,* pp. 20–26; see generally "Joint AMA-ABA Guidelines: Present Status of Serologic Testing in Problems of Disputed Parentage," 10 *Family Law Quarterly* 247 (1976). The tests were commonly referred to as the Landsteimer series of red cell blood grouping tests. *Commonwealth v. Dillworth,* 431 Pa. 479, 246 A.2d 859 (1968). See Fifty-second Ann.Rep. of the County Ct. of Phila., 292 (1965) for numbers of those who pled guilty. *Donley v. State ex rel. Lewis,* 226 Ark. 49, 287 S.W.2d 886 (1956); *Dalton v. State,* 100 Ga.App. 732, 112 S.E.2d 446 (1959); *People v. Makar,* 25 Ill.App.2d 246, 166 N.E.2d 467 (1960).

48. G——, *Appellant v. G*——, *Appellee,* 604 S.W.2d 521 (1980).

49. Ibid.

50. *Wachter v. Ascero,* 379 Pa.Super. 618, 550 A.2d 1019 (1988).

51. Ibid.; see also *Moore v. McNamara,* 201 Conn. 16, 513 A.2d 660 (1986).

52. Ibid.; Shapiro, Reifler, Psome, "The DNA Paternity Test."

53. *People v. Rimicci,* 97 Ill.App.2d 470, 240 N.E.2d 195 (1968).

54. *State v. Hogan,* 32 Or.App. 89, 573 P.2d 328 (1977).

55. *Stanley v. Illinois,* 405 U.S. 645 (1972) (where contest is between a biological father and the state, the biological father wins custody whether he is married or not); Barbara Jean Pulaski, "Children of Adulterous Affairs: The Putative Father's Rights after *Michael H. et al. v. Gerald D.,*" 6 *Connecticut Probate Law Journal* 339 (1992) discusses *Michael H. v. Gerald D.* (1988), where the court held that the real father has no due process right concerning a child born within a marriage as a result of an adulterous affair.

56. *Robards v. Barlow,* 78 Mich.App. 707, 260 N.W.2d 896 (1977); *Robards v. Barlow,* 404 Mich. 216, 273 N.W.2d 35 (1978).

57. Ibid.

7 SUFFER THE CHILDREN

1. Maura Dougherty, "Evaluating Recovered Memories of Trauma as Evidence," 25 *Colorado Lawyer* 1 (January 1996), outlines the dangers and gives a checklist juries can use in deciding whether memories or testimony is fabricated. Judith Herman, *Trauma and Recovery: The Aftermath of Violence— From Domestic Abuse to Political Terror* (New York: Basic Books, 1992) supports the validity of recovered memories of abuse; but cf. Elizabeth Loftus, *The Myth of Repressed Memory: False Memories and the Accusations of Sexual Abuse* (New York: St. Martin's Press, 1994).

   Modern psychoanalysis was built on Freud's revised theories that women have unresolved "Oedipal" incestuous longings; as a result, he denied the reality of his clients' reported abuse. See the case history of the patient he called Dora in Sigmund Freud, *Dora: An Analysis of a Case of Hysteria*, P. Rieff, ed. (New York: Crowell-Collier, 1967).

2. *Anschicks v. State*, 45 Tex. 148 (1876); *Anschicks v. State*, 6 Tex.App. 524 (1879).

3. Ibid.

4. Ibid.

5. *Anschicks v. State*, 6 Tex.App. 524 (1879).

6. In a case involving African Americans, Andrew Davis was sentenced to hang for the rape of a ten-year-old child even though there was no evidence that there had been penetration or that Davis was ever alone with the child. His conviction was reversed in *Davis v. State*, 43 Tex. 189 (1875). Historian Donald Nieman argues that the prosecution occurred because an overzealous Republican prosecutor in Washington County, Texas, where blacks still held political power, was trying to use the case to make a name for himself and appeal to the community. Donald G. Nieman, "Black Political Power and Criminal Justice: Washington County, Texas, 1868–1884," *Journal of Southern History* 55, no. 3 (1989), pp. 391–420; see p. 413.

   See also *Smith v. Commonwealth*, 85 Va. 924 (1889); the defendant was pardoned in 1896. In *Lawrence v. Commonwealth*, 71 Va. 845 (1878); the defendant was pardoned nine days after his conviction; he really thought the girl was old enough and had consented. Samuel Pincus, "The Virginia Supreme Court, Blacks and the Law 1870–1902," Ph.D. diss., University of Virginia, 1978, p. 263. *Dawkins v. State*, 58 Ala. 376 (1877), conviction of black defendant for rape of white child reversed.

7. David Pivar, *Purity Crusade: Sexual Morality and Social Control 1868–1900* (Westport, Conn.: Greenwood Press, 1973), pp. 141–42. Between 1876 and 1885, Alabama's age of consent remained at ten; Arkansas's started at eighteen and decreased to sixteen (it was twelve in 1887); Florida started

at ten, increased to seventeen, and then went back down to ten. Georgia's went from ten to fourteen, Louisiana's from twelve up to eighteen and back down to twelve. North Carolina's and South Carolina's stayed at ten; Tennessee went from ten to sixteen to twelve; and Texas went from ten to fifteen.

8. *Anschicks v. State,* 6 Tex.App. 524 (1879); *State v. Henderson,* 19 Idaho 524, 114 P.30 (1908).

9. *State v. Dancy* 78 N.C. 437 (1878).

10. *Williams v. State,* 47 Miss. 609 (1873).

11. *Sharp v. State,* 15 Tex.Crim. 171 (1883).

12. Ibid.

13. Ibid.

14. Ibid.

15. Ibid.

16. *State v. Adams,* 247 Mo. 652, 153 S.W. 1046 (1913).

17. *Rowland v. Commonwealth,* 147 Va. 636, 136 S.E. 564 (Va. 1927); *State v. Priest,* 132 Wash. 580, 232 P. 353 (Wash. 1925).

18. *People v. Ritchie,* 401 Ill. 542, 82 N.E.2d 344 (1948); see also 399 Ill. 144, 77 N.E.2d 137.

19. Ibid.

20. Ibid.

21. *Williams v. State,* 164 Tex.Crim. 347, 298 S.W.2d 590 (1956); see also 283 S.W.2d 239 (1955). The second trial was held in Wharton County, the first in Matagorda County, next door.

22. Ibid.

23. Ibid.

24. *Nilsson v. State,* 477 S.W.2d 592 (1972); "G.I. Jailed on Charge of Assault," *San Antonio* (Tex.) *Express,* Nov. 15, 1967.

25. *Furman v. Georgia,* 408 U.S. 238, 92 S.Ct. 2726 (1972); *Gregg v. Georgia,* 428 U.S. 153 (1976). By 1955, only eighteen states and the District of Columbia allowed the death penalty for the rape of an adult woman. See the discussion in Carole Pateman, *The Sexual Contract* (Stanford, Cal.: University of California Press, 1988): the contractual character of modern patriarchy is sex-right, the power that men exercise over women. Men have the right to sexual access to females and domination of them, but not with respect to the females of other men.

26. Pateman, *The Sexual Contract,* chapter 3; see Drew Gilpin Faust, *James Henry Hammond and the Old South: A Design for Mastery* (Baton Rouge: Louisiana State University Press, 1982), pp. 232, 241, 243, 291, 314–15; Bryan Strong, "Toward a History of the Experiential Family: Sex and Incest in the Nineteenth-Century Family," *Journal of Marriage and the Family* 35, pp. 457–66 (1973); Peter Bardaglio, *Reconstructing the Household:*

Families, Sex, and the Law in the Nineteenth-Century South (Chapel Hill: University of North Carolina Press, 1996), pp. 39–41.

27. Linda Gordon, *Heroes of Their Own Lives: The Politics and History of Family Violence, Boston 1880–1960* (New York: Viking Penguin, 1988), pp. 204–210; Bardaglio, *Reconstructing the Household,* pp. 204–205.

28. Bardaglio, *Reconstructing the Household,* pp. 206–212.

29. *Chancellor v. State,* 47 Miss. 278 (1872).

30. *Smith v. State,* 46 Ala. 540 (1872). See *Johnson v. State,* 20 Tex.App. 609 (1886): a stepfather had his conviction for repeatedly forcing sex on his fifteen-year-old stepdaughter reversed. The race of the parties is not mentioned, but Kinnie, the complainant, testified that she "did not know who her father was, but had been told that he was a white man." Assuming that Kinnie was African American, her mother was also. Since interracial marriages were illegal, Johnson would not have been acknowledged as married to her by the court in 1885 if he were not black.

31. *Smith v. State,* 46 Ala. 540 (1872).

32. Ibid.

33. *Coates v. State,* 50 Ark. 330 (1888).

34. *Webb v. Commonwealth,* 99 S.W. 909, 30 Ky.Law.Rep. 841 (1907).

35. *Alley v. Commonwealth,* 231 Ky. 372; 21 S.W.2d 476 (1929).

36. *State v. Wright,* 43 S.E.2d 295, 130 W.Va. 336 (1947); *Skinner v. State,* 60 So.2d 363, 36 Ala.App. 434 (1952).

37. *State v. Wright,* 43 S.E.2d 295, 130 W.Va. 336 (1947).

38. Ibid.

39. *Browning v. Commonwealth,* 351 S.W.2d 499 (1961); *Campbell v. State,* 172 Tex.Crim. 431, 358 S.W.2d 376 (1962); *State v. McCall,* 425 S.W.2d 165 (1968); *People v. Brown,* 12 Cal.App.3d 600, 90 Cal.Rptr. 881 (1970); William E. Nelson, "Criminality and Sexual Morality in New York, 1920–1980," 5 *Yale Journal of Law and the Humanities* 265 (1993).

40. *Browning v. Commonwealth,* 351 S.W.2d 499 (1961).

41. *Campbell v. Texas,* 172 Tex.Crim. 431, 358 S.W.2d 376 (1962). See also *State v. McCall,* 425 S.W.2d 165 (1968). The Supreme Court of Missouri upheld Virgil McCall's conviction for incest and a sentence of five years' imprisonment. He did not challenge the charge of "having committed fornication with his natural daughter on April 29, 1967, in the family home in Poplar Bluff, Missouri."

42. *People v. Brown,* 12 Cal.App.3d 600, 90 Cal.Rptr. 881 (1970).

43. Ibid.

44. James Stephen O'Brien, "Television Trials and Fundamental Fairness: The Constitutionality of Louisiana's Child Shield Law," 61 *Tulane Law Review* 141 (1986).

45. Ibid.

46. *Brown v. State,* 175 Ga.App. 246, 333 S.E.2d 124 (1985); Clerk's Office, Forsyth County Superior Court, telephone inquiry, by author, May 18, 1995.
47. *People v. Fierro,* 199 Colo. 215, 606 P.2d 1291 (1980).
48. *State v. Hewett,* 93 N.C.App. 1, 376 S.E.2d 467 (1989).

8 THE PIG FARMER'S DAUGHTER

1. James Elbert Cutler, *Lynch-Law: An Investigation into the History of Lynching in the United States* (Montclair, N.J.: Patterson Smith, 1969; reprint of 1905 ed.), pp. 155–77; Ida Wells Barnett, *On Lynching* (New York: reprinted by the Arno Press, 1969), p. 5; Edward Ayers, *Vengeance and Justice* (New York: Oxford University Press, 1984), pp. 223–65; Jacquelyn Dowd Hall, *Revolt Against Chivalry: Jessie Daniel Ames and the Women's Campaign Against Lynching* (New York: Columbia University Press, 1979), pp. 131–35; Robert Zangrando, *The NAACP Crusade Against Lynching 1909–1950* (Philadelphia: Temple University Press, 1980), pp. 3–11; Joel Williamson, *The Crucible of Race: Black-White Relations in the American South Since Emancipation* (New York: Oxford University Press, 1984), pp. 112–15; see generally, W. Fitzhugh Brundage, *Lynching in the New South: Georgia and Virginia, 1880–1930* (Urbana, Ill.: University of Illinois, 1993); and George C. Wright, *Racial Violence in Kentucky 1865–1940 Lynchings Mob Rule and "Legal Lynchings"* (Baton Rouge: Louisiana State University Press, 1990); Diane Miller Somerville, "The Rape Myth in the Old South Reconsidered," *Journal of Southern History* 61 (Aug. 1995), pp. 481–518; Samuel Pincus, "The Virginia Supreme Court, Blacks and the Law, 1870–1902," Ph.D. diss., University of Virginia, 1978, pp. 388–89; Glenda E. Gilmore, *Gender and Jim Crow: Women and the Politics of White Supremacy in North Carolina, 1896–1920* (Chapel Hill: University of North Carolina Press, 1997), pp. 203, 205.

2. G. Franklin Lydston, "Clinical Lecture: Sexual, Satyriasis, and Nymphomania," 61 *Medical And Surgical Report* 253 (1889); An Open Correspondence Between Hunter McGuire MD LLd of Richmond, President of the AMA and past president of the southern Surgical and Gynecological Association, and G. Frank Lydston M.D. of Chicago, Professor of GenitoUrinary Surgery and Syphilogy Of the Chicago College of Physicians and Surgeons Cook County Hospital, 1893 (Louisville, Ky.: printed by Renz and Henry for Hunter McGuire). Copy in Moorland Spingarn Collection, Howard University Libraries.

3. *Johnson v. Texas,* 21 Tex.App. 368 (1886); Manuscript Census of the United States, 1880, vol. 33, sheet 48, line 20; 1900, vol. 3, sheet 5, line 75; Agricultural Census of the United States, 1880, Washington County, Texas, p. 19, National Archives, Washington, D.C.

4. *Johnson v. Texas,* 21 Tex.App. 368 (1886).

5. Lawrence D. Rice, *The Negro in Texas 1874–1900* (Baton Rouge: Louisiana State University Press, 1971), p. 119.

6. *Johnson v. Texas,* 21 Tex.App. 368 (1886). Washington County's population was a little over 50 percent black. Albert Johnson, an eighteen-year-old "mulatto," is described as a farmer in the 1880 Census for Washington County Micro Roll, 1331, ed 141, p. 54, Manuscript Census of the United States, 1880.

7. *Johnson v. State,* 27 Tex.App. 163 (1889); see also 21 Tex.App. 268 (1888).

8. *Jones v. State,* 18 Tex.App. 485 (1885); *Johnson v. State* 27 Tex.App. 163 (1889).

9. *Green v. State,* 67 Miss. 356 (1889): *State v. Neely,* 74 N.C. 343 (1875); Bardaglio, *Reconstructing the Household: Families, Sex and the Law in the Nineteenth-Century South* (Chapel Hill: University of North Carolina Press, 1996), p. 194.

10. Ibid.

11. Booker T. Washington, et al., *The Negro Problem* (New York: Reprinted by the Arno Press, 1969), p. 143. Smith practiced in Greenville in Washington County, Mississippi, and in the surrounding districts in the black belt.

12. *Underwood v. State,* 49 La.Ann 1599 (1897).

13. Matthew Hale, *Pleas of the Crown,* 2 vols. (Philadelphia: Robert H. Small, 1847), vol. 1, pp. 633–35.

14. *Thompson v. Commonwealth,* 61 VA. 724 (1870–71). Willis Thompson, a black "boy" (no age given), was convicted of rape and murder of a black "girl." Bardaglio, *Reconstructing the Household,* reports two cases (*Anschicks* and *Powell*) of white men accused of raping an African American female; he does not record the *Bryson* case discussed below. Gary D. LaFree, *Rape and Criminal Justice: The Social Construction of Sexual Assault* (Belmont, Cal.: Wadsworth Pub. Co., 1989), pp. 201–19 finds that jurors are less likely to believe black women who allege rape than they are to believe white women who allege rape.

15. *Favors v. State,* 20 Tex.App. 155 (1886). A. M. Jackson and A. M. Jackson Jr. were the reporters for the volume. Dick Ward is also called R. P. Ward.

16. Ibid. In *Sanders v. State* (148 Ala.603, 41 So. 466 [1908]), the prosecutor's instructions for the trial jury asked them to keep in mind "your common knowledge and observation of the habits and characteristics and natural proclivities of the colored race as a race, as bearing on the question of the probable consent of the woman to the act of intercourse." This could include that blacks "are of loose habits of virtue."

17. Ibid.

18. *Bryson v. State,* 20 Tex.App. 567 (1886).

19. *State v. Dowell,* 106 N.C. 722 (1890); *Haines v. State,* 51 La.Ann. 731 (1899); Bardaglio, *Reconstructing the Household,* p. 200.
20. *State v. Dowell,* 106 N.C. 722 (1890).
21. Ibid.
22. *Innis v. State,* 42 Ga. 473 (1871).
23. *Cortney Crockett v. State,* 49 Ga. 185 (1873); see also *Topolanck v. State,* 40 Tex. 160 (1874).
24. William E. Nelson, "Criminality and Sexual Morality in New York, 1920–1980," 5 *Yale Journal of Law and the Humanities* 265 (1993).
25. *State v. Neil,* 13 Idaho 539, 90 P. 860 (1907) 91 P. 318.
26. Robert Zangrando, *The NAACP Crusade Against Lynching, 1909–1950* (Philadelphia: Temple University Press), pp. 22–23.
27. "Hey, Skinny! Circus Is Here," *Duluth News Tribune,* June 14, 1920; "Three Lynchings in State Since 1885," *Duluth News Tribune,* June 17, 1920.
28. See the following articles from the *Duluth News Tribune:* "Defense Quizzes Girl's Escort in Negro Trial," June 16, 1920; "Attack on Girl Was Cause of Negro Lynching," Nov. 4, 1920; "Second of Lynch Cases May Go to Trial Jury Today," Sept. 3, 1920.
29. See the following articles from the *Duluth News Tribune:* "Duluth Mob Hangs Negroes," June 16, 1920; "Second of Lynch Cases May Go to Trial Jury Today," Sept. 3, 1920; "4-Hour Battle Waged by Mob to Get Victims," June 16, 1920; "Three More Riot Trials May Go to Jury Today," Sept. 16, 1920; "Defense Quizzes Girl's Escort in Negro Trial," Nov. 24, 1920; "Attack on Girl Was Cause of Negro Lynching," June 16, 1920; "Guardsmen Sent to Virginia for Negro Suspects," June 17, 1920.
30. See the following articles from the *Duluth News Tribune:* "Duluth Has Suffered a Disgrace, a Horrible Blot Upon Its Name That It Can Never Outlive" (editorial), June 17, 1920; "Police Warned of Lynch Plot in Advance," June 18, 1920; "Lynchers Flayed in Charge of Grand Jury," June 18, 1920; "Round Up of Lynchers Starts Today," June 17, 1920.
31. "Lynching Scored by Negro Women," June 22, 1920, *Duluth News Tribune.*
32. See the following articles from the *Duluth News Tribune:* "Will Give Fund to Indicted Men," July 2, 1920; "Jurymen Chosen in Special Venire," Aug. 18, 1920; "One Convicted, Two Acquitted of Riot Charge," Sept. 17, 1920; "Two Acquitted of Riot Charges in Trials of Alleged Lynchers," Sept. 12, 1920; "State Scores Second Conviction in Rioting," Sept. 11, 1920; "Henry Stephenson Was Last Week Convicted of Rioting," Sept. 3, 1920; "Hammaberg's Counsel to Ask New Trial New Phase in Lynch Cases May Develop," Sept. 19, 1920; "Seven Negroes File Petition to Quash Charges," July 24, 1920.
33. See the following articles from the *Duluth News Tribune:* "New Evidence in

Lynching Probe Prolongs Quiz, Girl Testifies," July 8, 1920; "Defense Quizzes Girl's Escort in Negro Trial," Nov. 24, 1920; "Attack on Girl Was Cause of Negro Lynching," June 16, 1920; "Attorneys End Pleas to Jury in Assault Case," Nov. 27, 1920.

34. *State v. Mason,* 152 Minn. 306, 189 N.W. 452 (1922).

35. Ibid.

36. U.S. Bureau of the Census, *Fourteenth Census of the United States Taken in the Year 1920, Population 1920: General Report and Analytical Tables* (Washington, D.C.: Government Printing Office, 1922), p. 67.

37. Mary Frances Berry and John W. Blassingame, *Long Memory: The Black Experience in America* (New York: Oxford University Press, 1982), p. 124.

38. James McGovern, *Anatomy of a Lynching: The Killing of Claude Neal* (Baton Rouge: Louisiana State University Press, 1982); Dan Carter, *Scottsboro: Tragedy of the American South* (Baton Rouge: Louisiana State University Press, 1974); Domenic Capeci, "The Lynching of Cleo Wright: Federal Protection of Constitutional Rights During World War II," *Journal of American History* 72 (March 1986), p. 859.

39. Carter, *Scottsboro,* pp. 123, 174; James Goodman, *Stories of Scottsboro: The Rape Case That Shocked 1930s America and Revived the Struggle for Equality* (New York: Pantheon, 1994), p. 15; *Powell v. Alabama,* 287 U.S. 45 (1932); *Norris v. Alabama,* 294 U.S. 587 (1935).

40. *McGee v. State,* 200 Miss. 592, 26 So.2d 680 (1946); 203 Miss. 592, 33 So.2d 843 (1948) 40 So.2d 160 (1949), certiorari denied, 338 U.S. 805 (1949); Carl Rowan, *South of Freedom* (New York: Knopf, 1952), pp. 174, 177–85; see discussion of McGee case in Susan Brownmiller, *Against Our Will: Men, Women and Rape* (New York: Bantam, 1976), pp. 263–70; Charles Martin, "The Civil Rights Congress and Southern Black Defendants," 71 *Georgia Historical Quarterly* 26 (1987); Herbert Shapiro, *White Violence and Black Response: From Reconstruction to Montgomery* (Amherst: University of Massachusetts Press, 1988), pp. 395–96.

41. Berry and Blassingame, *Long Memory,* p. 124. In 1947, the North Carolina Supreme Court decided that assaults such as "rape by leer" involving no touching were assaults and not rape. See also *State v. Johnson,* 84 S.C. 45, 65 S.E. 1023 (1909); *Gerrard v. State,* 34 So.2d 195 (1948). The court made a point of saying that Gerrard was a white man because this was an interracial case, and announced that he "was fortunate in escaping with a sentence of only one year, which was probably under consideration of his drunken condition at the time."

42. Jacquelyn Hall, " 'The Mind That Burns in Each Body': Women, Rape, and Racial Violence," in Ann Snitow, Christine Stansell, and Sharon Thompson, eds., *Powers of Desire: The Politics of Sexuality* (New York: Monthly Review

Press, 1983), pp. 328–49; Gary LaFree, "The Effect of Sexual Stratification by Race on Official Reactions to Rape," *American Sociological Review* 45 (1980), p. 842; *Furman v. Georgia,* 408 U.S. 238 (1972); Robert J. Hunter, et al., "The Death Sentencing of Rapists in Pre-*Furman* Texas, 1942–1971: The Racial Dimension," 20 *American Journal of Criminal Law* 313 (1993); Donald H. Partington, "The Incidence of the Death Penalty for Rape in Virginia," 22 *Washington and Lee Law Review* 43 (1965). Eighteen states, the District of Columbia, and the federal government had a death penalty for rape of an adult woman. Eric W. Rise, *The Martinsville Seven: Race, Rape, and Capital Punishment* (Charlottesville: University of Virginia Press, 1995), pp. 70–98; Charles Martin, "The Civil Rights Congress and Southern Black Defendants," *Georgia Historical Quarterly* 71 (1987), pp. 25–52. *Legions v. Commonwealth,* 181 Va. 89, 23 S.E.2d 764 (1943).

43. *Humphreys v. Maryland,* 227 Md. 115, 175 A.2d 777 (1961).
44. Ibid.
45. *Kennedy v. Cannon,* 229 Md. 92, 182 A.2d 54 (1962); *Humphreys v. Maryland,* 227 Md. 115, 175 A.2d 777 (1961).
46. Ibid.
47. *State v. Merchant,* 10 Md.App. 545, 271 A.2d 752 (1970).
48. Ibid. *Merchant v. State* 217 Md 61, 141 A.2d 487 (1958).
49. "Gus Merchant," Vernon L. Papersack to Governor Theodore McKeldin June 26, 1958, Governor's Files: *Maryland Hall of Records,* contains a state mental health report with reference to his death sentence describing Merchant as of dull normal intelligence and short stature, as lacking in self-esteem, and as "emotionally sick." Eldridge Cleaver, *Soul On Ice* (New York: McGraw-Hill, 1967).
50. *State v. Merchant,* 10 Md.App. 545, 271 A.2d 752 (1970).
51. Ibid.
52. Ibid.
53. Ibid.
54. William E. Nelson, "Criminality and Sexual Morality in New York, 1920–1980," 5 *Yale Journal of Law and The Humanities* 265 (1993), quoting Miller song.
55. *People v. Bakutis,* 377 Ill. 386, 36 N.E.2d (1941).
56. Ibid.
57. *People v. Gonzalez,* 414 Ill. 205, 111 N.E.2d 106 (1953).
58. Ibid.
59. *Iowa v. Pilcher,* 158 N.W.2d 631 (1968); *Iowa v. Pilcher,* 171 N.W.2d 251 (1969); *Rice v. State,* 9 Md.App. 552, 267 A.2d 261 (1970); State of Maryland, Indictment of George Edward Rice, Bill No. 6471, Oct. 25, 1968. Maryland State Archives, Annapolis.

60. *Vessels v. State,* 467 S.W.2d 259 (1971).

61. *Furman v. Georgia,* 408 U.S. 238 (1972); *Gregg v. Georgia,* 428 U.S. 153 (1976); Nelson, "Criminality and Sexual Morality in New York."

62. See generally: Susan Brownmiller, *Against Our Will: Men, Women and Rape* (New York: Simon & Schuster, 1975); Angela Y. Davis, *Women, Race and Class* (New York: Random House, 1981), pp. 196–200; and Alison Edwards, *Rape, Racism and the White Women's Movement: An Answer to Susan Brownmiller* (Chicago: Sojourner Truth Organization, n.d.).

63. Nelson, "Criminality and Sexual Morality in New York," pp. 324–25; Jason M. Price, "Constitutional Law—Sex, Lies and Rape Shield Statutes: The Constitutionality of Interpreting Rape Shield Statutes to Exclude Evidence Relating to the Victim's Motive to Fabricate," 18 *Western New England Law Review* 541 (1996), pp. 549–52.

64. *Furman v. Georgia,* 408 U.S. 238, 92 S.Ct. 2726 (1972). By 1955 only eighteen states and the District of Columbia and the federal government allowed the death penalty for the rape of an adult woman.

65. *Coker v. Georgia,* 433 U.S. 584 (1977); Jack Greenberg, *Crusaders in the Courts: How a Dedicated Band of Lawyers Fought for the Civil Rights Revolution* (New York: Basic Books, 1994), p. 454. On racial disparities in rape sentencing, see Hall, " 'The Mind That Burns in Each Body' "; LaFree, "The Effect of Sexual Stratification by Race"; Hunter et al., "The Death Sentencing of Rapists in Pre-*Furman* Texas, 1942–1971"; Partington, "The Incidence of the Death Penalty for Rape in Virginia."

66. Alice Vachss, *Sex Crimes* (New York: Random House, 1993), points out that rapists select those who appear easy to victimize. See, for example, *People v. Solheim,* 54 Ill.App.3d 379, 369 N.E.2d 308 (1977), in which a woman was raped after she left O'Hare Airport with two men who claimed they worked for an airline and could sell her a cheap ticket for her onward journey. In *Commonwealth v. Maxwell* (280 Pa.Super. 235, 421 A.2d 699 [1980]), a rapist became acquainted with a woman by calling her on the phone and imitating a salesman conducting a survey concerning household products. She agreed to attend a products demonstration that he pretended to have scheduled at the Howard Johnson's Restaurant in Chester. When she arrived at the restaurant, he abducted her.

67. *Swain v. Alabama,* 380 U.S. 202 (1965), overruled by *Batson v. Kentucky,* 426 U.S. 79 (1986). The 1965 U.S. Supreme Court decision in *Swain v. Alabama* held that in the single case before the court, peremptorily challenging blacks merely because of their race was not a denial of equal protection. *Batson v. Kentucky,* 426 U.S 79 (1986), decided that a defendant may establish a prima facie case of purposeful discrimination in selection of the jury solely on evidence that the prosecutor exercised peremptory challenges

to remove from the pool members of the defendant's race. The court acknowledged that peremptory challenges were used to allow "those to discriminate who are of a mind to discriminate." The defendant must show that these facts and any other relevant circumstances raise an inference that the prosecutor used that practice to exclude the potential jurors from the trial jury due to their race. See also *People v. Dabbs,* 192 A.D.2d 932, 596 N.Y.S.2d 893 (1993).

68. *State v. Porter,* 615 So.2d 507 (1993); *State v. Aubrey,* 609 So.2d 1183 (1992). The woman's name is fictitious; she was not named in the record.

69. Ibid. For rape and kidnapping, the maximum term was forty-five years plus a $5,000 fine. There were two alternate jurors, one black and one white.

70. *State v. Porter,* 615 So.2d 507 (1993). In 1994 the Louisiana court, citing *J.E.B. v. Alabama ex rel. T.B.,* 114 S.Ct. 1419, 128 L.Ed.2d 89 (1994), overruled the holding in Porter's case. See also *State v. Ford,* 643 So.2d 293 (1994). The appeals court ruled that Aubrey's similar claim of jury bias came too late.

71. *State v. Porter,* 615 So.2d 507 (1993). In sentencing Porter, the court recognized his "past history indicates that he is usually a law abiding, church going individual." However, his refusal to confess deserved severe punishment.

Acknowledgments

Thanks to a number of research assistants, including James Johnson, Robert Natalini, and Rhonda Williams, who helped to collect the cases and archival material. Ruben Sinins and Jesse Shapiro produced essential research on the backgrounds and careers of the judges.

I also thank my faculty colleagues at Penn who commented on this work in its early stages, and my Truro and Big Sky "reading groups," especially Carroll Smith-Rosenberg, Alvia Golden, Joan Hoff, and Marian Yeates, for their aid and comfort. Smith-Rosenberg's work on sexuality and the tensions between gender, class, and race in the development of identity was essential to my subject. Conversations with Genna Rae McNeil, Blanche Wiesen Cook, Clare Coss, Dewayne Wickham, Roger Wilkins, Peter Bardaglio, T. J. Davis, V. P. Franklin, and Diane Miller Somerville helped immeasurably. John Hope Franklin's admonition to conclude my ten years of research because "you already know more about these materials than anyone else" encouraged me to publish, whether he is right or not.

I am grateful, as always, to my executive assistant, Krishna Toolsie, who minimized the distractions. Thanks to my agent, Charlotte Sheedy, for believing in my work, and to my editor, Victoria Wilson, who forced me to keep rewriting.

Mary Frances Berry,
Washington, D.C.
1999

Index

abortion, 70, 71, 152–62; class and availability of, 154–5; criminalization of, 154; legalization of, 13, 159, 168 (*see also Roe v. Wade*); parental consent for, 160; violence against providers of, 161–2

Abrahamson, Shirley, 106, 260*n2*

Access to Clinics Act (1994), 162

Adams case (1913), 187

adoption, 171–3, 177

adultery, 136, 145; interracial, 21–3; murder and, 9; *see also* fornication

affirmative action, 45, 239

African Americans, 3–8, 10–12, 20, 21, 127, 248*n24*, 252*n45*; abortion and, 152, 155, 159, 160; claims of inferiority of, 45; class and enforcement of unlawful cohabitation statutes against, 36–8; contraception for, 155; death penalty and, 237; gay and lesbian, 51–2, 55, 67–8, 78, 256*n32*; incest and child sexual abuse and, 180–3, 189, 191, 193–5; infanticide among, 163, 165–6; inheritance disputes of, 80–95, 102–3, 258*n8, n9*; and intelligence tests, 41–2; laws against marriage of whites and, *see* miscegenation statutes; marriage of, 28–9; myths about sexuality of, 27–9, 41, 45, 48; out-of-wedlock births of, 169–74; politics of respectability of, 16; prostitution and, 104–7, 110–14, 117, 118, 120–1; rape cases involving, 11, 28, 202–16, 218–33, 237–42, 272*n6*, 276*n14*; seduction cases involving, 131–5, 137, 151, 265*n19*; under slavery, 24–6

Aid to Dependent Children (ADC), 172, 173

AIDS, 46, 47, 72, 122, 161

Alabama, 254*n4*, 272*n7*; abortion clinic bombing in, 162; incest in, 193–4; infanticide in, 163–4, 166; inheritance disputes in, 85, 92–3, 258*n9*; miscegenation statute in, 22–3, 30, 32–5, 251*n23*, 251*n30*; out-of-wedlock births in, 170; rape in, 226; seduction cases in, 136, 139, 266*n38*

Allen v. Harris (1869), 270*n40*

American Civil Liberties Union, 126

American Medical Association, 154, 204

American Psychiatric Association, 66

Anschicks v. State (1876), 180–3, 189

anticommunism, 61–2

Ardizzonne, Heidi, 265*n19*

Arizona, 252*n44*; inheritance dispute in, 100

Arkansas, 251*n25*, 258*n9*, 272*n7*; gays in, 77; incest in, 194; interracial fornication in, 36–8; miscegenation

A Note on the Type

The text of this book was set in a typeface called
Times New Roman, designed by Stanley Morison
(1889–1967) for *The Times* (London) and first
introduced by that newspaper in 1932.
Among typographers and designers of the twentieth
century, Stanley Morison was a strong forming
influence—as a typographical adviser to the
Monotype Corporation, as a director of two
distinguished publishing houses, and as a writer of
sensibility, erudition, and keen practical sense.

Composed by Creative Graphics,
Allentown, Pennsylvania
Printed and bound by Quebecor Printing,
Martinsburg, West Virginia
Designed by Anthea Lingeman